GEORGE B. DAVIS

THE ELEMENTS OF LAW

AN INTRODUCTION TO THE STUDY OF THE CONSTITUTIONAL AND MILITARY LAW OF THE UNITED STATES

Elibron Classics

www. elibron.com

Elibron Classics series.

ISBN 0-543-89780-X (paperback)
ISBN 0-543-89779-6 (hardcover)

This Elibron Classics book contains the complete text of the edition published in 1897 by John Wiley & Sons, New York.

PREFACE

It has been my purpose in the preparation of this work to present so much, and only so much, of the elements of law and of the science of government as is necessary to enable one, not a student of the law, to study intelligently the constitutional law of the United States and to understand and appreciate the serious duties and obligations of citizenship. To that end the subject has been presented in a somewhat meager outline, and many important matters have been omitted which are essential to a formal study of the law, with which, as such, this book has nothing to do.

West Point, New York, *April* 13,1897.

CHAPTER I

THE STATE

The State: Source of its Sovereignty.— A *State* is a society of persons having a permanent political organization and exercising within a certain territory the usual functions of government. The chief purposes of the organization are to secure the common defense by an exercise of the combined strength of all, and to assure to each member of the body politic the quiet enjoyment of his personal and property rights and the greatest freedom of movement, occupation, and opinion that is consistent with a similar enjoyment on the part of others. While some modern States do not expressly recognize the great body of their citizens, or subjects, as the ultimate source of sovereign power and authority, the fact is none the less true; and there is no State now in existence in which the people, if such be their desire, cannot insist upon the recognition of their sovereignty and the establishment of a government in conformity to the popular will.

CONSTITUTIONS

Constitution.— The *constitution* of a State is its organic, or fundamental, law, to which acts done in its behalf must strictly conform; statutes in excess of the law-making power conferred upon the legislature have no binding force, and executive or judicial acts not in conformity to its provisions are void and of no effect. The Constitution of a State emanates from its supreme sovereign authority; if that authority be a monarch, it takes the form of a *charter* in which the sovereign concedes, or parts, with a portion of his power; if it be the people of the State, and the instrument be voluntarily adopted by them, it is called a *Constitution;* in either case it can be changed or modified only by the authority that called it into being. The *constitution* of a State prescribes the form of government, creates its several departments, endows each of the departments so created with appropriate powers, and prescribes certain limits within which those powers shall be exercised.

Written and unwritten Constitutions.— A constitution may be a formal instrument, solemnly enacted, or adopted, by the people of the State, acting through properly constituted delegates, or it may be gleaned from separate charters, statutes, or other public acts, enacted or granted at different times, extending through long periods of years; some of its provisions being ancient charters or grants of privileges, and others statutes or laws of later date. The former is called a *written* and the latter an *unwritten constitution;* the Constitution of the United States, that of the French Republic, and those of the several States of the Federal Union are examples of the former class, while the English Constitution is an example of the latter.

Constitutions are sometimes said to be *unwritten* when they do not consist of a single formal instrument. In the strict sense of the term, however, DO modern constitution can be said to be unwritten. The several provisions of the instrument may be traced to different sources, widely separated in point of time, but all of them, however they may differ in character and sanction, still exist as written records and, as such, may be examined and consulted. In England, for example, the Magna Charta, a concession wrested from King John in 1215, the Petition of Right,[1] a Parliamentary declaration of the liberties of the English people, assented to by Charles I. in

[1] 3 Charles I., Chap. I (1638).

1628, and the recent Acts of Parliament extending the suffrage, are all provisions of the British Constitution. What are called unwritten constitutions differ from formally enacted instruments chiefly in respect to the manner in which they may be amended; the former class containing no provision for such changes, while the latter usually prescribe a form of procedure for that purpose. The Constitution of the United States, for example, provides for two methods of amendment and can be changed in *no* other way; the English Constitution, on the other hand, can be amended, or modified, by an Act of Parliament, and is so amended in fact whenever an enactment of that body is found to be inconsistent with an existing provision of the Constitution. The most recent instances of such modification are to be found in the statutes extending the right of suffrage.

Unconstitutional Laws.— As the constitution of a State is its fundamental law, it follows that the laws or statutes enacted by its legislature must, in order to be binding, be in strict accordance with its provisions. A law or statute which fails to conform, wholly or in part, to the constitution of the State is called an *unconstitutional law.* If the constitution be written, some method of determining the validity of laws passed by the legislative body is provided in the instrument itself. The Constitution of the United States, and those of the several States of the Union, vest this important power in their highest judicial tribunals, or Supreme Courts. In States having unwritten constitutions it has been seen that enactments not in conformity to their constitutions operate to amend them. If the amendment be not satisfactory to the people of the State, it is within their power, by changing their representatives, to restore the old provision; on the other hand, if an amendment be desired by them, it is equally within their power to bring about such a modification by choosing representatives who will make the popular will in this regard effective.

Conditions of Success.— A constitution, to be successful in its workings, should consist of fundamental rules and should not contain matter coining within the domain of ordinary legislation; it should create the several agencies for the exercise of governmental powers, define the limits within which those powers shall be exercised, and prescribe such limitations upon them as will prevent an undue or tyrannical exercise of authority on the part of any of the agencies so created. The constitution of a State is thus seen to reflect the conditions of its political life at any instant of its existence. As those conditions change, the constitution itself should change, and such an instrument is successful in proportion as it accurately reflects those conditions and conforms to their gradual development. If it can be too easily amended, the temptation is to engraft upon it provisions which should properly be made the subject of ordinary legislation; if it be too difficult of amendment, the tendency of the instrument is to, fall behind the times and to prove inadequate as an instrument of government, or to fall into disrepute and to invite revolutionary changes and so to hinder, rather than assist, the political development of the State to which it belongs.[2]

GOVERNMENTS; CLASSIFICATION OF POWERS

The Government of a State.— The *government* of a State is the visible expression of its sovereignty and the organ through which its sovereign powers are exercised. It

---

[2] Cooley, Constitutional Law, 21 ; Ordronaux, Cons. Leg , 208 ; Pomeroy, Const. Law,. §§ 16-31.

speaks and acts through agents, called *public officers,* whose powers and duties are exercised, in behalf of the community at large, in strict accordance with the constitution and laws.

Classification of Powers.— In order that it may accomplish the purposes for which it is established, a State is endowed with certain rights and powers and becomes charged with corresponding duties and obligations. These powers and duties, which are usually defined and enumerated in the constitution, or fundamental law, are necessarily numerous, but are susceptible of arrangement under the three heads of *legislative, executive,* and *judicial.* The sovereign powers, as thus classified, differ materially in respect to the subjects with which they deal and the agencies through which they are exercised. In point of time the legislative power deals with the future, the executive with the present, and the judicial with the past.

Relations of the Several Departments.— The three branches of governmental power may be dependent on, or independent of, each other; or, as in the United States, may be equal and coordinate, each being supreme within the sphere of operations assigned to it in the Constitution.

The Legislative Power.— The *legislative power* represents, more immediately and directly than any other, the sovereign will of the people. It regulates and determines the personal and property rights of individuals, and secures them against wrongful infringement; it defines public and private wrongs, and endeavors, by the imposition of appropriate penalties, to prevent their occurrence; it creates duties and imposes obligations upon citizens and others residing within its territorial jurisdiction, and, by suitable enactments, secures respect for, and obedience to, its mandates.

The Executive Power.— The *executive power* is charged with the duty of carrying into effect the legislative will, with the maintenance of internal order and external peace, and, when properly declared, with the conduct of war and the direction of military operations, through agents of its own selection. It also represents the State in its foreign relations, superintends the collection and disbursement of the public revenues, and is charged with the general administration of internal affairs.

The Judiciary — Interpretation of Laws.— The *judicial power,* through the agency of *courts of justice,* hears and determines controversies arising under the laws, decides appeals, and, by the execution of the criminal laws, secures to individuals an immunity from injury as to their persons and property. In the United States the power of determining whether a particular enactment is, or is not, in accordance with the Constitution is also vested in the judiciary. As the legislature rarely explains or interprets its own enactments, the duty of interpreting the laws, or of determining their true meaning, is vested in the judiciary, and is exercised in accordance with certain well-defined maxims called *rules of interpretation.*

Classification of Governments.— Governments are classified according to the source of sovereign power, or the manner in which it is exercised in each.

A *monarchy* is a government in which the sovereign powers are concentrated in a single person. An *absolute monarchy,* of which the present government of Russia is an example, is one in which the concentration of sovereign powers is real. A *limited monarchy, is* one in which the royal authority is restricted in its exercise, usually by representative institutions of some kind. These restrictions may be so extensive in character as to reduce the sovereign to the condition of an hereditary executive. This is the case in England.

An *aristocracy* is a government in which the sovereign powers are held to reside in a class. If the ruling class constitutes a small proportion of the population the resulting government is called an *oligarchy.*

A *democracy* is a government in which the sovereign powers are held to-reside in all the people, and are exercised by them directly.

A *republic,* or, as it is sometimes called, a *democratic republic,* is a government in which the sovereign power resides in the people, but is exercised by representatives elected by them for that purpose. The Government of the United States, under the Constitution, and those of the several States of the Union are examples of republics.

CITIZENS

Citizens.— A *citizen* or *subject* of a State is an individual member of the body politic, owing it allegiance and entitled to its protection in person and property. The terms citizen and subject, in a legal sense, have precisely the same meaning. They apply to all the inhabitants of a State, of both sexes, and of all ages and conditions. The term *citizen* is usually applied in States having republican forms of government; the term *subject* in those having monarchical institutions. It is not an essential condition of citizenship that an individual subject or citizen should have any share in the government of a State; indeed, as a matter of fact, the great majority of citizens in most modern States, including women, children of immature age, persons of unsound mind, and those who have committed certain serious crimes, are debarred from participation in the suffrage.

PARTICIPATION OF CITIZENS IN GOVERNMENT; THE SUFFRAGE

Suffrage.— In States having constitutional governments, especially in those having republican institutions, the participation of the citizen in government is secured by the existence of the *right of suffrage.* The extent and character of the suffrage in a particular State is determined by its constitution and laws; in some States, Russia, Persia, and China, for example, it does not exist, in others it is greatly restricted, in none does it include the whole body of citizens, and in all it is subject, as has been seen, to considerable restrictions. Where it exists it is a right conferred by law and is based upon sex, age, intelligence, and, at times, upon the possession of a certain amount of property; it is acquired by naturalization and is forfeited by expatriation, by a failure to conform to its legal conditions, and by participation in certain crimes, especially in those affecting the allegiance of the citizen, such as treason, desertion in time of war, and participation in insurrection or rebellion.[3] In most States a conviction of felony works a forfeiture of the elective franchise.

References.— The oldest and most authoritative text-books oh the Constitution are those of Chancellor Kent and Judge Story. Although written at a relatively early period in our constitutional history, they are still standard authorities. Too much cannot be said of the excellent text-book on Constitutional Law prepared by Professor Cooley of the University of Michigan. The value of this work is due, in part, to the fact that the

---

[3] Cooley, Const. Law, 248, 249-263; Pomeroy, 132, 183. For a general discussion of the rights of citizenship, see the chapter entitled "Personal and Property Rights."

subject is treated from the historical point of view, having been written after nearly a century of governmental experience, and in part to the great importance attached by the author to the theory of limitations. Judge Cooley's book should be studied in connection with his exhaustive work on Constitutional Limitations. The admirable handbook of Judge Paschal is indispensable for general reference, and will be found of great use to the student as a guide in reading and study. Another work of the highest value will be found in the Lectures on Constitutional Law delivered by the late Justice Miller of the Supreme Court to the students of the National Law School in Washington. In connection with the study of the works above referred to, the original sources of authority should be consulted, either in the cases themselves, or in the excellent collection of Cases in Constitutional Law, Parts I, II, and III, which has been compiled and arranged for the use of law students by Professor Thayer of Harvard University. Although not intended for the technical use of law students, You Hoist's Constitutional Law and Bryce's American Commonwealth, together with the histories of Bancroft, Hildreth, Schouler, and Fiske, are indispensable to a proper understanding of our constitutional history. Among other works on the subject of the Constitution may be mentioned those of Pomeroy, Farrar, Black, Flanders, and Hare, which, with the more elementary work of Professor Andrews, may be consulted with advantage. The Digests of Danforth, Clarke, Kinney, Thatcher, and Abbott, Myers' Federal Decisions, and the recent Digests of the Federal Reporter will be found useful for purposes of reference.

Elementary Study.— Of books designed for elementary study, the following may be mentioned as especially worthy of attention. The oldest American textbooks are Hoffman's Legal Outlines, and the Course of

Legal Studies, by the same author, both published in 1836. Bishop's First Book of the Law and Walker's American Law are both excellent works for preliminary study. Robertson's and Smith's Elementary Law and Ewell's Essentials of the Law will also be found extremely useful, especially to students who are attending law lectures. The standard works on the general subject of law are Blackstone (Sharswood's, Cooley's, or Hammond's editions), the great work of Chancellor Kent (Lane's edition), and Walker, whose American Law leaves little to be desired in point of concise and logical treatment and clearness of statement. The presentations of the Common Law from the historical point of view by Crabbe, Brown, and Holmes will serve to make clear much that is obscure in the works of the earlier writers. Shirley's and Lawson's Leading Cases may be read with advantage in connection with any of the text-books above mentioned.

CHAPTER II

THE LEGISLATURE

The legislative Department — Statutes.— It has been seen that the *legislative department* represents and gives statutory expression to the popular will upon all subjects of general interest or public policy. A *law* or *statute,* may therefore be defined as the written will of the legislature expressed, in accordance with the constitution, in the forms necessary to constitute it the law of the State.

Classification of Laws and Statutes.— When we speak of the law of a State, however, the term includes, besides the statutory enactments of the legislature, a large body of unwritten but none the less binding provisions, derived partly from customs, rigidly adhered to for long periods of time, and partly from maxims, presumptions, and judicial decisions which explain and declare parts otherwise obscure or not easily understood. The terms *statutes* and *statutory law* are generally applied to the formal acts of the legislature, in order to distinguish them from the large body of unwritten law to which allusion has been made and which will presently be explained. In point of form, therefore, the law of a State may be classified into —

1. The Written Law, including the constitution of the State and all enactments of the legislature, or law-making power, which have been made in accordance therewith.

Treaties.— The Constitution of the United States also provides that "this Constitution and the laws of the United States which shall be made in pursuance thereof, and all treaties made, or which shall be made, under the authority of the United States, shall be the supreme law of the land; and the judges in every State shall be bound thereby, anything in the constitution or laws of any State to the contrary not with standing."[4] The effect of this provision is to give to *treaties* the binding force of laws. If, therefore, a clause in a treaty conflicts with a prior law, or the reverse, the provision latest in point of time will prevail in every case.

2. The Unwritten Law, including that part of the law of the State which is not expressed in statutory form. Under the head of unwritten law the most important branch is that known as

(a) The Common Law.— This system has controlled and regulated the business and domestic relations of the English people from the earliest times. It contains provisions respecting the course and descent of lands; the nature, extent, and qualification of estates; the acquisition, transfer, and testamentary disposition of real and personal property; the preparation, execution, and interpretation of contracts, together with remedies for public and private wrongs, the preservation of the peace and the punishment of crimes, and the forms of action and procedure in civil and criminal cases. The *Common Law* may therefore be defined as a collection of customs and maxims which derive their sanction and the force of law from immemorial usage, coupled with the express sanction or tacit consent of the legislature. As it is the business of the courts to define these customs, and to declare what are good and what are not, and to apply them in particular cases, their decisions acquire the force and authority of law, and, being recorded in the books of reports, form a part of the common law.

---

[4] Constitution of the United States, Art. VI. Sec. 2.

Application of the Common Law in the Several States.— The common law is the common jurisprudence of the people of the United States, and was brought with them as colonists from England and established here, so far as it was adapted to our institutions and circumstances. To that extent it has been recognized and adopted, as one entire system, by the constitutions of some of the States; and it has been assumed by the courts, or declared by statute, with the like modifications, to be the law of the land in every State. In most of the States, also, the English statutes passed before the emigration of the colonists, being applicable to our situation and in amendment of the common law, constitute a part of our common law.[5]

The Common Law in federal Jurisprudence.— In the jurisprudence of the United States the common law occupies a place of peculiar importance. The Government under the Constitution being one of limited and enumerated powers, and no grant of common-law jurisdiction having been made in that instrument, it has been repeatedly decided that the Federal Government, as such, has no common-law jurisdiction.[6] The operations of its several departments are carried on in obedience to laws passed by Congress in accordance with the Constitution and it is only when it becomes necessary to *interpret* Federal statutes that. the rules of the common law are applied to ascertain and determine their true meaning.[7]

---

[5] Kent's Commentaries, 473; Van Ness *vs.* Pacard, 2 Pet. 144 ; Wheaton *vs.* Peters, 8 Pet. 658, 659; The Lackawanna, 21 Wall. 572.

[6] Wheaton *vs.* Peters, 8 Pet. 658, 659 ; Penn. *vs.* Wheeling Bridge Co., 13 How. 568.

[7] Rice *vs.* Minn. and N. W. R. R. Co., 1 Black. 374; Charles River Bridges. The Warren Bridge, 11 Pet. 545.

Murder, arson, and larceny, for example, being felonies at common law, are punishable, as such, in most of the States; to be offenses against the Federal Government, however, in places over which it exercises exclusive jurisdiction, they must have been made such by statute, and jurisdiction to try and punish them must have been conferred upon some branch of the Federal judiciary. In the absence of such a statute those offenses are not punishable by the courts of the United States.

(6) *Customs and Usages.*— Another form of the unwritten law is that embodied in customs. It has been seen that the Common Law itself is largely customary in character, that is, composed of such usages as have become so fixed in their definition and operation as to have acquired the force of general customs or written laws. Customs vary considerably in respect to their acceptance and binding force, some, by long and uninterrupted usage, having acquired the obligatory force of laws, and others being still in process of formation. Some customs, also, are general in their Operation, while others are limited in their application to particular trades or occupations or to particular localities. To acquire legal sanction and recognition a usage or custom must conform to the following conditions:

1. It must be of long standing; that is, it must have been used so long that "the memory of man runneth not to the contrary."

2. It must have been continuous; that is, it must have existed without interruption.

3. It must have been peaceable and acquiesced in, not subject to contention and dispute.

4. It must be reasonable; or, rather, taken negatively, it must not be unreasonable.

5. It must be certain; that is, it must be generally understood both as to its meaning and application.

6. It must be compulsory. Customs, though established by consent, must, when established, be compulsory, and not left to the opinion of every man whether he will use them or no.

7. Customs must be consistent with each other: one custom cannot be set up in opposition to another.[8]

8. Finally, a custom to be obligatory in character must not contravene a statute; as a statute, having the higher sanction, must prevail in every case of conflict.

(c) *Other Forms of Unwritten Law.*— International Law, that is, the rules regulating the intercourse of sovereign States, and the Admiralty and Maritime Law of the world, are also parts of the unwritten law in the sense that they have no direct legislative sanction.

CLASSIFICATION OF STATUTES

A. By their Relation to the Common Law.— As the common law covers the ordinary field of jurisprudence so completely, it follows that much of the legislation of the several States must have for its purpose to amend or modify its provisions, or to adapt them to the peculiar circumstances of time and place. Indeed, this is the case to such an extent that the classification of statutes is largely based upon their relation to that system of law. Statutes are therefore classified according to their relation to the common law into —

1. *Declaratory Statutes.*— A *declaratory statute* is one enacted with a view to define, or make clear, a provision of the common law, or to explain the meaning

[8] Blackstone's Commentaries ; Int. Sec. 8, p. 77.

of another statute. When they relate to the common law they usually declare what it is and ever has been. The common law being unwritten, the effect of a declaratory statute is to give to one of its provisions the character of written or statutory law.[9]

---

[9] As the Government under the Constitution has no common-law jurisdiction, the cases in which that government finds it necessary to enact statutes declaratory of the common law are extremely rare. In the statute cited below, however. Congress has been compelled to resort to a declaratory statute in order to make clear the law of descents in the District of Columbia, a place within its exclusive jurisdiction. CHAP. 49.—An act declaratory of the law relating to descents and inheritance in the District of Columbia in certain cases. *Be it enacted by the Senate and House of Representatives of the United States of America in Congress assembled.* That the issue of any marriage of colored persons, contracted and entered into according to any custom prevailing at the time in any of the States wherein the same occurred, shall, for all purposes of descent and inheritance and the transmission of both real and personal property within the District of Columbia, be deemed and held to be legitimate, and capable of inheriting and transmitting inheritance, and taking as next of kin and distributee according to law, from and to their parents, or either of them, and from and to those from whom such parents, or either of them, may inherit or transmit inheritance, anything in the laws of such State to the contrary notwithstanding : Provided, That nothing herein shall be construed as implying that any such marriage is not valid, or such issue legitimate for all other purposes. Sec 2. This act shall take effect and be in force from and after its passage.

[9] Approved, February 6, 1879. The following is an

2. *Remedial Statutes — Remedies.*— As all personal and property rights are secured by law, of which they are the offspring, it follows that, when the deprivation of a right is complained of, it is the duty of the State to provide some method for its vindication or restoration. The method thus provided for the legal righting of a particular wrong is called a *remedy*. Many remedies for the wrongs

---

example of a statute declaratory of the meaning of a prior statute: CHAP. 158.—An act to declare the true Intent and meaning of " An act to reimburse the State of Kentucky for moneys expended for the United States in enrolling, subsisting, clothing, supplying arming, equipping, paying and transporting militia forces to aid in suppressing the rebellion," approved June eighth, eighteen hundred and-seventy two. *Be it enacted by the Senate and House of Representatives of the United States of America in Congress assembled.* That in adjusting the claim of the State of Kentucky the term "equipment" shall be construed to mean and include the arming of said forces, as an essential part of their equipments, and the word "supplying" shall include forage and fuel, and tlio transportation shall be embraced, as indicated in the title of the act, it being the intention of Congress in the passage of said act to settle and adjust said accounts.

[9] Approved, March 3, 1881.The following resolution is declaratory only in respect to the will of Congress in relation to its revenue policy : [No. 11.] Joint resolution declaring that a reduction of the tax on distilled spirits is inexpedient.

[9]*Be it resolved by the Senate and House of Representatives of the United States of America in Congress assembled.* That a reduction of the tax on distilled spirits is inexpedient. Approved, February 18, 1878.

of individuals are provided by the common law others are supplied by statute ill the several States. In every civilized State there should be no wrong without an appropriate remedy, and the remedies afforded by its laws should be prompt, adequate, and easy of application. *Remedial statutes,* therefore, are those enacted for the purpose of curing defects in prior statutes, or to modify the common law and adapt its provisions to changes of time and circumstances and to the needs of particular localities.[10] That system being to a great extent customary in character, it follows that, as the views and customs upon which it is based undergo a change, the law which embodies and represents them must undergo a corresponding change. These modifications are brought about in part by judicial decisions, and in part by remedial legislation. When such enactments operate to extend the common law, they are called *enlarging statutes;* when the opposite effect is aimed at they are called *restraining*

---

[10] The following enactment is an example of a remedial statute For a reason already stated (see note 1, page 10), such statutes should be looked for in the legislation of the several States rather than in those of the United States. CHAP. 81.—An act to relieve certain legal disabilities of women. *Be it enacted by the Senate and House of Representatives of the United States of America in Congress assembled.* That any woman who shall have been a member of the bar of the highest court of any State or Territory or of the Supreme Court of the District of Columbia for the space of three years, and shall have maintained a good standing before such court, and who shall be a person of good moral character, shall, on motion, and the production of such record, be admitted to practice before the Supreme Court of the United States.

[10] Approved, February 15, 1879.

statutes. B. By their Form.— Statutes are classified according to their form into —

1. *Affirmative or Permissive Statutes.*— An *affirmative* or *permissive* statute is one enacted in affirmative terms which authorizes certain acts or things to be done, without commanding them. When the provisions of such an enactment have been accepted or complied with by an individual, the rights acquired are protected and guaranteed by the terms of the statute.[11]

---

[11] The following are examples of affirmative statutes :[No. 35] Joint resolution authorizing the Secretary of War to turn over to the governor of Alabama such tents, poles and pins as he may require for the use of the volunteers of the State at their summer encampment. *Resolved by the Senate and House of Representatives of the United States of America in Congress assembled.* That the Secretary of War be and he is hereby directed to turn over to the governor of Alabama such tents, poles and pins as he may require for the use of the volunteers of said State at their summer encampment for eighteen hundred and seventy-eight, providing the same can be spared without detriment to the public service. The Secretary of War shall take a good and sufficient bond for the return of such property in good condition after such encampment. Approved, June 18, 1878. CHAP. 314.—An act for the relief of settlers on the public lands. *Be it enacted by the Senate and House of Representatives of the United States of America in Congress assembled.* That the provisions of an act of Congress, approved March third, eighteen hundred and seventy-seven, entitled " An act for the relief of settlers on the public lands ", are hereby extended to those settlers whose crops were destroyed or seriously injured by the grasshoppers during the year eighteen hundred and seventy-six. Approved, June 19, 1878.

2. *Negative Statutes.*— A *negative statute* is one stated in negative terms which forbids a thing to be done. The effect of these statutes upon the common law is not the same. An affirmative statute does not, in general, have the effect of setting aside or repealing the corresponding provisions of the common law. A negative statute usually has such a result, and so controls the common law that it has no effect in opposition to the statute. For example, a statute authorizing the registration of wills, and giving properly authenticated copies a particular evidential value, would not operate to invalidate a will not so registered. A statute forbidding leases of real estate for a longer term than twenty-one years is negative in character and would operate to destroy the validity of a common-law lease for a longer period of time.[12]

---

[12] The following are examples of negative statutes : CHAP. 10.—An act relating to the disqualification of registers and receivers of the United States land offices, and making provision in case of such disqualification. *Be it enacted by the Senate and House of Representatives of the United States of America in Congress assembled.* That 110 register or receiver shall receive evidence in, hear or determine any cause pending in any district land office in which cause lie is interested directly or indirectly, or has been of counsel, or where he is related to any of the parties in interest by consanguinity or affinity within the fourth degree, computing by the rules adopted by the common law. Sec 2. That it shall be the duty of every register or receiver so disqualified to report the fact of his disqualification to the Commissioner of the General Land Office, as soon as he shall ascertain it, and before the hearing of such cause, who thereupon, with the approval of the Secretary of the Interior, shall designate some other register, receiver, or special agent of the Land Department

3. *Penal Statutes.— Penal statutes* are those which prohibit an act and impose a penalty, or forfeiture, for its occurrence. The penalty may be in the nature of imprisonment or corporal punishment, or may be pecuniary in character and in the nature of a fine or forfeiture. In the latter case, the forfeiture is generally recoverable by the State, or by the party injured, or by an informer. An action for the recovery of a penalty or forfeiture is called a *penal action;* where a part of the forfeiture is awarded to the State and a part to the informer it is called a *qui tam action.*[13]

---

to act in the place of the disqualified officer, and the same authority is conferred on the officer so designated which such register or receiver would otherwise have possessed to act in such case. Approved, January 11, 1894. CHAP. 329.—An act to prevent the recording of subdivisions of land in the District of Columbia in the office of the recorder of deeds. *Be it enacted by the Senate and House of Representatives of the United States of America in Congress assembled.* That hereafter it shall not be lawful for any person or persons to record any map or plat of the subdivision of land in the District of Columbia in the office of the recorder of deeds for said District, whether such map or plat be attached to a deed or other document or is offered separately for record. Approved, August 24, 1894

[13] The following are examples of penal statutes : CHAP. 138.—An act relating to the punishment of the crime of manslaughter. *Be it enacted by the Senate and House of Representatives of the United States of America in Congress assembled.* That whoever shall herreafter be convicted of manslaughter, in any court of the United States, in any State or Territory, including the District of Columbia, shall be imprisoned not exceeding ten years,

and fined not exceeding one thousand dollars : *Provided,* That this act shall not affect or apply to any prosecution now pending, or the prosecution of any offense already committed. SEC. 3. That all acts or parts of acts inconsistent with this act are hereby repealed: *Provided,* That said acts shall remain in force for the punishment of all persons who have heretofore committed the crime of manslaughter." Approved, March 3, 1875. It will be observed that the above statute contains no definition of the crime of manslaughter: for such a definition the common law will have to be consulted and the offense made punishable in the statute cited in that known as manslaughter at common law. CHAP. 103.—An act establishing post roads and for other purposes. *Be it enacted,* etc., etc.

* * * * * * * * *

SEC. 5. That it shall be lawful to transmit through the mail, free of postage, any letters, packages, or other matters relating exclusively to the business of the Government of the United States: *Provided,* That every such letter or package to entitle it to pass free shall bear over the words " Official business " an endorsement showing also the name of the Department, and, if from a bureau or office, the names of the Department and bureau or office, as the case may be, whence transmitted. And if any person shall make use of any such official envelope to avoid the payment of postage on his private letter, package, or other matter in the mail, the person so offending shall be deemed guilty of a misdemeanor, and subject to a fine of three hundred dollars, to be prosecuted in any court of competent jurisdiction.

* * * * * * * * * *

Approved, March 3, 1877.

C. By their Scope.— Statutes are again classified in reference to their scope, or extent of operation, into public and private statutes.

1. *Public Statutes.*— A *public statute* is one which operates uniformly throughout the entire territory of a State, and applies to all citizens or other persons within its jurisdiction.

3. *Private or Local Statutes.*— A *private* or *local statute* is one which applies to an individual, or to a limited class of individuals, to private concerns, or to a particular locality, and does not have uniform or general operation throughout the entire jurisdiction.[14]

The distinction between *public and private statutes* has chiefly to do with their use in pleading in actions at law. As courts take judicial notice of the public statutes of the State in which they sit, neither the contents nor the substance of such a statute need be set forth or recited in a pleading. This is not the case, however, with private statutes, and such parts of them as are material to an action must be stated in the pleadings. In point of binding force both forms are of equal value. The rule above stated has

---

[14] The following is an example of a private statute : CHAP. 157.—An act authorizing Commander C. H. Davis, United States Navy, to accept a decoration from the King of Spain. *Be it enacted by the Senate and House of Representatives of the United States of America in Congress assembled.* That Commander C. H. Davis, of the United States Navy, be, and he is hereby, authorized to accept the decoration of " Comandador de numero de la Real Orden de Isabel la Catolica " conferred upon him by the King of Spain in recognition of his services while detailed to attend the Infanta of Spain during her visit to this country.' Approved, July 83, 1894.

been materially changed in most of the States, the common-law rule having been so modified, by statute, as to permit the pleading of a private statute by a mere reference to its title and the date of its passage.

D. Classification by Nature of Compliance.—Statutes are again classified, in accordance with the kind and amount of compliance required, into mandatory, directory, and prohibitory statutes.

1. A *Mandatory* or *Imperative Statute* is one framed in specific language and requiring a thing to be done in exact compliance with its provisions; the requirements of such an enactment must be strictly complied with by those charged with its execution, or whose conduct is to be regulated by it, and cannot be departed from in any respect.[15]

---

[15] The following are examples of mandatory statutes : CHAP. 287.--An act fixing the salaries of the several judges of the United States district courts at five thousand dollars per annum. *Be it enacted by the Senate and House of Representatives of the. United States of America in Congress assembled.* That the salaries of the several judges of the district courts of the United States shall hereafter be at the rate of five thousand dollars per annum. Approved, February 24, 1891. CHAP. 550.—An act to revise the wages of certain employees in the Government Printing Office. *Be it enacted by the Senate and House of Representatives of the United Stales of America in Congress assembled,* That the pay of all the employees of the Government Printing Office engaged on night work (between the hours of five o'clock postmeridian and eight o'clock antemeridian) shall be twenty per centum in addition to the amount paid for day labor. SEC. 2. That all acts and parts of acts conflicting herewith are hereby repealed. Approved, March 3, 1891.

2. A *Directory Statute* is one enjoining a thing to be done, but leaving to the executive some discretion as to the time or method of compliance.[16]

3. A *Prohibitory Statute* is one both negative and mandatory in character and which forbids an act or thing to be done in positive terms. If the act be one injurious to society or to individuals, what is called a *penal clause* is often annexed, and the act becomes penal, if not criminal, in character; if the thing done be not injurious to others, the statute makes it void, and no legal rights can accrue upon its performance.[17]

---

[16] The following is an example of a directory statute : CHAP. 688.—An act to provide for the examination and survey of a breakwater to form a harbor of safety and refuge in Lynnhaven Bay, near Cape Henry, at the foot of Chesapeake Bay, Virginia. *Be it enacted by the Senate and House of Representatives of the United States of America in Congress assembled,* That the Secretary of War is hereby directed to cause examination and survey to be made, and the estimated cost of improvement to be estimated for a breakwater to form a harbor of safety and refuge in Lynnhaven Bay, near Cape Henry, at the foot of Chesapeake Bay, Virginia. Approved, March 3, 1891.

[17] The following is an example of a prohibitory statute. CHAP. 385.—An act to prohibit the granting of liquor licenses within one mile of the Soldiers' Home. *Be it enacted by the Senate and House of Representatives of the United States of America in Congress assembled.* That *on* and after the passage of this act no license for the sale of Intoxicating liquor at any place within one mile of the Soldiers' Home property in the District of Columbia shall be granted. Approved, February 28, 1891.

E. Classification by Continuity of Operation.— Statutes are also divided according to their continuity of operation into —

1. *Permanent Statutes.*— These are to remain in force without limitation as to time. Permanent provisions may be incorporated in statutes otherwise temporary in character if preceded by the words " hereafter," " from and after the passage of this act," or words of like import.[18]

---

[18] The following are examples of permanent statutes; it will be observed that the first statute cited is both prohibitory and penal in character, while the second conforms to the definition of a private or local statute. Both are examples of statutes which are prospective in their operation. CHAP, 117.—An act to prohibit the sale of tobacco to minors under sixteen years of age in the District of Columbia. *Be it enacted by the Senate and House of Representatives of the United States of America in Congress assembled.* That hereafter no person in the District of Columbia shall sell, give, or furnish any cigar, cigarette, or tobacco in any of its forms to any minor under sixteen years of age; and for each and every violation of this section the offender shall, on conviction, be fined not less than two dollars nor more than ten dollars, or be imprisoned for not less than five days nor more than twenty days. Approved, February 7, 1891. CHAP. 79.—An act authorizing the Secretary of War to grant to tlie trustees of the Maine Insane Asylum, Augusta, Maine, a license to construct a roadway through the United States arsenal grounds at Augusta, Maine, and allow the same to be used by the public. *Be it enacted by the Senate and House of Representatives of the United States of America in Congress assembled.* That the Secretary of War be, and he hereby is, authorized to grant to the trustees of the Maine Insane Asylum, Augusta,

2. *Temporary Statutes* are those which are limited in duration or application by terms of limitation contained in the statute itself. The annual appropriation bills of Congress and those of the legislatures of the several States are examples of temporary enactments.

3. *Prospective Statutes* are those which operate in the future and deal with or regulate events occurring subsequent to their enactment.

4. *Retrospective Statutes* are those which relate to past events.[19] Such statutes are exceptional and are

---

Maine, a license to construct a roadway through the United States arsenal grounds in Augusta, Maine, for driving purposes, to be used by the public in traveling to and from the Insane Asylum, but not for purposes of traffic or teaming. The said license shall be upon such terms and conditions as the Secretary of War may prescribe, and may be revoked by him whenever in his opinion it is desirable to do so. Approved, January 19, 1891.

[19] The following are examples of retrospective statutes : CHAP. 327.—An act to legalize the collection of head-moneys already paid. *Be it enacted by the Senate and House of Representatives of the United States of America in Congress assembled.* That the acts of every State and municipal officer or corporation of the several States of the United States in the collection of head-moneys prior to the first day of January, eighteen hundred and seventy-seven, from the master, consignee, or owner of any vessel bringing passengers to the United States from a foreign port, pursuant to the then existing laws of the several States, shall be valid, and no action shall be maintained against any such State or municipal officer or corporation for the recovery of any moneys so paid or collected prior to said date. Approved, June 19, 1878. February 15,

disfavored as tending to impair rights already vested. When they relate to criminal matters, they are called *ex post facto* laws and, as such, are forbidden in the Constitution. By an *ex post facto* law is meant one which imposes a punishment for an act; which was not punishable at the time of, its commission; or imposes punishment additional to that then prescribed; or changes the rules of evidence in such a way that less or different testimony is sufficient to convict than was then required. Another class of retrospective statutes — those impairing the obligation of contracts — is expressly forbidden, in the Constitution, to be passed by the legislatures of the several States. There are some instances, however, in which an appropriate remedy can only be applied by the passage of a retroactive law in some form. To this class belong what are called indemnity laws, together with statutes relating to remedies and forms of procedure, and statutes affecting the rules of evidence in a manner favorable to an accused person. A law permitting a

---

1881.—CHAP. 47.—An act to restore the lands included in the Fort Reading and Fort Crook military reservations, in the State of California, to the public domain, and for other purposes. *Be it enacted by the Senate and House of Representatives of the United States of America in Congress assembled.* That the lands included in the Fort Reading military reservation and in the Port Crook military reservation in the State of California are hereby restored to the public domain. SEC. 2. That all patents heretofore issued to any lands within the Port Reading military reservation and Fort Crook military reservation are hereby confirmed. SEC 3. That the rights of all settlers on said reservations, to acquire title under the homestead and preemption laws, are hereby recognized and affirmed to the extent such settlers would have acquired by settling on public lands. Approved, February 15, 1881.

prisoner to testify in his own behalf, or one giving a more adequate remedy, or one more easily applied, is an example of a retrospective statute which is said to have beneficial operation.

STATUTES OF LIMITATION

An important class of statutes remains to be described called statutes of limitation.

Statutes of Limitation.— A *statute of limitation* is an enactment depriving an individual of the benefit of a statutory or common-law remedy after a lapse of time sufficient to create the presumption that a particular obligation has been satisfied.[20] Two theories have been

---

[20] The following are examples of statutes of limitation; the first relates to a particular class of civil actions, the second to criminal prosecutions. CHAP. 186.—An act to authorize suits for damages where death results from the wrongful act or neglect of any person or corporation in the District of Columbia. *Be it enacted by the Senate and House of Representatives of the United States of America in Congress assembled,* That whenever, by an injury done or happening within the limits of the District of Columbia, the death of a person shall be caused by the wrongful act, neglect, or default of any person or corporation, and the act, neglect, or default is such AS would, if death had not ensued, have entitled the party injured, or, if the person injured be a married woman, have entitled her husband, either separately or by joining with the wife, to maintain an action and recover damages, the person who or corporation which would have been liable if death had not ensued shall be liable to an action for damages for such death, notwithstanding the death of the person injured, even though the death shall have been

advanced to account for their existence: one that they are statutes of repose, enacted for the purpose of discouraging

---

caused under circumstances which constitute a felony: and such damages shall be assessed with reference to the injury resulting from such act. neglect, or default causing such death, to the widow and next of kin of such deceased person. *Provided,* That in no case shall the recovery under this act exceed the sum of ten thousand dollars. *And provided further.* That no action shall be maintained under this act in any case when the party injured by such wrongful act, neglect, or default has recovered damages therefor during the life of such party. Sac. 2. That every such action shall be brought by and in the name of the personal representative of such deceased person, and within one year after the death of the party Injured. SEC. 3. That the damages recovered in such action shall not be appropriated to the payment of the debts or liabilities of such deceased person, but shall inure to the benefit of his or her family, and be distributed according to the provisions of the statute of distributions in force in the said District of Columbia. Approved, February 17, 1885. CHAP. 56.—An act to amend section 10)4 of the Revised Statutes relating to limitations in criminal cases. *Be it enacted by the Senate and House of Representatives of the United States of America in Congress assembled,* That section one thousand and forty-four of the Revised Statutes of the United States be amended so as to read as follows: No person shall be prosecuted, tried, or punished for any offense, not capital, except as provided in section one thousand and forty-six, unless the indictment is found, or the Information is instituted, within three years next after such offense shall have been committed. But this act shall not have effect to authorize the prosecution, trial, or punishment for any offense barred by the provisions of existing laws. Approved, April 13, 1876.

litigation over what are known in law as stale claims; the other, based upon the self-interest of the individual, takes the view that a creditor will not rest upon a just claim, but will within a reasonable time enforce it against his debtor. When a reasonable time has elapsed, therefore, since a particular cause of action accrued, the original claim is: presumed to have been adjusted, or the obligation upon which it was based has been satisfied or has otherwise ceased to exist.

Limitations at Common Law.— At the common law there was a presumption that a debt, evidenced by a bond, or other instrument under seal, had *been* paid after the expiration of twenty years from its date of execution. In the same way, adverse possession and enjoyment of an estate for the same period created a similar presumption of title in behalf of the adverse occupant. These were presumptions, however, not limitations, and could be rebutted by the testimony of witnesses. The doctrine of limitations was of slow growth in England, and it was not until the year 1623 that the first statute of limitations was passed by Parliament to operate as a bar to the prosecution of actions at common law. This statute was in force in the American colonies prior to the Revolution, and has been made the basis of similar enactments in several of the States of the Federal Union.

Application to Civil and Criminal Cases.— Limitations upon actions, as above described, are always statutory in character and apply in criminal as well as civil actions, except in capital cases — murder, and desertion in time of war, for example — in which, from the peculiar character of the offense, no limitation is imposed, and prosecution may be brought whenever the offender comes within the proper jurisdiction. Statutes of limitation apply to remedies, which they destroy or render unavailable to one in whose favor a cause of action has accrued; as a rule, they apply to individuals only and not to the State which enacts them. The lapse of time that shall constitute a limitation in any case, civil or criminal, is determined by the law of the State where the action is brought, and varies in the several States from two to six years in civil cases and from sixty days to five years in criminal cases. When the conditions prescribed in the statute have been complied with the statute is said to begin to run, and when the time named therein has elapsed the action is forever barred.

Suspension of Operation.— The running of a statute is suspended by the existence of certain conditions, or by the performance of certain acts by a party, the suspension continuing during the period of their existence. The principal of these causes of suspension are, in civil actions, the existence of war, the minority of a party, absence from the jurisdiction in certain cases, and, in general, any act or admission of a party defendant which recognizes the existence of the obligation, or renews it or extends its operation. The death of a party, in certain personal actions, operates as a bar to their further prosecution. Absence from the jurisdiction and fraudulent evasion or concealment suspend the operation of a statute, during their continuance, in criminal cases. When the obstacle ceases to exist, in any case, the statute begins to run, and the burden of proof that its operation has been suspended lies upon the party who alleges it in pleading.

When Operative.— It is a well-settled rule that a statute of limitation does not begin to run until a particular cause of action has accrued. It may therefore be said, in general, that in actions of contract the cause of action accrues when there is a breach of contract; in cases of tort, the statute begins to run from the date of the tort. Where a demand is necessary to perfect a right of action, the statute runs from the date of the demand, as in case of a note payable on demand. Where money is payable in installments, the statute applies, as to each installment, from the failure of the debtor to pay it. Where a contract takes effect upon some contingency or upon the happening of some event, the statute runs from the performance the condition or the occurrence of the contingency.

Limitations in Equity.— Courts of equity, though not within the terms the statute, have nevertheless uniformly conformed to its spirit, and have, l a general rule, been governed by its provisions, unless special circumstances of fraud or the like require, in the interests of justice, that they should be disregarded. In some cases when claims are not barred by the statute, courts of equity will refuse to interfere on the ground of public policy and the difficulty of doing entire justice between the parties when the original transaction may have become obscure by the lapse of time and the evidence lost.

ENACTMENT OF STATUTES BY LEGISLATIVE BODIES

Bills — Introduction; Amendments.— Subjects of legislation are usually ought to the attention of legislative bodies in the form of bills introduced individual members. They retain this character during all of the subsequent stages of their progress through the different branches of the legislature. Bills relating to any subject of public interest or policy may be introduced by any member, and in either house, unless a constitutional provision requires bills of a particular character to be introduced in a particular house. This principle is illustrated by what are called "revenue bills," which, by the Federal Constitution,[21] must originate in the House of

---

[21] Constitution of the United States, Sec. VII. Art. 1.

Representatives. The details of passage, reference to committees, and the like, are regulated by all legislative bodies as incidents of their procedure. A bill may be amended or rejected in either house, and its consideration may be indefinitely postponed in either branch of the legislature.

Passage; Conference.— When a bill has passed the house in which it was introduced it is signed by the presiding officer and transmitted to the other branch of the legislature. If it be not passed by the second house in the same form in which it was received, it is returned to the house in which it originated, where the amendments that have been added, are concurred in or rejected. In the event of non-concurrence the bill is referred to a committee of conference, composed of members representing both houses. If an agreement is reached by this committee, a report is submitted to each house by its conferees, the adoption of which perfects the measure so far as the legislature is concerned. When a bill has passed both houses, and has been signed by their presiding officers, it is submitted to the executive for examination.

Approval by Executive; Veto Power.— If the measure receives executive approval, he makes it operative by affixing his signature; or he may, by an exercise of the *veto power,*[22] return it to the house in which it originated with a message of disapproval. This exercise of power on the part of the executive is strictly legislative in character, and his reasons for disapproval may be such as seem to him wise or expedient. The vote necessary to pass a bill over a qualified veto is usually stated explicitly in the constitution of the State. While in the hands of the executive a bill may be recalled, by the joint action of both houses, with a view to its

[22] *Ibid.,* Art. 2.

reconsideration or correction. The return of the measure, however, is a matter of executive discretion.

When Operative.— A bill becomes a law and begins to operate as such upon receiving the executive approval, unless it is to become effective on a day named in the future.[23] If a bill be returned by the executive without approval and be passed over his veto, it becomes operative from the date of its final passage; if it be retained by the executive for a longer period than is allowed in the constitution, it becomes a law on the expiration of the period fixed for such purpose in that instrument.

ESSENTIAL PARTS OF A STATUTE

Essential Parts.— In the matter of form and verbiage, legislative bodies are guided by the provisions of their respective constitutions, which must be complied with in all respects. A statute consists of the following essential parts:

I. *The Title.*— This indicates the subject of the enactment, the scope of its operation, and serves to identify it in pleadings in cases arising under it in courts of justice. A brief and concise statement, to indicate the nature and purpose of the act, is all that is usually regarded as necessary.

II. *The Preamble.*— This term refers to the introductory words or phrases of a statute which recite the intention of the legislature in its enactment. The particular wrong which the statute is to remedy is sometimes set forth in the preamble, which in most cases begins with the word "whereas." The title and preamble are not, in strictness, parts of the statute, and for this reason are

[23] *Ibid.*, Art. 2.

useful only as showing its subject and the intention of the legislature in its enactment.

III. *The Enacting Clause.*— This phrase is essential to the validity of a statute, as it gives it the binding force of law. Its form is either prescribed in the constitution, or is made the subject of directory legislation. The following examples are cited as indicating their general character: "Be it enacted by the general assembly of the State of Indiana;" "The people of the State of Nevada, represented in senate and assembly, do enact;" "Be it enacted by the Senate and House of Representatives of the United States of America in Congress assembled," etc. After the enacting clause follow the several paragraphs or provisions of the statute, arranged in logical sequence so as to be easily understood. The paragraphs, or sections, are numbered serial order; if they are numerous, they are arranged in groups or subdivisions, under appropriate headings.[24]

---

[24] The following statute illustrates the form of a legislative enactment: [No.9.] Joint resolution authorizing the Secretary of War to expend a sum of money heretofore : appropriated for the erection of a storehouse and depot building at the city of Omaha, in the-State of Nebraska. Whereas, by act of Congress approved June twenty-third, eighteen hundred and seventy-nine, the sum of thirty thousand dollars was appropriated for the purpose of erecting a military storehouse and depot building at the city of Omaha, in the State of Nebraska, providing that no part of said sum should be expended for the purchase of ground: and Whereas the citizens of said city of Omaha have donated to the Government of the United States five acres of land, the title having been approved by the Attorney-General, Whereon said building or buildings are to be erected; and Whereas the legislature of the State of

IV. *The Repealing Clause.*— If it be the purpose of the enactment to repeal or replace a prior enactment, a final clause is inserted, called, the repealing clause, the effect of which is to repeal, or deprive of legal sanction, all laws or parts of laws in conflict therewith. That part of the enactment between the enacting and repealing clauses is called the " purview " of the statute; and when a thing is said to come within the purview of a statute, it is held to be affected by it, or to come within the field or scope of Site operation. Each separate statute is usually entitled a chapter, and is given a serial number in the volumes containing the legislation of a particular session, or legislative year. An excepting clause in a statute is called a proviso, and begins with the words *"provided that* "; if there is more than one, the second begins with *provided also* "; the third *"and provided also*," or " *provided further.* "

Field of Operation — Binding Force.— Subject to a few exceptions, to be explained hereafter, statutes have no

---

Nebraska does not convene until January, eighteen hundred and eighty-one, so as to fulfill the requirements of section three hundred and fifty-five of the Revised Statutes touching the expenditure of said money; and Whereas the necessities of the government demand the immediate erection of said building or buildings; Therefore, *Resolved by the Senate and House of Representatives of the United States of America in Congress assembled,* That the Secretary of War be. and is hereby, empowered and directed to expend the said sum of thirty thousand dollars, or so much thereof as may be necessary, for the erection of said building or buildings. That all acts or parts of acts now in force which are inconsistent with the provisions of this act be, and the same are hereby, repealed. Approved, February 5, 1880.

extra-territorial effect; within the territory and jurisdiction of the State in whose name they are enacted, however, they are supreme, when operating within the limits prescribed in the constitution, and regulate the conduct of all persons within such territorial Jurisdiction.

PUBLICATION OF LAWS

Publication — Laws of the United States.— As all persons are presumed to know the law, it is not only necessary that they be enacted by the supreme legislative power, but that they be published and thus made known to the people whose conduct is to be regulated by them. The methods in which this is done may vary, but, whatever mode is adopted, it should be such as to afford a reasonable opportunity to all persons to become familiar with their provisions as soon after their enactment as possible. The laws of each Congress, covering a period of two years, are published in a volume entitled " Statutes at Large." Each volume bears a serial number, and contains all the acts and resolutions which became laws during the existence of the Congress whose number it bears. The acts and resolves of the legislatures of the several States are similarly published, usually in annual volumes, so entitled as to show their authority and source, and the year of their enactment.

Digests — Revised Statutes.— As the Federal Government and the governments of some of the older States have been in operation for more than a century, their legislation has become so voluminous, in many cases, as to make it necessary to authorize the preparation and publication of *digests,* or *compilations,* of their legislation extending over long periods of years. These volumes are intended to contain all permanent enactments that were passed during the periods to which they relate which are thus re-enacted or given a special legislative sanction. The Revised Statutes of the United States, enacted on December 1, 1873, and finally published m its present form in 1878, contains all of the permanent legislation of Congress which was enacted between 1789 and 1873, when the work of revision was authorized. Similar compilations have been prepared in many of the States; in some a like purpose has been accomplished by the preparation of civil and criminal codes and codes of procedure.[25]

---

[25] The following list contains the latest editions of the revised or compiled statutes of the several States and Territories :

Alabama...... Revised Code, 1887, 2 vols.

Arizona ... .. Compiled Laws, 1887, 1 vol.

Arkansas....... Mansfield's Digest of Statutes, 1884,1 vol. Oliphant's Dig., 1898, 2 v. California ..... Deering's Annotated Statutes. 1893, 6 vols.

Colorado .. ....General Statutes, 1890, 2 vols.

Connecticut ...Revised Statutes, 1887, 1 vol.

Dakota Ter. .. .Compiled Laws, 1887, 1 vol.

Delaware .... .Revised Code, 1893, 1 vol.

Dist. Columbia.. Revised Statutes of the United States relating to the District of Columbia, 1 vol.

Florida.. ...... Revised Statutes, 1892, 1 vol.

Georgia .... Code of Georgia, 188-3, I vol.

Idaho... ....Revised Laws, 2 vols.

Illinois..........Revised Statutes, 1893,1 vol.

Indiana..... .... Revised Statutes, 1894, 3 vols.

Iowa............Mc Clain's Annotated Statutes, 1893, 3 vols.

Kansas……General Statutes, 1889, 2 vols.

Kentucky…. General Statutes, 1984, 1 vol.

Louisiana….Revised Laws, 1884, 1 vol.

Maine…. Revised Statutes, 1883, 1 vol.

Maryland…. Maryland Code, 1888, 4 vol.

Massachusetts…. Revised Statutes, 1888, 2 vol.

Michigan….Howell's Annotated Statutes, 1890, 3 vol.

Minnesota......Minnesota Statutes, 1894, 2 vols.

Mississippi. .. Revised Code, 1893, 1 vol.

Missouri .... Missouri Statutes, 1889, 2 vols.

Montana........ Compiled Statutes, 1887, 1 vol.

Nebraska...... Revised Statutes, 1893, 1 vol.

Nevada .. .. .General Statutes, 1885, 1 vol.

Nebraska…. Revised Statutes, 1893, 1 vol.

Nevada…. General Statutes, 1885, 1 vol.

New Hampshire Public Statutes, 1891, 1 vol.

New Jersey. . .Revised Statutes, 1887, 2 vols.

New Mexico.... Compiled Laws, 1884, 1 vol.

New York .. ..Revised Statutes, 1892, 6 vols.

North Carolina. North Carolina Code, 188S, 2 vols.

North Dakota.. Levisee's Revised Code, 1885, 2 v.

Ohio .... Giauque's Revised Statutes, 1894, 3 vols.

REPEAL AND AMENDMENT OF STATUTES

Amendments.— Statutes once enacted may be amended by the same or a succeeding legislature, and may be repealed by the same authority.

An *amendatory statute* is one which modifies the terms of a prior enactment, with a view to cure its defects, or to extend or restrict the scope of its operation. They usually refer, by title and date, to the statute to be amended, and the change contemplated should be fully set

---

Oklahoma..... .Territorial Statutes, 1893 1 vol.

Oregon. ... .Hill's Code, 1891, 2 vols.

Pennsylvania... Purdon's Digest of Laws l894, 2 v.

Rhode Island. Revised Statutes, 1882, 1 vol.

South Carolina. Revised Statutes. 1893 8 vols.

South Dakota … .Levisee's Revised Code, 1885 2 v.

Tennessee ..... .Code of Laws, 1893 2 vols.

Texas ....Civil Statutes, 1894, 1 vol.

Criminal Statutes. 1894. 1 vol.

Utah........... Compiled Laws, 1888, 2 vols.

Vermont........ Revised Statutes. 1880, 1 vol.

Virginia ...... .Revised Code, 1887, 1 vol.

Washington .... General Statutes and Codes, 1891, 2 vols.

West Virginia . .Warth's Code, 1891, 1 vol.

Wisconsin . ....Sandborn and Berryman's Annotated Revised Statutes, 18S9, 2 v

Wyoming .... Compiled Laws, 1887, 1 vol.

forth in the amendatory statute. This may be accomplished by striking out words or clauses, and substituting therefor the amendatory matter; or the amending act may declare that the preceding statute shall be "amended to read as follows," substituting therefor the corresponding clauses of the new or amendatory matter. In this case it has been held that, when the same clauses appear in the old and new statutes, the old clauses shall not be considered as repealed and re-enacted, but as having been in force from the date of the original enactment.[26]

Express Repeals.— *Repealing statutes* are those which nullify, wholly or in part, preceding statutes, or provisions of the common law.[27] They are generally

---

[26] The following are illustrations of amendatory statutes (see also p. 17, note I): CHAP 37 —An act to amend an act entitled " An act making appropriations for sundry civil expenses of the government for the fiscal year ending June thirtieth, eighteen hundred and seventy-nine, and for other purposes," approved June twentieth, eighteen hundred and seventy-eight. *Be it enacted by the Senate and Souse of Representatives of the United Slates of America in Congress assembled,* That the act entitled "An act making appropriations for sundry civil expenses of the government for the fiscal year ending June thirtieth, eighteen hundred and seventy-nine, and for other purposes," approved June twentieth, eighteen hundred and seventy-eight, be, and the same is hereby, amended by adding to the clause of said act relating to the binding of books for the departments of the government, after the words " Congressional Library," the following words: "nor to the Library of the Surgeon-General's Office." Approved, January 27, 1879.

[27] The following is an example of a repealing statute : CHAP. 34.—An act to repeal section twelve hundred and

enacted with a view to such repeal, and are framed in language calculated to produce that effect. A statute so nullified or deprived of its legal sanction is said to be *expressly* repealed. "When enacted with a view to modify the common law the old rule was that the common-law provision remained in abeyance during the life of the repealing statute, but was revived by its repeal. A contrary rule now prevails in most of the States, and the rule has never applied to the repeal legislation of Congress, as the Federal Government, as such, has never had what is known as common-law jurisdiction.

Repeals by Implication.— In some instances legislative enactments outline a course of action which is inconsistent with existing law, in which event they operate to supersede or replace such provisions of the old law as are repugnant to the new enactment, and are then said to repeal them *by implication.*[28] Repeals by implication, however, are not favored by the courts. It must be presumed that a given law was enacted by the legislature with accurate knowledge, *on* its part, of the language and scope of the previous legislation on the same subject. If there was an intention to repeal or modify the prior statute, it must be presumed that direct terms for that purpose would have been employed. Ill the absence of direct words of repeal, it is the duty of the courts to give effect to the prior statute if it is possible to do so. Unless the

---

thirty-three of the Revised Statutes relating to company cookes in the Army. *Be it enacted by the Senate and House of Representatives of the United States of America in Congress assembled.* That section twelve hundred and thirty-three of the Revised Statutes be, and the same is hereby, repealed. Approved, January 39, 1879.

[28] United States vs. Tynen, 11 Wall., 88; Red Rock vs. Henry, 106 U.S., 596.

repugnancy between the subsequent and prior statutes is so absolute and palpable as to be recognized at once, without the aid of ingenious argument, it must be assumed that the legislature intended both statutes to stand.[29]

INTERPRETATION AND CONSTRUCTION OF STATUTE

Interpretation and Construction.— The terms "interpretation" and "construction" are not synonymous. It is the province of interpretation to ascertain the true meaning of a word or clause in a statute by a reference to the context, or by the application of certain principles deduced from experience called *rules of interpretation.* It is the province of construction to determine whether a statute does or does not apply to a case arising under it. This is done by comparison with earlier legislation upon the same subject, or with other sources of authority. Interpretation is therefore restricted in its operation to the text of the statute, and ceases, as such, where construction begins. Interpretation relates to the words and clauses of a statute, construction to their effects, and is resorted to with a view to determine whether a particular case falls within its scope.

RULES OF INTERPRETATION

1. General Rule.— In the interpretation and construction of statutes, "courts are to give the words their ordinary meaning; to presume that they were used, by the legislature, in their ordinary sense; neither to enlarge nor

---

[29] U. S. Vs. Cook Co. Nat., Bank, 4 Biss 60; Bishop on the Written Laws, 655; Bruce vs. Schuyler, 4 Gilman (III.), 221; 7 Myers Fed. Dec., § 2984.

unduly restrict their signification, and, if possible, give every word its full meaning, and, when that is impossible, to give such construction as best to carry out the intention of the legislature as gathered from the whole act."

2. Meanings of Words.— The words and clauses of a statute are to be given the meaning assigned them in common use at the date of its enactment; and the ordinary rules of grammar are to prevail in determining the relations of the several parts, or clauses, of a paragraph or sentence. Until relatively recent times punctuation played but little part in the interpretation of statutes. This for the reason that the enactments of a legislative body, being read orally while under consideration, address themselves to the ear rather than the eye, in legislation; the punctuation being rather the work of Jerks and transcribers than that of the legislature itself. The rolls containing the originals of the acts of Parliament are not punctuated, although some marks appear in the printed copies which are published by its authority.

3. Context.— In determining the true meaning of a word or clause, the context is to be consulted, and its use, in a particular clause, is to be ascertained by a comparison with other parts of the same statute, or with other statutes of similar character and purpose. For example, the word "mutiny," as used in Section 5359 of the Revised Statutes of the United States, in a description of the offense of inciting to revolt or mutiny, is not there defined; the succeeding section, however, contains a definition of the line of mutiny which would prevail in the interpretation of the word as used in Section 5359.

4. Technical Words and Phrases.— Words and phrases having a technical meaning or a meaning peculiar to an art or trade are to be given that mean-in statutes relating to that art or trade. The word " duties," for

example, as used in the revenue laws of the United States, relates in some sense to imposts upon imported goods, and in others to certain statutory rules of conduct imposed upon collectors of ports and their subordinates. Its meaning, in any particular case, would be determined by the context, or in the obvious intent of the clause in question.

5. The Common Law.— Words and clauses of a statute which have a technical meaning at common law are to be given that meaning in interpretation. This is a rule of great importance and of very general application, as the language used by legislative bodies, in their enactments, is in great part borrowed from the common law, in which system particular meanings *We* been assigned, to words, partly as a result of customary use and partly in consequence of judicial interpretation. Although the United States has, as such, no common-law jurisdiction, the enactments of Congress are usually expressed in terms borrowed from the common law and are intended, by the national legislature, to have such interpretation. The crime of murder, for example, when committed in territory over which the Federal Government has exclusive jurisdiction, is not defined in Section 5339 of the Revised "Statutes, which prescribes a punishment for that offense. It was the evident intention of Congress, however, that the offense there made punishable would be the one known as murder at the common law. In a similar manner, none of the offenses made punishable in the fifty-eighth article of war are defined therein, and we must look to the common law for definitions of the crimes over which courts-martial are given jurisdiction in time of war, insurrection, and rebellion.

6. Strict and Liberal Interpretation.— Strict interpretation gives to the words and clauses of a statute their exact and literal meaning, keeping always within the

clear intent of the legislature, as expressed in a particular enactment. Liberal interpretation gives to words a somewhat broader and more comprehensive meaning, and one more in accordance with the spirit and purpose of the statute.

7. Harsh and Liberal Clauses.— Harsh clauses are interpreted strictly, with a view to restrict their operation to the smallest number of cases. Clauses have this character which restrict remedies, impair vested rights, or impose restraints upon individuals. Clauses which recognize rights and privileges or extend their operation, or which create remedies, or make them more easily available, are construed liberally. It is a well-known maxim of interpretation that criminal laws are to be construed strictly ill all those parts which make against an accused person, but liberally as to those parts which make in his favor.

8. Extensive and Restrictive Interpretation.— Extensive interpretation gives to a word or clause a more comprehensive meaning than that assigned to it by the ordinary rules of grammatical construction. When carried to an extreme, it is called extravagant interpretation, and is rejected. Restrictive interpretation, on the other hand, avoids giving full meaning to words, in order not to go beyond the clear intent of the legislature.

9. True Meaning.— A word or clause in a statute can have but one true meaning, and that meaning, when ascertained, must be given it wherever it occurs.

10. Earlier and Later Clauses.— In determining the true meaning of a word, its meaning in a earlier or later clause of the same statute may be applied in interpretation. In some cases the use of the term in earlier or later statutes, on the same or similar subjects, will also assist in such determination.

11. Inoperative Interpretation.— An interpretation of a clause which makes a statute inoperative is to be rejected, as it was the intent of the legislature to make it effective in all its parts.

12. Executive and Judicial Interpretations.— An interpretation long acquiesced in by the courts will be deemed correct. Great weight will also be attached to the interpretation given to a word or clause of a statute by the executive agent charged with its administration. In a similar manner an officer of the executive will be bound by the interpretation of his predecessor, if such interpretation be not plainly contrary to the tenor of the statute in question.[30]

References.— The subjects of interpretation and construction are discussed at some length in the works of Blackstone and Kent, already referred to. The principal separate works on this subject are: Bishop on the Written Laws; Sedgwick's Statute and Constitutional Law; Endlich on Interpretation; and Sutherland oil Statutory Construction. Broome's Legal Maxims, Lawson's Concordance, and Hughes' Technology of the Law may also be consulted with advantage in this connection.

---

[30] U. S. *vs*. Healey, 160 U. S., 186.

CHAPTER III

THE EXECUTIVE

Powers of the Executive.— The general powers of the Executive, which have already been described, are derived in part from the Constitution and are, in part, created or imposed by law. In the performance of some of his duties, in which he directly represents the sovereign people, as in communications with foreign nations, in receiving ambassadors, and in his capacity as commander-in-chief, his independent action is guaranteed in the Constitution; other powers are shared with the entire Legislature — the veto lover, for example — or with a single branch of it, as is the case with the lower to make treaties or appointments to office.

Execution of the Laws.— The most important of the executive duties, however, have to do with the *execution of the laws,* in respect to which the auctions of the Executive are strictly administrative in character, and his responsibility ends with a rigid enforcement of the law as it emanates from the Legislature. If a statute be defective in any respect, the responsibility therefor rests with the Legislature which enacted it, as it is the duty of the Executive to execute the laws as he finds them, and he has no power to annul or suspend them, or to modify their operation in any particular.

Executive Departments.— As the President speaks and acts through the Heads of Departments in reference to the business committed to them, the action of the heads of the several Executive Departments, in matters which the President is authorized to direct, is presumed to have been directed by him.[31] Where, however, duties are explicitly imposed by law upon the head of a Department, or upon any other officer of the executive, the duty of such officer is determined by the law which creates the duty or imposes the obligation.[32] The *Department of State* is the organ by means of which the official utterances of the President, in the nature of proclamations and the Mice, are made known to the public at large. Such of his correspondence, aIso, as does not relate directly to the business of any of the other Executive Departments is carried on through the same agency.[33]

Executive Duties, How Performed.— Of the several duties imposed upon the Executive by the Constitution and laws, some are performed by him in person, others by officers or agents selected by him or his principal subordinates. The duties of these officers are defined and their performance regulated by the statutes creating the several offices or departments of which the Executive is composed. The offices of judges, magistrates, sheriffs, and coroners were recognized by the common law, but their duties have been added to or modified by statute in the several States, while those pertaining to the Federal Government are created either by the Constitution or by enactments of Congress in accordance therewith.

---

[31] Wilcox *vs.* Jackson, 13 Pet., 498, 513; Lapeyre *vs. V. S.,* 17 Wall., 191; Wolsey *vs.* Chapman, 101 U. S., 755; Runkle *vs. V.* S., 123 U. S., 548, 557.

[32] Kendall *vs.* United States, 12 Peters, 524; 7 Opin. Att. Cten., 453.

[33] Lockington vs. Smith, Peters C. Ct.. 460; Lapeyre *vs. V. S.,* 17 Wall., 191.

PUBLIC OFFICE

Public Office.— A *Public office*[34] is an employment exercised by an individual in behalf of the community at large, the tenure, duties, and emoluments of which are defined by law. The law creating an office is not, in general, in the nature of a statutory contract; office is rather a trust or agency arising from an exercise of the legislative power, and, unless the constitution of the State directs otherwise, it maybe abolished, or its duties, emoluments, or conditions of tenure may be changed, at any time, by the authority which created it.

Public Officers.— A *Public officer* is the incumbent of a public office who has been elected or appointed to the same in accordance with law. Only the higher grades of employees are regarded as public officers in the strict sense of the term, their powers being conferred by statute and their duties performed under the sanction of an oath of office. Other services, some of them of the highest importance, are obtained *by contract,* but to these no political or administrative responsibilities are attached, and they are secured by the State in the same manner as similar services are obtained by corporations or by private individuals.

---

[34] An office is a public station, or employment, conferred by the appointment of Government. The term embraces the ideas of tenure, emolument, and duties. * * * The duties are continuing and permanent, not occasional and transitory, and are defined by *rules* prescribed by Government and not by contract. U. S. *vs.* Hartwell, 6 Wall., 385-394. See, also, U. S. *vs.* Maurice. 3 Brockenbrough, 103; Sheboygan Co. *vs.* Parker, 3 Wall., 93-96; U. S. *vs.* Hartwell, 6 Wall., 385; U. 8. *vs.* Mouat, 134 U. S. 303, 307;*V. S. vs.* Germaine, 99 U. S., 508-510.

CHAPTER III

QUALIFICATIONS FOR OFFICE

Qualifications for Office.— The qualifications for office are, in general, those necessary to an exercise of the right of suffrage. An officer of a State must, as a rule, be a citizen, voter, or resident of the jurisdiction in which he is elected or appointed to office. From the nature of the operations of the Federal Government this rule is, in many cases, impossible of application; it is observed, however, as to offices in the postal service and some others the duties of which are local in character. An officer must also be over twenty-one years of age, and must fulfill such conditions as to education, professional attainments, and property qualifications as are or may be attached by law to the office to which he has been appointed or elected. Preference in appointment to office, or in selection for public employment, may be shown to a class — as, to discharged soldiers or sailors, or those who have passed a competitive examination — and a special tenure may attach to appointments so made. Aliens, women, infants, and persons mentally or physically incapacitated are, as a rule, incapable of lading office, unless specially authorized to do so by statute. Bribery, Hid, false representations, and conviction of treason, felony, and of some statutory crimes are also causes of disqualification for office.

The term and the tenure of office, that is, the conditions under which it is held, are regulated by statute in the several States. The term of office may be for good behavior — that is, for life — or for a period of years.

Tenure.— In the absence of statutory regulation an officer may be removed at the will of the appointing power, and, with the same qualification, may resign office at any time and for any reason.[35] In other words, the tenure of public office, unless the law directs otherwise, is at the will of either party, and the relation may be so terminated at any time.

DUTIES

Duties — Ministerial and Discretionary Duties.— The *duties* attached to a public office are determined, in character and amount, by the statute which created it, and in respect to their nature are either ministerial or discretionary. *Ministerial duties* are those performed in strict conformity to the terms of a statute or in obedience to the orders of a superior. *Discretionary panties* are those requiring in their execution an exercise of prudence or judgment, or a choice of means within the limits of the law regulating their performance. The performance of ministerial duties may be compelled by the writ of mandamus,[36] the operation of which cannot, in general, be extended to compel the performance of an act of discretion.[37] "When the law requires a ministerial act to be

---

[35] U. S. *vs.* Wright, 1 McLean, 509; *Ex parte* Hennen, 13 Pet., 258; *V. S. vs.* Guthrie, 17 How., 284; Mimmack *vs. V. S.,* 97 U. S., 436; Blake *vs. V. S.,* 13 Otto, 227; Gratiot *vs. U.* S., 1 Ct. Claims, 258; U. S. *vs.* Avery, 1 Deady, 204, 3 Story Com. on Const., §§ 1538-44; Du Barry's Case, 4 Opin. Att. Gen., 1; Lansing's Case, 6 *ibid.,* 4, 8 *ibid.,* 283, 12 *ibid.,* 424, 15 *ibid.,* 421.

[36] Kendall vs. U. S., 12 Pet., 521; Tracy vs. Swartwout, 10 Pet., 80; Amy vs. Supervisors, 11 Wall.. 136; Bispham *vs.* Taylor, 2 McLean, 408; Pierce CT. Strickland, 2 Story, 292.

[37] Marbury *vs.* Madison, 11 Cranch, 137; Martin *vs.* Mott, 12 Wheaton, 31; Kendall *vs.* Stokes, 3 How., 87;

done by an officer and he neglects or refuses to do such act, he may be compelled to respond in damages to the extent of the injury arising from his conduct. A mistake as to his duty and honest intention will not excuse the offender."[38] " If the officer acts in good faith, however, he is not liable in exemplary damages for a wrong done in the performance of his duty." [39]

Rule of Diligence.— An officer is bound to use that care and diligence in the discharge of his duties that a conscientious and prudent man, acting under a just sense of his obligations, would exercise under the particular case, and if he fails and neglects to do so he is culpable.[40]

Principle of Agency.— The principles regulating the relations of principal and agent apply with peculiar force to public officers in the performance of their duties. This for the reason that "all the officers of the Government, from the highest to the lowest, are but agents with delegated powers, and if they act beyond the scope of their delegated powers their acts do not bind the principal."[41] From this principle it follows "that an officer can bind the Government only by acts which come within a just exercise of his official power." [42]

Wilkes *vs.* Dinsman, 71 How., 89, 132; U. S. *vs.* Guthrie, 17 How., 284; Gaines *vs.* Thompson, 7 Wall., 347.

[38] Amy *vs.* The Supervisors, 11 Wall., 136.

[39] Tracy *vs.* Swartwout, 10 Pet., 80.

[40] U. S. *vs.* Baldridge, 11 Fed. Fed., 552; Buck *vs.* Colbath, 3 Wall., 334;Haffin *vs.* Mason, 15 Wall., 671.

[41] U. S. *vs.* The Maxwell Grant, 21 Fed. Rep., 19.

[42] Hunter *vs. V. S.,* 5 Pet., 173, 178; The Floyd Acceptances, 7 Wall., 666; State *vs.* Hastings, 12 Wis., 596.

Office, How Acquired.— Office may be acquired by election, by succession, or promotion, and by appointment, with or without the approval, or concurrence, of some portion of the Legislature. It may be terminated by the death, resignation, removal, or dismissal of the incumbent, by the expiration of a statutory term of office, or by the discontinuance of the office itself. While an incumbent may resign office at pleasure, the duties and responsibilities of the situation do not cease until his resignation has been accepted or a successor appointed.[43]

Termination of Office — Removal.— The *tenure of office,* in so far as its legal termination is concerned, has already been described. It may also be terminated for misconduct on the part of the official, or for incapacity to perform its duties, at the discretion of the appointing power. For misconduct act, or for actual crime, on the part of a public officer, other and more effective remedies are provided. For political misconduct he may be impeached and, if found guilty, may be removed from office, and disqualified to hold office thereafter in the State in which the impeachment proceedings were had. If he holds office unlawfully, his right thereto may be inquired into by a legal proceeding, to be explained hereafter, known as an *information in the nature of a quo warrantor.*[44] In the performance of ministerial duties he is subject, as has been seen, to the control of the courts, by means of the wits of mandamus and injunction. Nor does his office shield him from punishment for crime committed in violation of the personal or property rights of another, since public

---

[43] Edwards *vs. V.* S., 13 Otto, 471; Thompson *vs. V.* S., *ibid.,* 480; U. S. *vs.* Wright, 1 McLean, 509; *V. S. vs.* Justices of Lauderdale Co., 10 Fed. Rep., 460, 10 Opin. Att. Gen., 229, 14 *ibid.,* 209.

[44] See page 50, *post*

officers, as a class, are amenable to the Jurisdiction of the courts in the same manner and to the same extent as other citizens of the State.

EXECUTION OF LAWS.EXECUTIVE INTERPRETATION. EXECUTIVE REGULATIONS

Executive Interpretation — Regulations.— In the execution of laws, the first duty of the executive agent charged with their administration is to place an interpretation upon them unless they are self-executing, and to supplement them, if need be, by such regulations as are necessary to carry them into effect. "The construction given to a statute by those charged with the duty of executing it is always entitled to the most respectful consideration, and ought not to be overruled without cogent reasons. The officers concerned are usually able men and masters of the subject; not infrequently they are the draftsmen of the laws they are afterwards called upon to interpret."[45] The authority to prepare regulations may be expressly conferred by statute, or may be implied as necessary to make the legislation effective.[46] For example, a statute may authorize enlisted men to purchase their discharges, under such regulations as the Secretary of War may prescribe; or the same officer may be authorized, by statute, to construct a work of river improvement, to be thrown open to the public use in accordance with such regulations as he may deem necessary. In both of these

---

[45] *U.* S. *vs.* Moore, 95 *V. S.*, 760, 763

[46] *U.* S. vs. Eliason, 16 Pet., 291; *V. S. vs.* Maurice, 2 Brockenbrough, 96. See also sections 161, 465, and 1753, Revised Statutes, and the Act of March 1, 1875 (18 Stat. at Large, 337).

cases the power to make regulations is expressly conferred. Or, the army ration being fixed by statute as to the amount and variety of its components, the President may, by appropriate regulations, prescribe the times and places of issue and the conditions under which the several components shall be used. In this case the power to make regulations is conferred by implication. Regulations to have binding force must be in strict conformity to the statute and in furtherance of it. Regulations supplemental to statutes, or otherwise, can contain nothing contrary to the tenor of such statutes, and officers, in cases arising under the laws, must be guided by them, and not by the instructions or requirements of the Departments which are in conflict therewith.[47]

RULES FOR THE EXERCISE OF EXECUTIVE POWERS

The following rules are recognized as governing the Executive and his subordinate agents in the performance of their duties:

1. Acts of Executive Binding upon his Successors.— Acts done or questions decided by the executive or his principal subordinates are binding upon and not subject to review by his successors in office. The purpose of this rule, which has not always been strictly adhered to in practice, is to secure order, certainty, and finality in the administration of the laws The right of the head of an executive department to review a predecessor's decisions extends to mistakes in matters of fact arising from errors in calculation and to cases of rejected claims

[47] Teal *vs.* Felton, 13 How., 289.

in which material testimony is afterwards discovered and produced.[48]

2. Executive Authority, How Exercised.—The authority pertaining to an office must be exercised in strict conformity to law; and no public officer has power to vary the terms of the law in any respect. This for the reason that public statutes must receive uniform execution throughout the territorial jurisdiction to which they apply. As regulations must be drawn in accordance with law, an officer must follow the law, rather than the regulation, whenever there is a variation between them.[49]

3. Delegation of Powers-Ratification.— In the course of administration some duties must be performed by the incumbent, while others may be per formed by deputies or others, subject to ratification by the proper superior As a rule, ministerial duties only may thus be delegated, the performance of duties involving discretion not being proper subjects of delegation. An unlawful act or one in its nature void cannot be authorized by ratification.

4. Presumptions of Authority and Good Faith.— The acts of a public officer are presumed to be within his

---

[48] United States *vs.* Bank of the Metropolis, 15 Pet., 377, 401; Lavalette *us US* 1 Ct CIs., 147, 2 Op. Alt. Gen., 8, 110, 331: *ibid.,* 110, *6 ibid.* 603.

[49] *U.* S. *vs.* Eliason. 16 Pet.. 291, 302: Harvey *vs. V.* S., 3 C. CIs., 38, 42- Landram *vs U.* S., 16 C. CIs., 75; U. 8 *vs.* Freeman, 3 How., 536; V. 8. *vs.* Symonds 120 U 8 46' 59; *V. S. va* Bishop, *id.,* 51: U. *S. vs.* Davis, 132 U S., 334.

authority, and a similar presumption of good faith attends the performance of all public duties.[50]

5. Public Officers Act in the Name of the State — Contracts.— Public officers act in the name of the State. Contracts entered into by them are the contracts of the State, to whose benefit they accrue; and the officer charged with their execution, so long as he observes the rule of good faith, incurs no legal responsibility therefor. A contrary doctrine would be productive of the most injurious consequences to the public as well as to individuals. The government is incapable of acting otherwise than by its agents, and no prudent man would consent to become a public agent if he should be made personally responsible for contracts on the public account.[51]

6. Measure of Power to Contract.— The measure of an officer's power to contract is found in the statute authorizing the contract to be made; and he cannot incur a liability in behalf of the United States in excess of the authority so conferred.[52]

---

[50] Marbury vs. Madison. 1 Cranch, 116, 170: United States *vs.* Arredondo 6 Pet 691 729: Lowell *vs.* Flint, 20 Me.. 501: Russell *vs.* Beebe. 1 Hempstead 704; Garcia *vs. Lee* 12 Pet.. 511; Williams *vs.* Suffolk Ins. Co., 13 Pet., 415; U. *S. vs.* Humason, 5 Sawyer, 537; Dunlop *vs.* Munroe, 1 Cranch C. C., 536; Alyord *vs. U.* S., 13 Blatchford 279 Cornett *vs.* Williams, 20 Wall., 226; Cofield v*s.* McClelland, 16 Wall., 331; U. S.' *Vs* Crusell 14 Wall., 1; U. S. *vs.* Cambuston, 7 Sawyer, 575; Den *vs.* Hill, 1 McAllister 480; Bottomley vs. U. S., 1 Story, 135.

[51] Hodgin *vs.* Dexter, 1 Cranch, 362, 364; Parks *vs.* Boss, 11 How., 363.

[52] U. S. *vs.* Maurice, 2 Marshall, 96; U. S. *vs.* City

References.— The powers and duties of the Executive under the Constitution are quite fully discussed in the works on constitutional law to which allusion has already been made. Conkling on the Executive Powers, Mechem's Public Officers, Throop's Officers and Agents, and Crocker on Sheriffs are the most recent works on this subject.

Bank, 6 McLean, 130; Whitesides *vs. U. S.*, 3 Otto, 247; Bancroft *vs.* Thayer, 5 Sawyer, 509; Bennett *vs. U. S.,* 5 Ct. CIs., 109; Ryan *vs.* U. S., 8 *ibid.,* 274; Spencer *vs.* U. S., *ibid.,* 293; Savage *vs.* U. S.. *ibid.,* 653; Noble vs. U. S., 11 *ibid.,* 620; Thompson *vs. U.* S., 9 Ct. CIs. 197.

CHAPTER IV

THE JUDICIARY

The Judicial Power.— The judicial power is exercised through tribunals, created by law, called *courts of justice.* These courts are called into being by an exercise of legislative authority, which endows them with jurisdiction to hear and determine cases arising under the Constitution and laws, and to issue such writs, orders, and decrees as are necessary thereto.

JURISDICTION

Jurisdiction.— The *jurisdiction* of a court is its power to hear and determine a case and to carry into effect its judgment thereon, after a trial had in due form of law in which all parties to the action have had an opportunity to appear and present their claims.[53] The exercise of jurisdiction in a particular case includes the power to take cognizance of the subject-matter of the action, and, by the issue and service of proper writs and processes, to compel the appearance of the parties and witnesses, and to assume control of the subject of litigation, or to require security therefor pending a decision thereon.[54]

Classification of Jurisdiction.— Jurisdiction is classified according to its extent and authority, and is said to be original or appellate, exclusive or concurrent, final or intermediate. A court is said to have *original jurisdiction* when, under the law, it is the first tribunal into

---

[53] Rhode Island *vs.* Massachusetts, 12 Pet., 657.

[54] Boswell *vs.* Otis, 9 How., 836 ; Kendall *vs.* *U. S.*, 12 Pet., 554.

which a particular case can be brought for trial; when there is but a single court into which a case may be brought, its jurisdiction is said to be *exclusive.* When two or more courts may take cognizance of the same case they are said to have *concurrent jurisdiction.*

Appellate jurisdiction is a power exercised by superior courts of examining the proceedings of inferior tribunals at the instance of parties who, for reasons stated, are not satisfied with the decision of the court below and desire to obtain a review of its proceedings or a retrial of the case. The jurisdiction of a court *is final* when there is no appeal from its decision, or when its decisions cannot be reviewed by a higher court; it is said to be *intermediate* when it may hear cases by way of appeal, subject to having its own judgments reviewed by a court of superior authority.

COURTS

Courts — Officers; Terms.— A *court* is a place where justice is judicially administered. It is composed of one or more judges, who are habitually referred to as *the court* to distinguish them from the subordinate officials attached thereto. Courts are provided with certain ministerial officers, called *sheriffs, clerks, marshals, criers,* etc., whose duty it is to prepare and execute writs and processes, to make and preserve a record of its proceedings, and to maintain order in its presence. Parties are assisted in the preparation and presentation of their cases by officers of the court called *attorneys* or *counselors at law.* The periods of the year set apart by statute for the sessions of particular courts are known as *terms.* These terms receive names in England from the festivals of the church; in the United States they are named from the month in the year in which their sittings begin.

Classification.— Courts are classified in accordance with the nature of their jurisdiction and the form of relief afforded by them into *courts of law* and *equity courts.* Courts of law hear and determine causes of action at common law or cases arising under statutes enacted by the legislature. If their jurisdiction extends to civil cases only, they are called *civil courts* to distinguish them from those having power to try criminal cases or public wrongs, called *criminal courts.* In most of the States the jurisdiction of the superior courts extends to and includes both civil and criminal cases. *Courts of equity* or *chancery* exercise a peculiar jurisdiction, in some respects supplemental to that exercised by courts of law, called *equity jurisdiction* or *jurisdiction in chancery.*[55]

Courts of General and Special Jurisdiction — Courts of Record — Summary Courts.— A *court of general jurisdiction* is one having a seal, whose proceedings are formally recorded, and which is given power to issue the ordinary writs and processes, to try both civil and criminal cases, and, sitting as a court of chancery, to administer chancery jurisdiction. This term is also applied, in some of the States, to a court having full common-law jurisdiction. A *court of special jurisdiction* is one whose power is restricted as to the kind or importance of the cases which may come before it for trial. The record of such a court must show, in every instance, that cases tried by it fall within its statutory jurisdiction. *Police* or *magistrates' courts* and *military* and *naval courts-martial* are examples of this class. *Courts of record* are those whose proceedings are formally recorded, which have power to

[55] For description of equity jurisdiction, see Chapter XII, *post.*

fine and imprison for contempt of their authority, and whose orders and decrees are authenticated by seals. *Summary courts* or *courts not of record* are those which are not required to make and preserve formal records of their proceedings. Their jurisdiction is generally original and is always narrowly limited ill extent.

Courts-martial and Military Commissions.—*Courts-martial* are *statutory* tribunals, composed of military officers, having power to try offenses against military law committed by persons in the military service; their sentences are subject to revision by the officer who convenes them, and do not become operative until they have been approved or confirmed by such convening authority. *Military commissions* are tribunals called into existence in time of war by generals commanding in the occupied territory of the enemy. The order creating a military commission confers authority to bear evidence ill a particular case, to determine questions of guilt or innocence, and to recommend an appropriate punishment. These tribunals are not statutory in character; their jurisdiction extends only to the particular case or cases referred to them for trial, and their proceedings and sentences, which are purely advisory in their nature, have no effect until they have been approved or adopted by the convening authority.

ACTIONS AT LAW

How Instituted — Appearance of Parties.—Proceedings in an *action at law* are instituted by an individual who, with a view to obtain redress for an alleged wrong, comes into court and states his grievance, or *cause of action,* in accordance with the forms of law and the rules of procedure in force in the particular court to which he appeals for redress. The court, having obtained jurisdiction over the plaintiff by such voluntary appearance, proceeds to acquire jurisdiction over the person of the defendant by means of *writs* or commands, issued in the name of the State and by its sovereign authority. These writs are served upon the defendant, informing him of the nature of the demand and commanding him to appear in court, on a day named, for the hearing of the case. By the issue of similar process the court may also obtain judicial possession of the subject of litigation, or its equivalent in money or property, such possession continuing until judgment has been rendered and execution had thereon, or an appeal taken to a higher court with a view to a rehearing or a retrial of the case.

Original Writs.— According to the common law, the king was regarded as the fountain of justice, and all judicial authority was presumed to be vested in and exercised by him, either directly or through the agency of the royal courts at Westminster. In ancient times all actions at law were begun by what were called *original writs* issued from the court of chancery. These writs contained not only a statement of the plaintiff's case and a demand for restitution for the wrong complained of, but conferred jurisdiction upon a particular court to hear and determine the case if such restitution were not made.

Forms of Action at Common Law.— Certain inflexible forms of action were provided, in accordance with which all demands had to be stated. If, for any reason, they were not susceptible of such statement, no remedy could be afforded by an action at law. To meet the hardship of such cases, a general form of action was devised, called the writ of *trespass on the case* — that is, the case stated by the plaintiff in his writ, which comprehended all causes of action which could not be reduced to any of the forms then ill *use,* the use of which will be presently explained.

Actions at Law.— An *action at law* may be defined as a proceeding carried on in a court of justice with a view to obtain redress for a private wrong. The *form of action* in any case is determined by the nature and character of the wrong complained of. If the claim be that of one individual against another, it is called a *civil action;* if it be undertaken by the State to obtain redress for a violation of a criminal law, it is called a *criminal action* or *trial.* The parties to a civil action are called the *plaintiff* and *defendant;* in all criminal cases the State is the plaintiff, and the person accused of crime is the defendant. Actions at law are classified according to their subject-matter into *real, personal,* and *mixed actions.*

Real actions are those brought for the specific recovery of lauds, tenements, and hereditaments. *Mixed actions* are those involving the title to real estate in connection with other claims, or demands, for damages for injuries done thereto. *Personal actions* are those brought for the specific recovery of chattels, for all breaches of contract, or with a view to obtain compensation, in the nature of damages, for injuries to person or property. Indeed, all actions not relating directly to the acquisition, ownership, or disposition of real property fall under the head of personal actions. Personal actions are classified, in accordance with the nature of the injury complained of, into —

Actions of contract (ex contractu), including all actions for the recovery of debts or damages for the breach or non-performance of contracts and agreements, and for the recovery of amounts due thereon. *Actions of fort (ex delicto),* including all suits for the recovery of personalty wrongfully withheld, or for damages for a wrong not in its nature a breach of contract.

FORMS OF ACTION

Real Actions.— The principal Real Actions at Common Law were *Dower, Quare Impedit,* and *Ejectment.* The action of Dower applied to the claim of a widow to recover her dower, that is, a specific recovery of a life interest in one-third of the lands of which her husband had been seized during coverture. If no dower had been assigned, the action was called the *Writ of Dower;* if a residue only remained unassigned, the action was called a *Writ of Right of Dower.*

The action of *Quare Impedit* was one brought to recover the presentation to a benefice. This action is obsolete if, indeed, it ever existed in the United States.

The action of *Ejectment* is one brought for the specific recovery of lands. In its original form the action was brought for the recovery of damages for a term of years during which the plaintiff had been forcibly ejected. The courts decided, however, that the plaintiff was entitled to recover not only the damages claimed by the action, but, by way of collateral relief, was entitled to recover, also, the possession of the land itself for the term of years for which he had been ousted or dispossessed. This action has come to be the usual method of trying titles to land.

A *Mixed Action* is one resembling a real action, in that the specific recovery of lands is sought, but which partakes of the character of a personal action in that damages are demanded for a wrong sustained.[56]

Personal Actions.— The personal actions at Common Law were *Debt, Covenant, Assumpsit, Replevin, Detinue, Trover, Trespass,* and *Trespass on the Case.* Of these the actions of *debt, covenant,* and *assumpsit,* being

---

[56] Hall *vs.* Decker, 48 Me., 255.

founded on promises, were called *actions of contract;* while *replevin, detinue, trover, trespass,* and *trespass on the case,* being founded on injuries done, property withheld, etc., were called *actions of tort.*

The *Action of Debt* lay for the specific recovery of a specific sum due, as on a bond, bill, or note, and, in general, applied to all cases in which the amount due was a fixed and definite sum.

The *Action of Covenant* lay for a breach of the conditions of a covenant, that is, of a contract under seal.

The *Action of Assumpsit,* which was, in its origin, a form of action on the case, lay for the recovery of damages for the breach of the conditions of a simple or parol contract. It is a form of action of very extensive application, as it affords a remedy for breach of all contracts or agreements, whether express or implied, which are not, in form, contracts under seal.

The *Action of Replevin* lay for the wrongful taking of personal property by the execution of a distress warrant, the purpose of the action being to recover the particular thing taken pending the adjudication of the case. It has been extended to apply to the recovery of all personal property unlawfully taken or unlawfully detained.

The *Action of Detinue* lay for the recovery of goods unlawfully detained, the original taking being lawful. This action is practically obsolete, the form of action by replevin having been so extended in its scope as to cover the unlawful taking, or detaining, of the goods of another. This action is practically obsolete in most of the States.

The *Action of Trover,* originally, like assumpsit, a form of action on the case, lay for the recovery of damages for goods alleged to have been found by another and wrongfully converted to his own use. As the alleged finding soon came to be regarded as a fiction, and as the conversion constituted the real injury in the case, proof of finding has been generally dispensed with by statute, leaving only the fact of wrongful conversion to be established by the evidence submitted to the jury in the trial of the case.

The *Action of Trespass* lay to recover damages for any injury to the person, property, or rights of another, accompanied by force, either express or implied. Of actual violence an assault and battery is an example; of implied violence, a peaceful but wrongful entry upon another's land.

The Action of Trespass on the Case.— At a very early period in the development of the common-law procedure the forms of action above described became so fixed in character that, if a cause of action arose which could not be stated in accordance with any one of them, the common-law courts were unable to afford relief to the injured party. To remedy this state of affairs a new form of action was devised called *Trespass on the Case,* that is, on the case stated by the plaintiff in his declaration, which was intended to cover all causes of action which were not susceptible of statement in accordance with any of the forms then recognized at common law. It is now regarded as the appropriate remedy for all injuries committed without force, in which the damages sustained are collateral or consequential in character and are ascertained and assessed by a jury.

Forms of Action in the United States.— The practice of the several States in respect to the old forms of action at common law has not been uniform. In some they have been retained with but little change, in others they have undergone extensive modification, in still others they have been abolished by statute, and replaced by a single form of action at law. They continue to have value, however, in all jurisdictions, to the extent of furnishing a standard with which the facts constituting a particular case may be compared,— this with a view to determine whether they do, or do not, present a cause of action under the statute or the common law, and if so, to determine the proper form of remedy that should be applied.[57]

Local and Transitory Actions.— Actions are also classified, in accordance with the jurisdiction in which they must be brought for trial, into *local* and *transitory actions. Local actions* are those brought to recover real estate or involving the title to or possession of the same, and must be brought in the jurisdiction in which the property is situated. *Transitory actions* relate to breaches of contract or to injuries which might have happened anywhere; they follow the person of the defendant wherever he may go, and may be brought wherever service may be had upon him.

PROCEDURE

Procedure.— In the trial of cases and in the general administration of justice, courts are controlled in the conduct of business before them by a system of rules called *procedure.* These rules are in part statutory and in part composed of regulations adopted by the courts themselves with a view to the orderly transaction of judicial business. If the system applies in the trial of actions at law, it is called *civil procedure;* if to the trial of criminal cases, it is known as *criminal procedure;* if to

---

[57] Gudger vs. Western N. C. R. R. Co.. 21 Fed. Rep., 81; Lubert *vs.* Chauviteau, 3 Cal., 458; Lorraine *vs.* Long, 6 *ibid.,* 452; Goulet *vs.* Asseler, 83 N. Y., 225; Cropsey *vs.* Sweeney, 27 Barber (N. Y.), 310.

equity proceedings, it is called *procedure in equity* or *chancery procedure.* When, as is often the case, the same tribunal has both law and equity jurisdiction, questions of *law* and *equity* procedure are said to pertain to the *law* or *equity side* of the court in question.[58]

Actions at Law, How Brought — Declaration; Summons — Return Day.— The manner of bringing an action at law varies in each of the several States of the Union; some retaining the original writ, or a modification thereof; others prescribing, by statute, a simpler and more direct method of stating the demand. In all jurisdictions, however, there is agreement as to two fundamental requirements: (1) the plaintiff must appear and state his grievance, or cause of action, in accordance with the provisions of the local law; this statement is called the *declaration*[59] and is filed in the court having jurisdiction to try the case; (2) upon the filing of the plaintiff's declaration, the court will issue a *summons* commanding the defendant to appear in court on a day named, and make answer or show cause why the plaintiff's claim should not be allowed. The day so fixed is called the *return day,* on which the defendant must make his appearance in court, either in person or by attorney, and recognize, in due form of law, the tendency of the suit and his willingness to abide by the result of the trial.

---

[58] The outline of procedure which follows is based upon a number of text-books on pleading to which it has not been deemed necessary to make special reference. The excellent manual of Judge Cox, "Common-Law Practice," has been largely used in this connection

[59] In States having codes of civil procedure this paper is called the plaintiff's *petition,* or *complaint.*

Security — Bail.— In former times the defendant was required to give security not only for his appearance in court, but also that the judgment awarded would be paid or otherwise satisfied. This security was called *bail to the action,* and the defendant, if unable to furnish it, was restrained of his liberty until bail was obtained or the judgment satisfied. As this restraint upon liberty was, in fact, imprisonment, the result was that a creditor, aside from the remedy afforded by an action at law, was able to cause his debtor to be imprisoned until his debt was paid. This practice gave rise to such serious abuses and was the occasion of so much hardship and injustice that it has been abolished, by constitutional prohibition or by statute, in most of the States of the Union. In those jurisdictions in which the practice is retained, imprisonment is permitted only in cases in which there is a strong presumption of fraud which give to the act of the debtor a quasi-criminal character. Since the abolition of imprisonment for debt this requirement has been greatly modified, and is regulated in its exercise, wherever it exists, in strict accordance with statutes which prescribe the cases in which bail to the action may be demanded and arrest made in default thereof. In criminal cases, however, *bail* is still required, and is determined, in the discretion of the court, by the gravity of the charge and, to some extent, by the character of the accused and the other circumstances of the case.

Importance.— With a view to give the defendant time to obtain witnesses and prepare his case for trial, it was provided by the common law that the trial should take place during the second term of court following that in which the action was brought and return of service upon the defendant made. The intermediate term was called the *importance term,* during which an opportunity was afforded to the litigant parties to settle their difference out of court. This delay is no longer generally recognized in the United States, and the statutes of the State in which the action is brought determine the time within which all cases shall be brought to trial.

Pleadings.— The plaintiff having filed his declaration, the defendant was given a short time, usually from four to eight days, in which to reply to the case stated in the declaration. This answer was called the *plea,* and was one of a series of alternate allegations and replies, called *pleadings,* which fulfilled an important office in the trial of an action at common law and will now be explained.

Jury Trial.— All actions at common law involving issues of fact were tried in the presence of a jury composed of twelve impartial men, whose conclusions, after hearing the testimony submitted on either side, were embodied in a verdict, which, unless appealed from, was final as to all questions of fact involved. The jury being composed of persons not learned in the law, it was desirable that the issue referred to it for trial should be the simplest possible, involving, in most cases, the existence or non-existence of a single proposition of fact. It was the purpose of the system of pleading, therefore, to reduce the various questions of fact which constituted a particular cause of action to a single issue of fact, in support or denial of which all the evidence submitted was to apply as simply and directly as possible.

Purpose of Pleading.— The office, or function, of the rules of pleading at common law was to provide for the orderly introduction of successive allegations of fact by the parties to the action, with a view to bring about an issue which could be easily understood and intelligently tried by the jury. The first pleading in the case was, as we have seen, the plaintiff's *declaration,* in which his legal demand, or cause of action, was stated. The next pleading in order was the defendant's *plea,* which was followed by the plaintiff's answer, called the *replication;* this was answered by the defendant, and the parties continued to plead in succession until an issue was reached. In each successive pleading it was required that the party answering should admit the correctness of all the facts which had been correctly and sufficiently pleaded by the opposite party. The result was to eliminate all subordinate issues of fact, until a single one remained which was referred to the jury for trial.

Demurrers — Issues of Law and Fact.— It has thus far been seen that a party must, under the rules of pleading, reply to his adversary's pleading only by an allegation of fact; now, it frequently happened that one of the parties desired to reply, not by art allegation of fact, but by an objection to the legal sufficiency of the facts alleged by his adversary. This purpose was accomplished by a form of reply called a *demurrer,* in which the party admitted the facts to be as stated in the opposite pleading, but denied that the law, as applied to those facts, gave his opponent a cause of action, or constituted the injury alleged in the declaration. This gave rise to an *issue of law,* as distinguished from the *issue of fact* which has already been described. The issue of law thus raised on demurrer was decided by the court and not by the jury, as was the case with questions of fact; and judgment was given by the court, without jury trial, to the party who, in view of the whole record, was best entitled to the judgment.

Issues of Law and Fact.— It is thus seen that the result of the successive pleadings was to raise either an *issue of fact,* which was tried by the jury, or an *issue of law* on *demurrer,* which was decided by the court on the facts as admitted of record. In the former case the jury, after hearing the evidence on both sides, embodied its conclusion of fact in a *verdict;* in the latter the court, an issue of law having been raised, applied the law to the facts as they appeared of record, and gave *judgment* to him who was best entitled thereto upon all of the facts in the case.

THE JURY

The Function of the Jury — Verdicts.— The application of the rules of pleading having brought about a single issue, represented by a proposition of fact affirmed by one party and denied by the other, the issue so presented is tried in accordance with one of the forms provided by law,[60] of which the most common and usual is that known as trial by jury. It is the function of the jury to hear and weigh the evidence submitted in proof, or disproof, of the facts constituting the issue, and to determine the result by a finding of fact called a *verdict.* In an action at law mere preponderance of proof is sufficient; this is not the case, however, in a criminal trial, where, as has been seen, a finding adverse to an accused person can only be reached when the evidence is such as to prove his guilt beyond a reasonable doubt.

History, of the Jury Trial.— In the earliest form of trial known to the common law, the jury was composed of witnesses who, having themselves observed the facts, were sworn to do justice between man and man. By a

---

[60] There were seven different forms of trial known to the common law — i.e., trial by record, by certificate, by witnesses, by inspection, by wager of battle, by wager of law, and, finally, by jury as above described. The forms of trial other than by jury are practically obsolete m the United States.

gradual process of change, acting through a long period of years, witnesses ceased to be eligible, as such, to serve as jurors and began to form a class apart, until, at present, juries are composed of persons who have no direct acquaintance with the facts in a case, but gain the knowledge, or evidence, upon which to base their verdict from the testimony of witnesses, or from documentary evidence obtained in accordance with a system of principles, presently to be described, called *rules of evidence.* So strictly, indeed, is this rule applied at the present time that the possession of knowledge of a case derived from any other source is regarded as a prime cause of disqualification to serve as a juror.

Composition of Jury — Challenges.— After the pleadings have been completed and an *issue of fact* has been reached, the office of the jury begins. The *jury* is composed of twelve men whose impartiality has been secured by an exercise of the *right of challenge,* in behalf of both parties, which results in the exclusion from the panel of all those who, from personally acquired knowledge of the cause, interest in the subject of litigation, relationship to either of the parties, or from bias or prejudice, as proven by their own admissions or by the testimony of witnesses, are disqualified to assist in the trial of the case. The jury having been impaneled and sworn to well and truly try the cause before it, the plaintiff, through his attorney, addresses the court, stating the case which he expects to prove, and then produces the witnesses upon whose testimony he relies to establish his claim.

The Trial and its Incidents.— It has been seen that the chief purpose in reducing the facts to a single issue was to render the task of the jury as simple and untechnical as possible. To this end, such evidence only as tends directly to prove or disprove the facts in issue is permitted to go to the jury. Experience has shown that all these precautions are necessary in order to obtain a verdict that shall be correct in point of fact and insure a just determination of the action on its merits. Each witness, after being sworn, is questioned first by the party in whose behalf he appears, and is then cross-examined by the opposite party. When all the witnesses for the prosecution have testified, those for the defense are produced and examined in the same manner; the testimony for the defense being introduced by a statement by the defendant's attorney, in which his case is presented and the line of defense disclosed. When the testimony on both sides has been beard, the counsel address the jury, the right of opening and closing being given usually to the plaintiff, but always to the one upon whom the burden of proof rests.

Charge to the Jury.— The court then charges the jury in a final address, in which he sums up the evidence in the case and instructs them as to the rules of law which apply to the various facts composing the issue, and which they should observe in reaching their verdict. The *charge* is in the nature of instructions to the jury and is intended to assist them in reaching a verdict. It may and usually does relate to the application of the law to the facts established in evidence, but may consist in an instruction as to matters of fact only. The court cannot in such charge usurp the function of the jury, or take from it the right of weighing the evidence or of determining what weight it shall have. In the performance of this duty, the matter of the charge may originate with the court itself, or the parties to the action may submit requests that the jury be specially instructed upon certain points. The granting of these requests is discretionary with the court, but, in the event of a refusal to charge, the party submitting the request may note an exception to the ruling of the court.

Verdict — Disagreement.— After receiving the instructions contained in the charge the jury retires, and when a unanimous verdict has been reached returns to the presence of the court and announces, through its foreman, its verdict or disagreement. In the latter event the jury may be again sent out, with new or additional instructions, upon which a verdict may be based. Verdicts are either general or special; a *general verdict* is one covering all the issues of law or fact referred to the jury by the court in its charge; a *special verdict* is one in which a finding of fact only is rendered, leaving the law to be applied by the court in deciding the case.

The Judgment.— The final step in an action at law is the *judgment,* of which there were several forms at common law. The most frequent of these was, in a case tried on its merits, " that the plaintiff recover his debt, damages, and costs," or "damages and costs" if the finding was for the plaintiff; or "that the plaintiff should take nothing by this writ, and that the defendant should go thereof without day and should recover against the plaintiff the costs and charges he had been at in his defense" if the judgment was for the defendant. If the judgment be for the plaintiff, the final proceeding in the action is the *execution.* This consists in the issue and execution of such writs as are necessary to cause the judgment to be satisfied out of the property or goods of the defendant.

APPELLATE PROCEEDINGS AND NEW TRIALS

Appellate Proceedings.— If the case be tried in a court having original or intermediate jurisdiction merely, one of the parties may not be satisfied with the result of the trial and may desire either a rehearing, amounting to a re-trial of the case, or he may wish to have the decision of the lower court reviewed by an appellate tribunal. The first purpose is accomplished by an appeal, or by a motion for a new trial. Appeals are regulated by statute and usually authorize a case tried by an inferior court, board, or commission to be re-tried by a court of higher grade and more general jurisdiction. They are addressed to the court having appellate jurisdiction, and are granted sometimes as a matter of right, at the mere request of the party, and sometimes at the discretion of the higher court. The parties to the proceedings in appeal are called the *appellant* and *appelle,* corresponding to the *plaintiff* and *defendant* in the original cause of action.

New Trials.— If a rehearing of the case before the same court is desired, the party desired it submits a motion for a new trial, which is granted or not at the discretion of the court. Motions for such rehearing are made for a number of reasons, as where the verdict of the jury has been against the weight of evidence, or contrary to law, or when inadequate damages have been awarded or illegal evidence admitted, or where new and material evidence has been discovered subsequent to the trial of the case, etc.

WRITS OF ERROR

Writs of Error — Bills of Exceptions.— A case decided by a lower court is carried to a higher court for review by the issue of a mandate from the appellate court called a *write of error,* the use of which will now be explained.

In the course of the trial court of original jurisdiction questions arise from time to time which can only be disposed of by a ruling or decision of the court. From these rulings the party adversely affected may desire to appeal in which event makes use of an agency called a *writ of error,* which the law places at his disposal for this purpose. An *exception* may, therefore be defined as an objection to a ruling or decision of a court, made during the progress *of* the trial, by the party who believes it to be erroneous and for that reason, to have affected the decision in a manner unfavorable to his interest. The objections so made are called *errors* and, when formally stated in an instrument known as a *bill of exceptions,* constitute the basis for an application for a *writ of error,* by means of which the judgment of the lower court is reviewed.

Parties to Writs *of* Error.— The party in whose behalf the appeal is made is called the *plaintiff in error;* the opposite party, who becomes the defendant in the appellate proceedings, is called the *defendant in error.* The effect of the allowance of the writ of error is to stay, or defer, execution of judgment in the court below, pending the result of the appeal. If no such action is taken however, and the period allowed by statute for taking an appeal is allowed to pass the judgment of the lower court becomes final and the case is forever barred.

Procedure in Appeal — The procedure in the appellate court consists in great part of the arguments of counsel upon the points raised in the bill of exceptions and is addressed to the errors of the court below. The court sits without a jury, no testimony is submitted, there is no re-trial, and the decision relates to the case of each party as presented in a summary of points and suggestions, together with the authorities cited in their support, called a *brief,* which is usually printed and submitted to the court in advance of the hearing in appeal. The result of the appellate proceedings is to affirm or reverse the judgment, or to remand the case to the court below for a new trial, in which event the case is re-tried from the beginning.

THE WRIT OF CERTIORARI

The Writ of Certiorari.— It has been seen that cases are carried to courts of appeal, as a general rule, by the agency of writs of error. The effect of the issue of a *writ of certiorari* is to remove a case from a court in which it is pending to a higher court or, in certain cases, to remove it to another tribunal of different and more extensive jurisdiction. This removal is effected by the issue of a mandate directing that the record in a particular case be certified to the court from which the writ has issued. The effect of the writ is to discontinue all proceedings in the court below and to transfer the case to the tribunal having jurisdiction to issue the writ. The chief purpose of the writ, which may issue in civil as well as criminal cases, is to inquire into the jurisdiction exercised by the court below in the particular case in respect to which its issue has been prayed for.[61] It is also resorted to for the purpose of reviewing the proceedings of boards, commissions, and other administrative bodies having jurisdiction, under statutes, to hear and determine questions of fact, to make awards and assessments, and to perform other executive duties of a similar character.

Judgment.— The judgment upon the writ, after hearing, is that the proceeding be quashed or confirmed, wholly or in part. If the higher court takes jurisdiction of the case, the proceedings are not continuous, but the trial is begun anew, upon declaration or indictment, depending upon whether the action is civil or criminal in character. The writ will not issue in cases in which an appeal or writ of error will properly lie, or to correct mere irregularities of procedure.

---

[61] For the use of the writ of *habeas corpus* in connection with certiorari proceedings, see page 49, *post.*

CHAPTER IV

CONTEMPT OF COURT

Contempt of Court — Forms of Contempt.— Contempt of court is an offense against the orderly administration of justice, and is punishable summarily by the court in whose presence or in defiance of whose authority it is committed. Contempts are either *direct* or *constructive. Direct contempt* consists in insulting or disrespectful language addressed to the court itself, in disobedience to its orders or decrees, or in disorderly conduct, or in affrays or assaults committed in its presence. *Constructive contempt* is committed out of the presence of the court, and consists in disobedience to the writs, orders, or decrees of a court having jurisdiction of the case in which they are issued, or in acts undertaken in defiance or contempt of its authority.

Procedure.— Contempts may be committed by parties to an action, or by witnesses or officers of the court, or by strangers, or bystanders in its presence. The proceedings in cases of direct contempt are usually summary in character, as they are committed in the presence and under the observation of the court itself. In cases of constructive contempt courts will, upon proper presentation of the facts, issue a rule directing the offender to appear and show cause why process of attachment should not issue against him. Upon the hearing which follows, if the person charged with contempt clears himself upon oath, he is said to *stand purged of his contempt,* and the attachment is discharged; if found guilty, the offender is usually punished by fine or imprisonment, or both, in the discretion of the court of whose authority he is in contempt.

ARBITRATION

Besides the remedy afforded by an action at law, another form of adjusting disputes remains to be described; it is peculiarly applicable to actions on contract and is called *arbitration.*

Arbitration.— *Arbitration* consists in the reference of a dispute or difference of any kind to one or more disinterested persons for decision. In many cases the reference is entirely private, and results from the voluntary act of the parties, who mutually agree to be bound by the decision of the tribunal of their own creation. In this event the law takes no cognizance of the matter unless the reference takes the form of a contract, in which case, if there be non-performance, an action at law may result. In some of the States the subject is regulated by statute and the decisions of arbitrators are enforced by the courts. Where such statutes exist the procedure of tribunals of arbitration must conform strictly to their terms, in order that the decision or award may have the obligatory force of a legal judgment.

The Tribunal — Awards.— The tribunal consists, usually, of from one to three members; if two are chosen, they are frequently given power to select an *umpire,* or third arbitrator. Evidence may be obtained from the testimony of witnesses, or the facts in the case, as agreed upon by the parties, may be submitted to the tribunal. The submission, unless the statute provides otherwise, is revocable at any time prior to award, and the decision, or *award,* as it is technically called, is binding upon all parties to the arbitration, and an appropriate method of enforcement is usually afforded by statute. The award can be impeached only for fraud, partiality, want of competency, or serious mistake in point of fact on the part of the arbitrators; or where the award covers matters not submitted, or where there has been a failure to make a complete and final determination of the matter submitted to the board for decision.

EXTRAORDINARY REMEDIES

Extraordinary Remedies.— The relief afforded by means of an action at law, the proceedings in which have just been described, constitutes the *ordinary remedy* which the law provides for the redress of individual wrongs. There are some occasions, however, in which, from the nature of the wrong complained of, an action at law does not afford adequate relief. In such cases certain *extraordinary remedies* are provided, which are applied by the courts having equity or chancery jurisdiction, upon evidence showing that a state of facts exists to which such a remedy will properly apply, and that adequate relief can be obtained in no other way.

Form of Remedy — Parties.— The relief above referred to is afforded by means of certain *extraordinary writs* which are issued in the discretion of the court, on presentation of sufficient evidence to show that a probable case exists to which the writ applies, and that the ends of justice can be attained in no other way. When the statute provides a plain and speedy remedy these writs will not be awarded. The parties to the writs are called, respectively, the *petitioner,* or *realtor,* arid the *respondent.* The *petitioner,* or *relator,* is the injured party, who appears in court and relates, or states under oath, the facts upon which he relies to obtain the relief prayed for. The *respondent* is the defendant, who replies, or responds, to the case stated by the petitioner, and who undertakes to show that the case so stated is not sufficient in law or in fact to warrant a resort to the remedy afforded by the writ in question, or that adequate relief can be obtained by the application of other and more appropriate remedies.

MANDAMUS

Mandamus.— A writ of *mandamus* is a command issuing from a superior court of competent jurisdiction, addressed to an inferior tribunal, or to a magistrate or public officer, commanding a thing to be done or a duty to be performed. The writ will also lie against boards, commissions, and other administrative bodies having power to hear and determine questions of fact — as to make awards, or adjust assessments, or the like — and against corporations, trustees, and other persons or bodies charged with the performance of legal duties. From the definition of the writ it will be seen that the action required is *affirmative* in character, action of a *negative* or *preventive* character being obtained by a proceeding in the nature of an injunction, which will presently be described. The prayer for the issue of the writ must show a *prima facie* case of right on the part of the petitioner, that the right has been denied, infringed, or trespassed upon, or that justice has been denied. Upon such a showing the court issues a rule to the respondent, in the alternative form, commanding him to appear in court on a day named and show cause why the mandamus should not issue. On the day so appointed the respondent appears and makes return to the writ, and the court, after a full hearing of all parties affected, dismisses or quashes the writ, or by an appropriate decree makes it final or permanent.

Effects.— Mandamus will issue to compel the performance of a plain legal duty owed by a court to a party before it, or of a similar duty owed by a public officer or individual. It will also lie to compel the performance of a statutory duty owed by a board, commission, or corporation to an individual or to another corporation. If addressed to a court, board, or commission, it will require the performance of a statutory duty, but will not point out the manner in which the duty is to be performed, unless a single method of performance is possible, as where the signing of a judgment only is prayed for, or when what is known as a ministerial duty[62] is to be performed. The writ will not, in general, lie to compel the performance of a discretionary duty, or one requiring the existence of certain facts to be determined, by a public officer, as a condition precedent to such performance; the purpose of the writ being to set machinery in motion to accomplish a result, rather than to attain that result by a particular course of action.

INJUNCTION

Injunction — Forms.— An *injunction* is a remedial writ, having a preventive or restorative effect, which issues from a superior to an inferior court, or to a public officer, or to a corporation or private individual, forbidding the doing of a particular act, or the continuance of an existing status or condition of affairs. It has been seen that by the use of the writ of mandamus affirmative action was obtained, or the performance of a particular act or duty required; the opposite or preventive effect is usually sought by a resort to the writ of injunction. An individual desiring to avail himself of this remedy in a proper case applies in the first instance for a preliminary injunction, the execution of which holds the rights of the respective parties in abeyance until a formal hearing can be had. At such hearing, if the party in whose behalf the preliminary writ issued makes out a case for relief, the

---

[62] For a description of ministerial and discretionary duties, see page 29. *ante.*

temporary injunction is made permanent and is given perpetual effect. An injunction is available to stay proceedings at law, to restrain the transfer of stocks, bills, notes, and other evidences of debt, to restrain the transfer of the titles to or possession of property, to restrain the infringement of patents, copyrights, and trade-marks, and to prevent the creation or continuance of a nuisance, or to restrain acts of waste.

HABEAS CORPUS

Habeas Corpus — Purpose of Writ.— The writ of *habeas corpus* is a mandate issuing from a superior to an inferior court, or to an officer or other individual holding a person in custody, commanding him to produce the body of the prisoner in court and to show cause why he should not be set at liberty. The purpose of the writ is to inquire into all cases in which it is alleged that an individual is unlawfully confined or restrained of his liberty and, in a proper case, to put an end to such unlawful restraint or confinement. The writ has nothing to do with what are known as the *merits of the case,* that is, with the guilt or innocence of the person in whose behalf it is issued. The *legality of the restraint* is the sole subject of inquiry, and the result of its issue may be to release a guilty person or to remand an innocent one to confinement. The writ is also used as a supplemental remedy in certiorari proceedings[63] where the production of the record alone is not sufficient and the presence of the prisoner himself is necessary to the ends of justice. The writ issues from both the State and Federal courts. From the latter, in a case of a prisoner held by or under color of the authority of the United States, or by the orders or process of a State court

---

[63] For a description of the writ of certiorari, see page 46, *ante*.

for an act done in pursuance of Federal authority. It is issued from the proper State court in all other cases.

Procedure — Return.— The procedure under the writ is as follows: The writ issues upon a petition showing facts sufficient to constitute a *prima facie* case of unlawful restraint. It is addressed to the officer holding the person in custody, commanding him to appear in court, on a day named, with the body of the prisoner, and show cause why he should not be released from custody. On the day set apart for the hearing the respondent appears and submits a return, or statement, in writing, setting forth the authority by which the prisoner is held. This return, or statement, may be traversed or denied by the opposite party. The judgment is that the prisoner be released, or that the writ be discharged and the prisoner be remanded to the custody of the respondent. The writ is sometimes resorted to when the restraint alleged does not amount to imprisonment, as in the case of married women, wards, and infants, or to determine questions relating to the custody of children.

The writ of *habeas corpus ad testificandum* may be issued by any court for the purpose of bringing a prisoner into court with a view to the taking of his testimony in a cause there pending. When the testimony of such prisoner has been given in, he is remanded, or returned to the custody of the sheriff.

QUO WARRANTO

Quo Warranto.— The writ of *quo warranto* was what was known as a prerogative writ at common law, because its issue involved an exercise or assertion of the sovereign power. It was addressed to a person who exercised a franchise or was the incumbent of an office, and commanded the respondent to show by what warrant or authority he acted. In England and the United States it has been generally replaced by a similar remedy called *an information in the nature of a quo warranto,* and is used to test the validity of an incumbent's right to a particular office, or the right of a person or corporation to exercise a particular franchise. The *information* may originate with a public officer or a private individual, and must be supported by evidence, in the form of an affidavit, showing that a proper case for its issue exists. Upon receipt of the information the court issues a rule to the respondent to show cause. The return to the rule sets forth the authority by which the office is held or the franchise exercised. The judgment in the case of an officer is of ouster; that is, to oust or remove the incumbent and to vacate the office, or to confirm his incumbency, as the case may be. In the case of a corporation the judgment is of ouster or of seizure, in which event the franchise revests in the State. As the information in the nature of.quo warranto is criminal in form, the pleadings are those of a criminal rather than a civil action.

NE EXEAT REPUBLICA

Ne Exeat Republica.— The writ of *ne exeat,* like that of quo warranto, is a prerogative writ, the purpose of which is, as its name implies, to prevent a person from leaving the State, district, or territorial jurisdiction of the court from which it issues. At present its issue is an incident of equity jurisdiction, and is restricted in its operation to prevent a person against whom an equitable demand exists, and who is believed to have sequestered his property, from leaving the jurisdiction of the court having authority to issue the mandate. The proceeding originates in a motion, supported by affidavit, showing that the case exists which is contemplated in the statute authorizing the issue of the writ. The operation of the writ, the issuing of which is discretionary, extends to any person within the jurisdiction of the court, and commands him not to go out of such territorial jurisdiction without its permission. Upon payment into court of the amount of the claim, or upon proof that such claim has no foundation in fact, the writ is discharged.

PROHIBITION

The *writ of prohibition* differs from those which have already been described in that it may be issued by a court having common-law as distinguished from equity jurisdiction. The object of a *writ of prohibition* is to prevent a court of limited or inferior jurisdiction from assuming jurisdiction of a matter beyond its legal cognizance. The writ will not lie unless it clearly appears that the inferior court is about to exceed its jurisdiction; nor will the writ be granted unless the want of jurisdiction shall have been brought to the attention of the court below, by plea, suggestion, or otherwise, but without avail. It cannot be made to serve the purpose of a writ of error or certiorari, to correct mistakes of that court in deciding any questions of law or fact within, its jurisdiction.[64] If the case can be carried up by way of appeal or by writ of error, the writ will not lie and the petitioner will be left to his ordinary remedy, or to the extraordinary relief afforded by the writs already described. The writ will also lie against minor legislative bodies, such as town councils and the like, and against

---

[64] Smith *vs.* Whitney, 116 U. S., 167, 176: U. S. *vs.* Peters, 3 Dallas, 121; *Ex parts* Easton, 95 U. S. 68; *Ex parte* Gordon, 104 U. S., 515; *Exports* Ferry, *ibid.,* 174; U. S. *vs.* Hoffman, 4 Wall., 158; *Ex parte* McMechen, 12 Ark., 70.

boards, commissions, courts martial,[65] and public officers whose acts are in excess of their statutory powers, especially when those acts have a quasi-judicial character. In some of the States, however, the operation of the writ is restricted, by statute, to courts of justice.

PLEADING

Origin of the System.— It has been seen that the common law provided a number of *writs,* or *forms of action,* in strict accordance with which all demands for the redress of private wrongs, or causes of action as they came to be called, had to be stated. The system of pleading was based upon the forms of action at common law and was devised for the purpose of eliminating from a case all questions of fact that were susceptible of answer, with a view to bring about a single issue of fact, affirmed by one party and denied by the other, which could be referred to a jury for trial. The system of pleading, which was contemporaneous in its origin with the common law, reached its development in the reign of Edward IV. and continued to prevail, without substantial change, until the reign of Queen Anne, when a serious innovation was made by the enactment of a statute which allowed a defendant to plead several matters of defense, and in this way to create as many issues as there were separate pleas.

Present Practice.— This legislation, which operated to produce confusion in the trial of cases by introducing a multiplicity of issues, continued in force until the year 1834, when the rules of the Hilary Term were adopted with a view to simplify the existing rules of pleading at

---

[65] Smith *vs.* Whitney, 116 U. S., 167; Grant *vs.* Gould, 2 H. Blackstone, 69; Washburn *vs.* Phillipps, 2 Metcalf, 296.

common law. These rules, as amended — the last time in 1883 — are now in force in England. In the United States there is considerable diversity of practice in this respect; and the subject of pleading, in both civil and criminal cases, is regulated by statute in the several States of the Federal Union. In some jurisdictions a modified form of the common-law rules prevails; in others the subject is regulated by codes of civil and criminal procedure.

Objects.— The chief objects of pleading are to bring the parties to an issue at the earliest moment, and to produce an issue that shall be material, single, and certain in its quality. These objects are attained by a series of alternate allegations of fact, each of which the opposite party answers by a corresponding statement of fact, or by an objection in law, until an issue is produced upon which the parties go to trial. If an answer to an opponent's pleading be by a statement of fact, it is called a *pleading;* if it be in the form of an objection ill law, it is called a *demurrer.*

Pleadings, Demurrers, etc.— Classification.— *Pleadings* may therefore be defined as allegations of fact, advanced in alternate succession by plaintiff and defendant, with a view of reaching an issue of fact to be tried, by a jury or otherwise, as the law may direct. Pleadings are classified, according to their nature and effect, *into pleas to the action* and *dilatory pleas.* The former meet the issue of fact raised by the plaintiff, in his declaration, in a manner hereafter to be explained; the latter raise a question as to the jurisdiction of the court, its power to try the particular case, or the ability of the parties to maintain the action; or are addressed to the form of action used, or to the remedy which is sought to be applied. Their effect is to delay the action rather than to try it on its merits, and, if allowed, the result is to give rise to a new cause of action which shall be free from the objections advanced in the dilatory plea.

Titles of Pleadings.— The first pleading in an action at law is the plaintiff's *declaration,* which contains a statement of the particular facts upon which he relies to maintain his action. The defendant's reply is called the *plea,* and the pleadings that follow in regular order are called the *replication, rejoinder, surrejoinder, rebutter,* and *surrebutter;* these names being given to distinguish them from each other, and to enable them to be referred to at subsequent stages of the case.

How Made.— Pleadings were originally made orally, in open court; they are now generally submitted in writing, and are made a part of the formal record in the case. The distinct and separate statements of the several causes of action in a declaration, indictment, or other pleading are called *counts,* the use of which has already been explained.[66] Pleadings begin and end with formal commencements and conclusions which are regulated by codes or by statute in the several States, or, in the absence of such statutory regulations, by the rules of pleading as recognized by the common law.

Demurrers.— It has been seen that, at any stage of the pleadings, either party may, in a proper case, regard his opponent's pleading as defective in form or insufficient in substance to constitute a cause of action, and he may therefore object or *demur* to answering by matter of fact, and thus raise an issue of law by showing that the pleading

---

[66] If a single cause of action be set forth in the declaration, it is referred to as a count, or as a declaration; if the declaration contain several distinct causes of notion, or if the facts constituting a cause of action be stated in different forms, each statement is called a count.

in question is defective in form or substance. By so doing he admits the facts to be as stilted in the several pleadings and undertakes to show that the law, as applied to such facts, does not make out a case for his opponent. The issue of law so raised is decided by the court on its merits, the facts being already admitted as of record. Such tender of issue in law is called a *demurrer.*

Pleas by Way of Traverse.— The answer of fact, of which every pleading must consist, is said to be made by way of *traverse,* or *in confession and avoidance. A* pleading is said to be by way of *traverse* when it denies the allegation of fact made by an adversary in his pleading and *tenders issue,* as it is called; that is, concludes with an offer to go to trial on the issue thus raised in the pleadings.

Pleas in Confession and Avoidance.— A party is said to plead by way of *confession and avoidance* when he admits or confesses the truth of the facts stated in his opponent's pleading, but replies thereto by stating new matter, the effect of which is to avoid the legal inference which would naturally be deduced or inferred from such admission. It is thus seen that a traverse implies an immediate joinder of issue, while a plea in confession and avoidance defers such joinder of issue to a later stage of the pleadings. Pleadings in confession and avoidance are said to be *by way of justification or excuse* when it is claimed that an act alleged in pleading was lawful, and that therefore no cause of action exists. They are said to be by way of *discharge* when they admit that a cause of action existed at one time, but that it has been released or discharged by an act of the opposite party.

Illustration.— The following case will illustrate the foregoing classification of pleadings in an action at law. A complains that he has been assaulted by B, the act having taken place on land belonging to B. This being an assault in which actual force was used, the form of action is that of trespass *vi et armis.* A brings suit and alleges ill his *declaration* that B assaulted him at a time and place named therein. B in his *plea* may simply *deny* or *traverse* the fact and declare his willingness to go to trial on the issue of fact thus raised. In this case B pleads by way of *traverse* and *tenders issue.* Instead of doing this, however, B in his plea may admit the fact of assault, but may say in reply that he resorted to force in self-defense. He thus admits the fact of the assault, as alleged by A, but pleads in *confession and avoidance by way of justification.* That is, he confesses the facts to be as stated by A, but avoids the legal inference therefrom by introducing new matter which, if true, tends to justify or excuse his act. A, in turn, may simply deny or *traverse,* and tender issue; or he may plead *in confession and avoidance* by alleging that he assaulted B to prevent him from taking away the goods of A. This also may be traversed by the defendant, or he may again plead *in confession and avoidance* by admitting-that the goods were on his land, and that he was in the act of removing them when he was assaulted by A. The plaintiff A may *traverse* the pleading of his opponent and tender issue thereon, or he may *confess and avoid* by admitting that the goods were there by the leave or license of the defendant. While it is very unlikely that the pleadings, in any action at law, however complicated, will ever reach this stage, it is apparent that in any case they will sooner or later reach a stage consisting of a single issue of fact, affirmed by one party and denied by the other, upon which issue is joined and the case seat to trial.

RULES OF PLEADING

General Rule.— From the nature and character of the process it is obvious that all facts should be pleaded with the greatest accuracy, certainty, and precision. Forms for the commencement and conclusion of pleadings are required by the common law, or by statute in those jurisdictions in which the common-law methods have been modified, or replaced, by codes of civil and criminal procedure. To secure accuracy, precision, and brevity in pleading, the following rules should be observed:

1. Every pleading must meet and answer or cover the whole of the opposite pleading, either by a *traverse,* or by a plea *in confession* and *avoidance,* or by a *demurrer.* If a defendant answers to a part only of the plaintiff's declaration, the latter may ask judgment on the part not answered; failing to do this, he is said to suffer a *discontinuance,* if the matter be material, as to the part not answered. That is, he waives, or abandons, so much of his case as has not been answered by the defendant in his pleading.

2. Tender of Issue.— Upon a plea by way of *traverse,* or *denial, issue* must be tendered; that is, the party must assert his readiness to go to trial upon the issue created by such traverse or denial.

3. Issue must be accepted.— Issue when tendered must be accepted. Such issue must be well tendered, however, and must not be subject to answer by matter of fact or open to demurrer. In other words, issue cannot be joined at an intermediate stage of the pleadings, but the process must continue until not only a single but an ultimate, or final, issue has been reached which can be referred to a jury for trial.

4. Materiality.— Every pleading must contain matter pertinent and material to the pleading to which it is an answer. It must also meet such pleading accurately, being neither too broad nor too narrow.

5. Duplicity — Repugnancy.— Pleadings must be neither double nor repugnant. Duplicity, or double pleading, consists in the allegation of two or more distinct defenses in the same pleading. As the purpose of pleading is to reach a single issue, duplicity is disfavored, as calculated to defeat the attainment of such purpose. Repugnancy exists when pleadings are inconsistent with, or opposed to, each other. Where a party takes up a particular ground in pleading and then changes to another and different ground, not in support of the former, there is said to be a *departure.* This is not regarded with favor, as it tends to defer and in some instances to defeat joinder of issue — the prime object of all pleading.

6. Argumentativeness.— Argumentativeness in pleading is to be avoided. A pleading, from its definition, should contain only *matter of fact* in answer to what has been pleaded by the opposite party; anything in the nature of reasoning upon the facts stated, or the drawing of conclusions therefrom, is subject to objection as argumentative, and, if the objection be well taken, the court will order the objectionable matter to be stricken out.

7. Certainty.— Pleadings must be *certain;* that is, must be so stated as to enable an adversary to know the precise nature of the demand to which be is expected to reply, or against which he must defend himself, if the charge be criminal in character. Allegations of title and ownership, statements of fact relating to the names and titles of office of persons, dates, names of places, descriptions of things in controversy and the like, fall under this head.

8. Party cannot Plead and Demur to the same Matter — Exception.— A party cannot plead and demur in answer to the same matter, but must answer by *allegation of fact,* by way of traverse, or in confession and

avoidance, or must answer by *demurrer* and thereby raise an issue of law. There is an exception to this rule when a party elects to demur and the court, in deciding the demurrer, orders him to plead over or, as it is called, to answer over. In the criminal procedure of the Federal courts it is required by statute "that the judgment upon any demurrer which is overruled shall be that the party shall answer over," that is, shall plead again, or, if he have no matter upon which to base a special plea, he shall plead the general issue of guilty or not guilty.[67]

ORDER OF PLEADING

Pleas are required to be submitted in the following order:

1. Order of Pleading.— Pleas to the Jurisdiction of the Court.— If there are sufficient grounds for such a course, it is proper, at the outset, to question the jurisdiction of the court, for if it be found that it has not power to try the case it is useless to carry the pleadings further.

2. Pleas in Abatement of the Action, or Dilatory Pleas.— If the court is found to have jurisdiction of the subject-matter of the case, the next point to be determined is whether the plaintiff has the right and capacity under the law to maintain the action. An infant or a married woman, for example, cannot sue alone unless specially authorized to do so by statute. Such are said to be pleas in *bar of the action* or in *bar of trial.* Next follow what are called pleas in abatement of the action. A *plea in abatement* alleges that, by reason of some defect, the action is not maintainable in its present form; that the proper persons have not been made parties; that there is some defect of

---

[67] Section 1026 Revised Statutes of the United States.

form or substance in the declaration, or that there has been a failure to serve process, etc. As pleas in abatement do not go to the merits of the case, but tend to delay the trial, and so to protract litigation, they are disfavored and it is required that they shall contain such matter as will enable the error to be corrected and a new action to be brought in due form of law. The judgment on a plea in abatement is, if for the plaintiff, that the defendant answer over; if for the defendant, that the writ be quashed or abated. When the dilatory pleas have been disposed of the parties are required to plead to the action in accordance with the foregoing rules.

REFERENCES.— Among the older works on this subject the American editions of Chitty and Archbold will be found useful for reference in those States which still retain the common-law forms of action and pleading. Tyler's edition of Stephen, Estee, Abbot, and the smaller works of Heard, Shipman, Evans, and McKelvey will be found useful for purposes of study and reference.

CRIMINAL TRIALS

Criminal Trials.— The proceedings in a criminal trial are substantially the same as those just described in an action at law, the theory in both cases being that an impartial tribunal is provided by the State for the trial of the cause, and that the parties are bound by the judgment of the tribunal so provided. The differences of procedure in criminal cases are due, in large measure, to the precautions taken to insure a fair and impartial trial.

General Incidents.— The pleadings are somewhat similar and begin with an *indictment,* in which the offense of the accused person is set forth, an issue is sooner obtained, a greater number of *peremptory challenges* is allowed than in an action at law, and somewhat more latitude is accorded in the matter of *challenges for cause;* the presumption of innocence until the contrary is proven attends the accused throughout the trial, and evidence to convict must convince the jury beyond a reasonable doubt.[68] In addition, such guarantees in respect to the rights of a person accused of crime as are contained in the Constitution must be strictly observed in respect to all the incidents of trial.

Criminal Prosecutions. How Instituted.— A criminal prosecution may be instituted in two ways; one private, at the instance of the party injured, the other public, at the instance of the grand jury. The person injured by the commission of a crime, or a peace officer, and, in some cases, a private citizen who has knowledge that an offense has been committed, may appear before a magistrate and make a *sworn complaint* against the offender. Upon this complaint a warrant for the arrest of the person charged with the commission of the offense is issued by the justice or magistrate to whom the complaint was addressed. Upon the arrest of the offender a preliminary hearing is had before the magistrate by whom the warrant was issued, for the purpose of determining whether an offense has been committed which will justify the holding of the prisoner for trial. If the complaint is found to be well grounded, the prisoner is committed for trial and held to await the action of the grand jury or, in a

---

[68] A reasonable doubt is an honest, substantial misgiving generated by insufficiency of proof. It is not a captious doubt, nor a doubt suggested by the ingenuity of counsel or jury and unwarranted by the testimony; nor is it a doubt born of a merciful inclination to permit the defendant to escape conviction, nor prompted by sympathy with him or those connected with him. (United States *vs.* Newton, 52 Fed. Rep., 275.)

proper case, is released upon the production of security for his appearance, called bail. If the facts as developed at the hearing do not warrant his holding, the accused person is released.

THE GRAND JURY. INDICTMENTS INFORMATIONS

The Grand Jury — Indictments.— At common law there were two methods by which a public prosecution could be instituted; these were: (1) by *indictment;* (2) by *information.* The *indictment,* or *presentment,* originated with the grand jury, the *information* with a law officer of the Crown. These methods still obtain as to criminal prosecutions in the several States of the Union; for violations of the criminal laws of the United States amounting to felony, the method by indictment, or presentment, by a grand jury is required by the Fifth Amendment to the Constitution.

Procedure.— The Grand Jury is composed of not less than 12 and not more than 23 members, who are chosen, usually by lot, from the residents of the county or judicial district. It is the duty of the grand jury to inquire into and investigate all crimes which have been committed within the jurisdiction of the court to which its presentments are made. In these indictments, or presentments, twelve jurors must concur. Before entering upon the investigation the members are sworn to the faithful performance of their duties and are instructed or *charged* by the court as to the nature and scope of their inquiry. Witnesses are summoned and examined, usually with the assistance of the district attorney, and upon the evidence thus obtained indictments are found and presented to the court. If sufficient cause appear to warrant prosecution, an indictment, or *true bill,* is returned; if the facts do not warrant a criminal prosecution, the bill is returned as *not true.* An *indictment* may, therefore, be defined as "a written accusation, presented on oath by at least twelve of a grand jury, charging a person named therein with a crime which it specifically defines, and returned by the grand jury into court, where it becomes a matter of record."[69]

Indictments and Presentments Distinguished.— At present the terms *indictment* and *presentment* have much the same meaning; the former, however, always relates to a formal accusation of crime, preferred against a particular person, or persons, if more than one were concerned in its commission. A *presentment* is a more general accusation and may relate to the prevalence of particular crimes in the community, or to neglect or misconduct in respect to their prevention or punishment. In some cases grand juries make a general presentment of evils and evil things, which they mention, for the purpose of calling the attention of the public, or the officers of the law, to them; not intending thereby to furnish instructions for any specific indictments.

It was, and is, the office of the grand jury at common law to institute prosecutions, and, save for the limited power of instituting prosecutions by *information,* presently to be explained, no person can be brought to trial without the concurrence and cooperation of the grand jurors, who, for this purpose, represent the freeholders, or voters of the county. The institution thus acted as a check upon the law officers of the Crown and protected the subject against prosecution at the instance of the sovereign. It still serves to prevent unfounded accusations from being brought to trial, to the detriment of innocent

---

[69] 1 Bishop Criminal Procedure, § 133.

persons and, where the evidence is not sufficient to convict, eaves the expense of useless trials. [70]

Prosecution by Information.— The method of prosecution by *information* had its origin in England, where it was set on foot at the suggestion of the Sovereign or Ministry or, on his own motion, by one of the principal law officers of the Crown. As such prosecutions were, at times, political in character, the practice of filing information has been restricted, by statute, in its application to the more serious criminal offenses, not only in England, but in the several States of the Union as well. The use of information, in the criminal procedure of the United States, is regulated by the Fifth Amendment to the Constitution, which requires that "no person shall be held to answer for a capital or otherwise infamous crime unless on a presentment or indictment of a grand jury, except in cases arising in the land or naval forces, or in the militia when in actual service in time of war or public danger."[71]

The Indictment — Counts.— The *indictment,* which has already been explained, corresponds exactly to the *declaration* in an action at law. It also serves to apprise the accused of the particular offense with which he is charged, and for which he must prepare to defend himself at the trial. Indictments may charge a single offense, or allege several offenses to have been committed; these separate

---

[70] 1 Bishop, § 138.

[71] As the provisions of the Fifth Amendment relate to "capital and otherwise infamous offenses," it has been held by the Federal courts that offenses not capital or infamous might be prosecuted by information. U. S. *vs.* Maxwell, 3 Dill., 275 ; U. S. *vs.* Shepard, 1 Abb. C. C., 431 ; U. S *vs.* Black, 4 Sawyer, 211 ; *V. S: vs.* Baugh, 1 Fed. Rep., 145.

allegations are called *counts.* In some cases the *counts* are distinct and unconnected charges, which might have been made the subject of separate indictments; in others they are different statements of the same offense, and are so charged in order to enable the jury to bring in a finding of guilty of a lesser kindred offense than that charged, when the evidence does not show that an offense of greater degree has been committed. An indictment charging murder, for example, may contain a count charging the same offense as manslaughter; in some jurisdictions a finding of guilty of an offense less than that charged, or of an attempt to commit the particular offense charged, is authorized by statute.[72]

The Arraignment — Pleadings — Demurrers.— The time set for the trial of the case having arrived, the prisoner is arraigned — that is, he is called upon to plead to the allegations contained in the indictment, a copy of which has been furnished to the accused previous to the trial. If the plea be *guilty,* judgment is entered, an. appropriate sentence is pronounced, and the trial ends. If the plea be otherwise than *guilty, the* further pleadings in the case are submitted as in civil actions. Either party may raise an issue of law by demurrer, but as such a course requires the defendant to admit the truth of all facts charged in the indictment that have been correctly pleaded, a, judgment of guilty would necessarily ensue upon the failure of the court to sustain his demurrer. To avoid this and enable the case to go to trial on its merits, it is required, by statute, in most jurisdictions that the judgment, in case a demurrer submitted in behalf of the

---

[72] See Section 1035 Revised Statutes of the United States.

accused be not sustained, shall be that he *answer over,* that is, that he plead anew to the indictment.[73]

The Petit Jury — Challenges.— The next step in a criminal trial is the formation of the *petit* or *trial jury.* This body is summoned by the sheriff in the State courts, and by the marshal in the criminal courts of the United States. With a view to secure an impartial jury, the right of *challenge is* exercised in behalf of both the Government and the accused.

Challenges are either *peremptory or for cause stated.* In making *peremptory* challenges no reason or ground of objection is stated, the number of such challenges being regulated by statute in the jurisdiction in which the trial takes place.[74] Challenges for cause are classified into *challenges to the array* and *challenges to the poll* or *individual challenges,* and in most of the States, are tried by *triers,* and in the courts of the United States by the court itself, without reference to triers.

Forms of Challenges.— A *challenge to the array* is directed against the whole body, or panel, of jurors, and is based upon some illegality in respect to their summons, or to fraud or partiality in their selection. Challenges to the poll are further classified as *principal challenges* and

---

[73] See Sec. 1036, Revised Statutes of the United States.

[74] This subject is regulated in the procedure of the Federal courts by Section 829 of the Revised Statutes, which entitles the accused in a capital case to twenty peremptory challenges and the United States to five. In a trial for a felony, not capital, the parties are entitled to ten and three respectively. In ail other cases, civil and criminal, each party is entitled to three. Similar provisions will be found in the statutes of the several States.

challenges to the favor. A *principal challenge* is one addressed to a juror for a cause which, when stated, operates to cause his discharge as a matter of course. This is the case where the juror has already sat in a previous trial of the same case, or has investigated the offense as a matter of official duty, or has had connection with it as an attorney, etc. A *challenge to the favor* is one based upon bias, prejudice, relationship to a party, etc. The presumption of competency exists in all cases, and the burden of proving incapacity rests upon the party who offers the challenge. Bias, etc., may be shown by the testimony of witnesses, or by the testimony of the juror himself obtained under the sanction of a peculiar form of oath called a "*voir dire.*" The challenging continues until the panel is completed, that is, until twelve jurors have been obtained for the trial of the case. The jurors are then sworn and the trial proceeds in accordance with the form already described in connection with the action at law.

THE LAW OF EVIDENCE

The Judicial Ascertainment of Facts.— The methods which are employed by courts of justice to ascertain the facts — that is, the truth — respecting any past transaction closely resemble those resorted to by an individual for a similar purpose. If he desires to ascertain whether a particular act did or did not take place, he addresses himself to those who were in a situation to witness the transaction itself, and so endeavors to obtain from each person present his version of the occurrence. From the testimony thus obtained he forms his conclusion as to whether or not the act took place. In the course of his investigation, however, he finds that all who were present and witnessed the transaction, as bystanders, do not give testimony of equal importance or value. Some, having greater powers of observation or better memories than others, give, in consequence, more valuable testimony. Some of the witnesses were children or persons of weak or unsound mind and so had not the requisite mental capacity to observe facts or to appreciate their relations to each other; others, by reason of their bad character, are not regarded as worthy of belief by their fellow citizens; others still were insane or, perhaps, under the influence of intoxicating liquor at the time of the occurrence, and so were incapacitated from observing. A therefore rejects some of the statements as entirely untrustworthy; to others he attaches weight in proportion to their worthiness of belief, and so endeavors to reach a conclusion as to the truth of the occurrence, or event, which was the original subject of his inquiry.

Evidence.— It has been seen that the chief purpose in reducing the facts to a single issue was to render the task of the jury as simple and untechnical as possible. To this end, such evidence only as tends directly to prove or disprove the facts in issue is permitted to go to the jury. Experience has shown that all these precautions are necessary in order to obtain a verdict that shall be correct in point of fact and insure a just determination of the action on its merits.

Definition of the Term.— The term *evidence* is, in general, applied to that which tends to render evident or clear;[75] in its legal acceptation the term may be defined as including and applying to all matters of fact which a court of justice permits to be submitted to the jury, in the trial of a case, with a view to prove or disprove the existence of a fact in issue.[76]

---

[75] ' Best on Evidence, 8, § 11.

[76] According to Professor Greenleaf the term includes "all the means by which any matter of fact, the truth of

How Obtained.— Evidence is obtained by the application of a system of rules, partly statutory and in part derived from the common law, called *rules of evidence.* The facts so presented are derived from the *testimony of witnesses* who have observed them, or from *documents* relating to the case, the production of which has been compelled by due process of law.

WITNESSES

Purpose of Rules of Evidence.— The *rules of evidence* have to do with determining what is called the *competency of witnesses;* that is, of deciding whether a particular person shall be permitted to testify at all; and with the exclusion of certain testimony from the consideration of the jury upon the ground that it is likely to mislead them and to confuse, rather than to make clear, the issue referred to them for trial. They also determine, to a certain extent, the *credibility of witnesses,* or the *weight* that is to be attached to their testimony.

Witnesses.— *Witnesses* are persons who appear in court in obedience to appropriate summons and there relate, under the sanction of an oath, such facts pertaining to a particular case as they have become cognizant of through the medium of their senses. The facts in a particular case, as established by the testimony of witnesses or the production of documents, constitute the evidence upon which the jury must base its findings.

Duty of Witness to Testify — Appearance.— The giving of testimony in an action at law is regarded as an important public duty, due from the individual to the State of which he is a citizen. In a criminal case every person

---

which is submitted to investigation, is established or disproved."

upon whom a subpœna has been duly served must appear and testify, or render himself liable to punishment for contempt. In a civil case, however, such appearance is not required of an individual unless his fees have been tendered, but when such tender has been properly made his attendance becomes compulsory. To obtain the attendance of a particular person as a witness a *writ of subpœna* is issued directing him to appear in court as a witness on a day named. If the witness has in his possession a book, paper, or other thing material to a cause as an instrument of evidence, a writ called a *subpœna duces tecum* issues commanding him to appear in court on a day certain, and to have with him the particular paper or other article named and described in the subpœna. If the witness be a prisoner in jail, his presence is secured by the issue of a peculiar form of the writ of habeas corpus called *habeas corpus ad testificandum,* the use of which has already been described.

Service of Summons.— All service of writs must be personal; that is, the writ must be actually delivered to the witness by the officer deputed to serve it; and the fact of service must be verified by indorsement on the duplicate writ, which is returned to the court as evidence that service has been made.

Attachment.— Should a witness who has been duly summoned fail to appear on the day named in the subpœna, his presence is compelled by the issue of *process of attachment,* which is, in substance, an order of court directing that the witness be arrested and brought into its presence. If the failure to appear be not explained to its satisfaction, the court will proceed summarily in the matter and may, in its discretion, impose sentence of fine or imprisonment upon the person so adjudged guilty of contempt.

CHAPTER IV

COMPETENCY OF WITNESSES CREDIBILITY

Competency of Witnesses.— The *competency* of a witness is his legal power to testify, and is determined by the common law, or by statute, in the State in which the trial takes place. *Competency* is always presumed and the burden of proving incompetency lies upon the party that asserts it in the case of a particular witness. The *credibility* of a witness is his worthiness of belief, and is determined by his character, by the acuteness of his powers of observation, by the accuracy and retentiveness of his memory, and by his capacity to give lucid expression to facts within his knowledge. Questions of competency are determined by the court, and if decided adversely the witness is not permitted to testify at all. Questions of credibility are always determined by the jury.

GROUNDS OF INCOMPETENCY

Grounds of Incompetency.— The principal grounds of incompetency at the common law are: (1) infamy; (2) want of religious belief; (3) interest in the subject of litigation, as a party or otherwise; (4) want of understanding.

Infamy.— The term *infamous* — without fame or good report — was applied at common law to certain crimes, upon conviction of which a person became incompetent to testify as a witness. This was upon the theory that a person would not commit a crime of such heinous character unless so depraved as to be wholly insensible to the obligation of an oath and, therefore, unworthy of credit. The crimes involving infamy are *treason, felony,* and the *erimen falsi.* As to whether all species of this last are infamous, there is disagreement among the authorities.[77]

Procedure in Case of Incompetency from Infamy.— *Incompetency from infamy* is established by the production or proof of the judgment itself, in the case of the person whose incompetency is alleged. A finding of guilt merely is not sufficient, but the judgment itself must be produced. Incompetency so established may be removed by reversal of judgment or by pardon. In the latter case, if the statute imposing the penalty is, in its nature, a rule of evidence and not a measure of punishment only, it has been held that a pardon will not operate to restore competency; the power to pardon being subordinate to the paramount authority of the legislature to prescribe rules of evidence as an incident of procedure in actions at law.

Treason.— *Treason* is defined in the Constitution of the United States, and "shall consist only in levying war against them, or in. adhering to their enemies, giving them aid and comfort." Similar definitions occur in the constitutions of the several States. The essence of the offense is a repudiation, on the part of the individual, of his allegiance to the State of which he is a citizen. A person convicted of so serious a crime forfeits, upon conviction, such rights as attach to citizenship. He denies the obligation of the laws, and properly forfeits the privileges and immunities conferred by them; one of the most important of which is that of testifying, as a witness, in a court of the State in which he occupies the status of a traitor.

---

[77] 1 Greenleaf, § 372 ; People *vs.* Whipple, 9 Cow. (N. Y.) 707 ; U. S. *vs.* Reid, 13 How., 361; Logan *vs. U.* S., 144 U. S., 263.

Felony.— When a person had been convicted of certain crimes at common law he occupied, in consequence of such conviction and the judgment had thereon, a peculiar status called *felony. Felony* was, therefore, in strictness, rather a result or consequence of crime than a crime itself. Any offense which at common law was punishable capitally or with a forfeiture of land and goods was a felony, and a person convicted thereof became infamous and forfeited a number of civil rights, among them the capacity to testify, as a witness, in a court of justice.

In the United States there is some confusion as to the precise meaning of the term felony, and, consequently, as to what offenses are felonious and, as such, involve incompetency to testify. In some of the States the rules of the common law still prevail; in others all grounds of incompetency have been swept away by statute; between these two extremes falls the practice of the several States of the Union in respect to felony as a cause of disqualification. The practice in a particular State can only be ascertained by an examination of its statutes relating to the competency and credibility of witnesses. In most of the States, however, it may be said that all statutory crimes not capital are classed as felonies or as misdemeanors accordingly as they are or are not punishable by imprisonment in a State prison or penitentiary. The competency of witnesses in the criminal courts of the United States is determined by the law of the State in which the case is tried, as it was when those courts were established by the Judiciary Act of 1789, subject, however, to such statutory modifications as are contained in subsequent enactments of Congress.[78]

---

[78] U. S. *vs.* Reid, 12 How., 361, 363, 366 ; Packet Co. *vs.* Clough, 20 Wall., 528 ; Logan *vs. U. S.*, 144 U. S. 263,

Practice of the United States Courts.— It has been seen that the United States Government, as such, has no common-law jurisdiction. There is, therefore, no status of felony under the laws of the United States unless an offense has been declared felonious or infamous by statute, or unless the punishment attached thereto is such as to render one who has undergone it infamous. "What punishments shall be considered as infamous may be affected by changes of public opinion from one age to another. For more than a century imprisonment at hard labor in the State prison or penitentiary has been considered as infamous punishment in England and America. Such imprisonment, with or without hard labor, is at present considered infamous punishment."[79]

Crimen Falsi.— The *crimen faisi,* at common law, "was any offense involving falsehood, and which might injuriously affect the administration of justice by the introduction of falsehood or fraud,"[80] and any person guilty of such an offense was properly regarded as incompetent to testify, in view of such willful disregard of truth and wanton contempt for the solemn sanction of an oath. The offenses included under this head are forgery, perjury, subornation of perjury, and the like; each of which involves the repudiation, on the part of the individual, of the sanction of an oath and a willful attempt to introduce falsehood and fraud into judicial proceedings, under the guise of testimony and with a view to subvert the ends of justice.

301.

[79] Mackin *vs.* The United States, 117 U. S., 350, 353 ; *Ex parte* Wilson, 114 U. S.. 117.

[80] 1 Greenleaf, § 373.

INTERESTS

Interest.— It was a rule of the common law that a party to the record, in a civil action, was permitted to testify against his interest, but was regarded as incompetent to give evidence in his own behalf. This by reason of his *interest* in the subject of the action, based upon the experience of mankind and the belief that any testimony given by a party would be colored by his relationship to the controversy. It was also regarded as expedient, from the point of view of an enlightened public policy, to remove from the path of a witness every temptation to commit perjury. To disqualify, the interest must be real and actual and not conditional merely; the particular degree of interest that will disqualify, in any case, being determined by the court; the test applied being whether the witness will "gain or lose by the legal operation of the judgment; or that the record will be legal evidence for or against him in some other action."[81]

Degree of Interest.— "The *degree of interest* is immaterial," for it is impossible to measure the influence which any given interest may exert. It is enough that the interest that the witness has in the subject is direct, certain, and vested, however small be its amount; for, interest being admitted as a disqualifying circumstance in any case, it must of necessity be so in every case, whatever be the character, rank, or fortune of the party interested."[82]

Application to Criminal Cases.— The rule that interest disqualifies applies in criminal as well as civil cases when the witness has a direct, certain, and immediate interest in the result of the prosecution. The

---

[81] *Ibid.*, § 390.

[82] 11 Greenleaf, § 391.

interest may be to recover a penalty, to obtain a reward or other benefit, or to secure immunity from prosecution; the disqualifying interest may also be that of an accomplice or co-defendant.[83]

Testimony against Interest.— A party is competent to testify voluntarily against himself at any time and in any case. He may do this under the sanction of an oath, or he may accomplish the same purpose in any indirect way, by means of declarations against interest, made oat of court in a matter relating to the subject of the action. It is proper to observe, in this connection, that this rule of disqualification, which has never been recognized in equity proceedings, has been removed or greatly modified as a ground of incompetency in many of the States, where provision is made by statute that any interest which a party may have in an action at law may be testified to with a view to affect his credibility with the jury.[84]

The Accused in a Criminal Case.— The party chiefly interested in a criminal prosecution is the accused himself, the prosecutor or plaintiff being always the State, which, for reasons of public policy, regards all criminal acts as directed against the peace and dignity of the Commonwealth. The party actually injured by the commission of a criminal offense, who is known as the prosecutor, or prosecuting witness, is always a competent, and in most cases a necessary witness. With a view to prevent what were known as inquisitorial trials, it has long been the rule of the common law not only to forbid an accused person to testify against himself (except by way of confession, as will presently be described), but to

---

[83] *Ibid.*. §§ 403, 404.

[84] *Ibid.,* §§ 329, 333. See also note to § 329, Vol. I. pp. 449-468.

deprive the prosecution of the power to compel such testimony. This right is guaranteed to persons accused of crime in the Constitution of the United States and in the constitutions of the several States of the Union. It is proper to observe, also, in this connection, that, while a party to a civil action may waive his privilege and testify, voluntarily, against his interest, either in open court or by way of admission against interest, he may not be compelled, in any case, to testify against himself.

HUSBAND AND WIFE

Husband and Wife — Exceptions.— The absolute identity of interest in the case of husband and wife, and the peculiar situation of dependence occupied by the latter, are recognized by the common law in a provision making either party to a marriage contract incompetent to testify for or against the other in any action, civil or criminal, to which the other is a party. It does not matter when the relation of marriage existed, or whether it exists at the time of the trial; it is only necessary that that marriage should have been lawful, and that the parties occupied that relation when the crime was committed or the cause of action accrued. An exception to the rule exists in the case of a crime committed by a husband against the person of the wife. In this case, in strictness, the State — not the wife — is the plaintiff; but the exception is made, not for this reason, which would be merely technical, but on the broad ground of public policy. For the reason above stated, the dying declaration of the wife is admissible against the husband, or the reverse, when he is charged with the murder of the declarant.

To this general rule of exclusion, which has been so strictly adhered to as to reject the testimony of the wife even with the consent of the husband, there are some necessary exceptions. It has been held that either party may testify in a case in which the other party is charged with treason; and the wife is allowed to testify in certain civil actions in which, from the nature of the case, she is the only possible witness. Either husband or wife may also "testify in collateral proceedings not immediately affecting their mutual interests, and this notwithstanding their testimony may tend to criminate, or may contradict, the other, or subject him to a legal demand."[85] The provisions of the common law on this subject have been materially modified by statute in many of the States, the tendency of the legislation being to place both parties on a footing of more nearly perfect equality, and to admit testimony formerly excluded, subject to objection as to its credibility.[86]

ACCOMPLICES, CO-DEFENDANTS, ETC

Accomplices and Co-defendants.— The testimony of accomplices, co-defendants, and the like is, as a rule, excluded. With a view to attain the ends of justice, however, it is sometimes necessary to obtain such testimony in a case in which a serious offense would otherwise go unpunished. An accomplice or co-defendant is incompetent for two reasons: first, because of infamy; second, because of interest. The first ground accrues upon conviction and judgment; the second, when an indictment has been obtained or a prosecution begun. If judgment be withheld or suspended, or if a *nolle prosequi* be entered in the case of an accomplice, he becomes competent, so far as infamy is concerned, and may testify for or against the principal or co-defendant. The credibility to be attached to

[85] 1 Greenleaf, § 342.

[86] Kingen *vs.* State, 50 Ind., 557 ; People *vs.* Simonds, 19 Cal., 275 ; State *vs.* Center,. 35 Vt., 378.

such testimony is a question for the jury, and great weight will not be given to it unless it is corroborated by other and better testimony, or strongly supported by facts otherwise established in evidence.

WANT OF UNDERSTANDING

Want of Understanding.— Deficiency of understanding becomes a ground of incompetency, because persons so afflicted are not only unable to appreciate the sanction of an oath, but are lacking also in capacity to observe facts accurately, to remember them or to testify to them lucidly, or with full understanding of their significance in a court of justice. Under this head fall young children, the deaf and dumb, idiots, the insane, and persons under the influence of drugs or intoxicating liquors. "It makes no difference from what cause this defect of understanding may have arisen, nor whether it be temporary and curable or permanent, whether the party be hopelessly an idiot, or maniac, or only occasionally insane, as a lunatic, or be intoxicated, or whether the defect arises from mere immaturity of intellect, as in the case of children. While a deficiency of understanding exists, be the cause of what nature soever, the person is not admissible to be sworn as a witness. But if the cause be temporary, and a lucid interval should occur, or a cure be effected, the competency is restored." [87]

CHILDREN

Children — Insane Persons.— In the case of children, the question is not so much of age as of intelligence and moral responsibility, which must be present in such a degree as to enable the child to observe

---

[87] 1 Greenleaf, § 365.

facts with accuracy, to testify to them correctly, and to realize the responsibility of an oath. Although the presumption is against the admission of the testimony of children under seven, there are instances in which children of peculiar intelligence and capacity have been permitted to testify below that age, but such cases constitute marked exceptions to a well-defined rule. If *insanity* is alleged, and the facts were observed and the testimony given during what are known as *lucid intervals,* competency will be presumed. The burden of proof of incompetency in such cases rests first upon the party who advances it as a ground of objection, to the extent of establishing the general ground of incompetency, and then upon the party producing the witness, of proving the case to be an exception to the rule. As in all other cases of incompetency, questions of mental incapacity are determined by the court.

RELIGIOUS BELIEF

Religious Belief.— The law regards the giving of testimony not only as an important duty, owed by a citizen to the State, but as an act of such serious importance as to require its performance to be accompanied by the solemn sanction of an oath. The administration of an oath is, therefore, not a mere ceremonial observance, but an act presuming religious belief of some kind on the part of the person taking it. If such person is wanting in religious belief, he is not regarded, at common law, as competent to testify as a witness in a court of justice. The particular form of religious belief cherished by a witness is not material, so long as it contemplates the existence of a Supreme Being to whom he acknowledges a moral accountability. An oath may therefore be defined as "an outward pledge given by the juror (or other person taking it) that his attestation or promise is made under an immediate sense of his responsibility to God."[88] A security to this extent, for the truth of testimony, is all that the law seems to have deemed necessary; and with less security than this it is believed that the purposes of justice cannot be accomplished."[89]

PROCEDURE IN CASES OF INCOMPETENCY

Procedure.— As has been said, the competency of a witness is presumed in all cases, and the burden of establishing the contrary falls upon him who alleges it to exist. The question of competency should, in general, be raised and decided before the witness is sworn, but may come up at any time when his incompetency becomes apparent. Being matters of law, or of the application of law to fact, questions of competency are always determined by the court. If the judgment be in favor of the witness, he is allowed to testify; if the contrary, he is not permitted to be sworn and is excused from further attendance upon the sessions of the court. The details of procedure, where incompetency is alleged, are regulated by the common law, or by statute in the several States of the Union. In some cases the fact of incompetency is apparent from some record or judgment, as from a judgment record where infamy is alleged; in others the facts tending to show incompetency are given in evidence, and the question is decided by the court after a full presentation of both sides of the case.

The Voir Dire.— When interest or want of religions belief is alleged as a ground of incompetency the fact may

---

[88] Tayler on Oaths,15

[89] I Greenleaf, § 328.

be established by the testimony of witnesses, or by the admission of the proposed witness, or by his own testimony, given under the sanction of a peculiar form of oath known as *voir dire.* Whether the election of one of these modes will preclude the party from afterwards resorting to the other is not clearly settled by the authorities. If the evidence offered *aliunde,* to prove the interest, is rejected as inadmissible, the witness may then be examined on the *voir dire.* And if the witness on the *voir dire* states that he does not know, or leaves it doubtful whether he is interested or not, his interest may be shown by other evidence. It has also been held that a resort to one of these modes to prove the interest of a witness on one ground does not preclude a resort to the other mode to prove the interest on another ground. But, subject to these modifications, the rule recognized and adopted by the general current of authorities is that where the objecting party has undertaken to prove the interest of the witness by interrogating him upon the *voir dire,* he shall not, upon failure of that mode, resort to the other to prove facts the existence of which was known when the witness was interrogated. The party appealing to the conscience of a witness offers him to the court as a credible witness; and it is contrary to the spirit of the law to permit him afterwards to say that the witness is not worthy to be believed. It would also violate another rule by its tendency to raise collateral issues. Nor is it deemed reasonable to permit a party to sport with the conscience of a witness when he has other proof of his interest.[90]

---

[90] 1 Greenleaf, § 423.

OPINIONS. EXPERT TESTIMONY

Opinion — Experts.— As a rule, testimony in the nature of opinion is excluded.[91] This for the reason that witnesses are required to testify to facts only, leaving to the jury the duty of deducing conclusions, or of forming opinions as to the effects or consequences of such facts. There are two exceptions to this rule, however, to which attention will now be drawn. In the first place, any intelligent witness may testify as to opinions which are themselves conclusions drawn from numerous facts within the daily observation and experience of all intelligent persons. Such relate to the appearance or demeanor of a person; his sanity, sobriety, or identity, or his resemblance to another; his physical condition, whether sick or well; his condition as regards emotion or passion, as to anger, hope or fear, joy or sorrow, excitement or coolness, and the like. These are matters of every-day occurrence as to which all thoughtful persons form conclusions of fact to which they are competent to testify in a proper case.[92]Second, the opinion of experts in an art, trade, or profession, in which they have attained especial proficiency may, at the discretion of the court and under its direction, be given in evidence.[93] This is permitted for

---

[91] Cameron *vs.* State, 14 Ala., 546 ; Corn. *m.* Mooney, 110 Mass., 99 ; Corn. *vs.* Sturtevant, 117 Mass., 122 ; Morse *vs.* State, 6 Conn., 9.

[92] Cameron *vs.* State, 14 Ala., 546 ; Corn. *m.* Mooney, 110 Mass., 99 ; Corn. *vs.* Sturtevant, 117 Mass., 122 ; Morse *vs.* State, 6 Conn., 9.

[93] Corn. *vs.* Sturtevant, 117 Mass., 122; Campbell *vs.* State, 23 Ala., 44; Evans *vs.* People, 12 Mich., 27 ; McLean *vs.* State, 16 Ala., 672; Messner *vs.* People. 45 N. Y., 1;People *vs.* Eastwood, 14 N. Y., 562.

the reason that the opinions in question are technical or scientific in character and are based upon experience that is beyond the knowledge or experience of the average juror. Under this head, for example, fall opinions as to the effects of particular poisons; that is, certain symptoms having been observed, expert opinion may be received as to the poisons that would produce such effects. In general, certain facts or effects having been established in evidence, the testimony of experts may be admitted as to the causes which would have produced such effects; or as to the laws of nature applicable to certain causes to produce particular effects.[94]

Procedure.— The party who introduces expert witnesses must show that they are experts in fact; that is, that they actually possess the technical or scientific knowledge which will assist the jury to a correct understanding of the facts in a case. Having established their competency and the necessity for their appearance, they may give opinions as to certain facts, or may testify in answer to a hypothetical question, agreed upon by the parties and approved by the court, the answer to which is calculated to afford the members of the jury the assistance of which they stand in need.

HEARSAY

Hearsay.— What is called hearsay testimony is inadmissible. *Hearsay testimony is* that obtained from a

---

[94] Milwaukee Railway Co. *vs.* Kellogg, 94 U. S., 409 ; Chicago *vs.* Greer, 9 Wall., 726: Dexter vs. Hall, 15 Wall., 9; Transportation Line *vs.* Hope. 95 U. S., 297; People *vs.* Bodine, 1 Denio, 282; Woodin *vs.* People, 1 Parker, 464; Cook *vs.* State, 4 Zabriskie, 843 ; State *vs.* Smith. 32 Mann., 369 ; 1 Green Crim. Reports, 241.

witness who has not himself observed the facts to which he testifies, but whose knowledge of them is gained from the statements of others. Hearsay is objectionable for several reasons: *first,* because it is secondary, and the law requires primary evidence — the best evidence attainable — in every case; *second,* the real witness is not testifying in court, under the sanction of an oath; and *third,* the opposite party, and especially the defendant in a criminal case, has no opportunity to be confronted with the witnesses against him or to exercise the right of cross-examination. There are some necessary exceptions to this rule, and there are some apparent exceptions which, upon close examination, will be found to relate to relevant facts and to be, as such, not liable to objection as hearsay. The principal exceptions are:

1. *Confessions or Admissions against Interest.—* These will presently be described. They may be made in open court, by the accused person, or may be testified to by those who heard them or to whom they were addressed.[95]

2. *Dying Declarations.—* In this case, which has been touched upon in the discussion of the subject of admissions, the question is of obtaining, from the declarant, an ante-mortem statement of the facts relating to the injury from which he is suffering. The statement is receivable in evidence in a trial for the murder or manslaughter of the declarant, and then only when made in view of impending death and when he no longer cherishes any hope of recovery. In this case the sense of impending death is held to replace the sanction of an oath, and for this reason the statement will not be received if it appears that the declarant cherishes any hope, however slight, of ultimate restoration to health. The competency of

[95] See page 66, *ante.* See also page 72, *post.*

the declarant as a witness, and the sufficiency of his statement are determined by the court, who, after hearing all the facts, admits the statement, or rejects it as not proper to be submitted to the jury.[96]

CONFESSIONS

Confessions.— One form of criminating testimony known as *confessions* has always been. received from accused persons in. criminal cases. The most common form of confession is that afforded by the plea of guilty, made by the accused in answer to an indictment, with full knowledge of the legal consequences that will ensue. Confessions may be made by a plea of guilty, as above described, or by a statement made in open court by, or in behalf of, the accused; if made elsewhere, they may be testified to by those who heard them, or to whom they were addressed, if made under such circumstances as to make it clear that the admissions of guilt were entirely voluntary. Any evidence going to show that a confession was extorted by means of threats or promises, or by the use of force, especially by a person in authority, will completely destroy its evidential value. When offered under the conditions above described, a confession must be received in its entirety, and weight must be attached to those parts which weigh for the accused as well as those which operate to his prejudice.[97]

---

[96] Johnson v*s*. State, 17 Ala., 618: Thompson *vs*. State, 24 Ga., 297 : People *vs*. Vernon, 35 Coe., 49 ; Com. *vs* Carey, 12 Gushing (Mass.), 246 ; Corn. *vs*. Cooper, 5 Alien (Mass.), 495 ; Nelson *vs*. State, 7 Humph. (Tenn.), 543 ; Smith *vs*. State, 9 *ibid., 9; U. S. vs*. Woods, 4 Cranch C. C., 484; People v*s*. Lee, 17 Cal., 76.

[97] Aikin *vs*. State, 35 Ala., 399 ; Corn. *vs*. King, 8

THE RULES OF EVIDENCE

Purpose of Rules of Evidence.— It has been seen that the *rules of evidence* have to do with determining what is called the competency of witnesses; that is, of deciding whether a particular person shall be permitted to testify at all; and with the exclusion of certain testimony from the consideration of the jury upon the ground that it is likely to mislead them and to confuse, rather than to make clear, the issue referred to them for trial. They also determine, to a certain extent, the credibility of witnesses, or the weight that is to be attached to their testimony.

Oral and Written Testimony.— An application of the rules of pleading having reduced the several elements constituting the cause of action to a single issue of fact, the case is referred to a jury for trial, the different steps or stages of which have already been described. Each party in turn submits the testimony of witnesses in proof or disproof of the facts composing the issue. The oral or written testimony offered in support of the case, on either side, makes up the evidence upon which the jury bases its verdict, which has been seen to be simply a finding of fact in accordance with the weight of evidence submitted. Testimony is classified, according to its form, as either oral or written. *Oral testimony* is that given *viva voce* in open court. *Written testimony* is composed of documents, which may be formal, sealed instruments, or it may consist of writings not under seal, and may appear in the shape of originals or copies.

Direct and Indirect — Hearsay — Real Evidence.— Oral testimony is classified according to its nature and

---

Gray (Mass.), 501 : Corn. *vs.* Dower, 4 Alien (Mass.). 297 ; Keenan *vs.* State, 8 Wis., 3 ; O'Brien *vs.* People, 48 Burton (N. Y.), 1274.

character, and is said to be *direct* or *original* when the witness testifies to facts observed by him through the medium of his senses. It is said to be indirect when the witness derives his knowledge as to particular facts from the observations of others and testifies to their declarations or statements concerning them. For this reason what is called *hearsay testimony is,* in most cases, inadmissible. *Real evidence* consists in the production in court of objects or articles that pertain to a case in hearing, in order that the jury may be enabled to make a personal examination or inspection of them, or that witnesses may identify them or illustrate their application or use in connection with a matter in issue. Evidence is also said to be *indirect* or, more properly speaking, *circumstantial* when the existence of a fact is inferred, by a process of reasoning, from the existence or nonexistence of other facts established in evidence by the testimony of witnesses or by the production of documents.[98]

RELEVANCY OF EVIDENCE

Relevancy.— Evidence must be *relevant;* that is, must bear directly upon the issue.[99] The issue here referred to is that obtained by an application of the rules of pleading, and the reason for the rule is simple. From the nature of pleading it is apparent that no testimony can be received which does not tend to prove or disprove the facts of which the issue is composed. This question alone

---

[98] People *vs.* Kendall, 32 N. Y., 141 ; Brig Struggle *vs. U. S.*, 9 Cranch, 71; Bank of *U. S. vs.* Corcoran, 2 Pet., 121.

[99] Turner *vs.* Tindall. 1 Cranch, 117; Stringer *vs.* Young, 3 Pet., 320 ; Winans *vs.* N. Y. & Erie R. R., 21 How., 88 ; U. S. *vs.* Gilbert, 2 Sumner, 19.

engages the attention of the court and jury, to the exclusion of every other, and it would be the veriest waste of time were the court to permit other testimony to be heard.

Relevancy of Facts.— A fact is said to be *relevant* when it is the cause or effect of another fact, or is the effect of the same cause, or is the cause of the same effect.[100] Particular testimony is said to tend to prove a fact when, taken in connection with other and similar testimony, it is calculated to establish such fact in evidence; each fact so testified to forming a link in the chain of proof submitted in support of the case of either party to the action. Testimony as to collateral facts is, as a rule, inadmissible, unless the burden rests upon a party of proving intent, or the existence of particular knowledge on the part of a person; or when good faith, malice, state of mind, or bodily health is in question. In a trial for desertion, for example, testimony that an accused purchased a ticket for a distant point, or attempted to dispose of his uniform, or to exchange it for civilian's dress, would be admissible to show the intent of not returning, which is essential to the offense of desertion. So the fact that a person charged with receiving stolen goods from A had received similar stolen goods from B or G, or had received stolen goods from A on a previous occasion, would be admissible as showing the guilty knowledge which is an essential ingredient of the offense of receiving stolen goods. Such testimony is therefore admitted, to a limited extent, to furnish the basis of fact from which the jury may deduce a just conclusion as to the particular intent with which an offense has been committed.

Character — Reputation.— The term *character,* as used at common law, is synonymous with *reputation;* this

---

[100] Stephen's Digest of the Law of Evidence, p. xii.

for the reason that the character of a person, using the term in relation to his disposition, cannot, from its nature, be established by the testimony of witnesses. Its outward manifestation, however, in the *reputation* which a person enjoys in the community, is a fact, and, like other facts, is susceptible of observation by neighbors and others who may testify as to such reputation in a proper case. Testimony as to *character* is, in general, inadmissible. In a civil action it rarely occurs that the character of a party is drawn in question; in a criminal trial, however, it may become an element of importance in two cases. First, when the evidence of guilt is not strong, testimony as to the good character of an accused may be admitted to strengthen the presumption of innocence;[101] and second, such testimony may be admitted where the punishment is discretionary with the court, with a view to mitigate the severity of the sentence imposed upon conviction.

Character, How Established.— As has been observed, the testimony offered in support of character is that of persons who know the reputation of the accused in the community in which he lives, and can testify as to the reputation which he there enjoys for sobriety, integrity, morality, and the like. Testimony so submitted should relate to character as indicated in the charge; if fraud or dishonesty be alleged, testimony as to integrity is appropriate; if a crime of violence be charged, testimony as to good disposition would be relevant. Testimony as to general good reputation would properly be submitted with a view to affect the discretion of the court in the matter of leniency.

---

[101] 1 State *vs.* Ford, 3 Strobh., 517, note; Fields *vs* State, 47 Ala., 603; Green's Crim. Reports, pp. 635, 640; Storrs *vs.* People, 56 N. Y., 315; People *vs.* Ashe, 44 Cal, 288.

Most States authorize, by statute, an increase of punishment for a second or third conviction of the same offense, and, in some cases, for repeated convictions of criminal offenses. While this is done largely as a measure of prevention, it amounts, in effect, to an admission of testimony as to bad character in determining the appropriate punishment for a particular offense.

Testimony as to previous convictions must be obtained from the judicial records of the convictions in question; for which purpose the originals or duly authenticated copies must be submitted in accordance with the rules regulating the production of documentary evidence.

RES GESTÆ

Res Gestæ.— A form of testimony remains to be described which conforms to the definition of hearsay, because it consists of the admissions, statements, and other utterances of accused persons, or interested parties, which are testified to by those who heard them. Such testimony, as will presently be shown, is not hearsay, or secondary, but primary, or original, in character.[102]

What Constitutes the Res Gestæ.— If the several acts or events which constitute a cause of action or a criminal offense be analyzed, or separated into their constituent elements, it will be seen that they consist in part of acts and in part of oral declarations or statements or, in some cases, of exclamations, or other expressions of emotion or feeling. These utterances are us essential to the

---

[102] Beavor *vs.* Taylor, 1 Wall., 637; lns. Co. *vs.* Mosley, 8 Wall., 397; Ins. Co. *vs.* Weide, 9 Wall., 677; James *vs.* Wharton, 3 McLean, 492; Bacon *vs.* Charlton, 7 Cush., 586; Smith vs. Shoemaker, 17 Wall., 630.

crime, or cause of action, as are the other acts of which it is composed. They are, indeed, *verbal facts,* and, as such, may be testified to by witnesses who observed them, or in whose presence or hearing they were uttered. They consist in general of oral declarations or admissions, but may take the form of written entries in certain cases to be explained hereafter.[103]

When Admissible.— The rule applies to the statements of a partner whose declarations bind the firm of which he is a member; to the representations of an agent, which, within the scope of his agency, are binding upon his principal, to the confessions of accused persons, and to the utterances of a conspirator which, if made m furtherance of the common purpose, are binding upon co-conspirators. It also applies to the case in which the fact in question is as to whether a particular statement was or was not made, its truth or falsehood being a matter of secondary importance. The rule has an extensive application in criminal cases. For example: A, by accident, discharges a pistol and wounds B; A gives expression to an exclamation of horror the instant that the result of his act is made known to him. Such exclamation is a verbal fact, and, as such, forms an essential part of the transaction. B stabs C, and, as he inflicts the wound, exclaims, "Take that," or "Now we are even," or words of similar effect; in this case, also, the exclamation is an essential ingredient of the offense. If, however, A shoots and kills B, and some time after the event, when he has had time to concert a theory of defense, expresses regret at the occurrence, it is obvious that such expression of regret, if offered ill evidence, should be rejected.[104]

---

[103] James vs. Wharton, 3 McLean, 492; Ins. Co. *vs.* Weide, 9 Wall., 677; 1 Greenleaf Evid., § 143.

[104] People vs. McMahon, 15 N. Y., 384: Phillips *vs.*

The rule governing the admission of such statements is that they are receivable when they are strictly contemporaneous with, and form an essential part of, the event to which they relate, and not otherwise. Whether they are or are not contemporaneous is a question for the court to decide. Under this head falls testimony as to the information under which a person acts; statements or declarations in regard to bodily health, expressions of feeling; statements in regard to pedigree or relationship, or to the facts in regard to birth, marriage, or death; declarations of a testator, inscriptions on monuments or tombstones, entries in family Bibles, charts, pedigrees, or the like. The court in every case will determine the question of admissibility, and will satisfy itself that the testimony offered is the best obtainable before allowing it to be given to the jury.

Written Matter as Res Gestæ.— Certain written matter may now be considered as falling within the exception above stated to hearsay testimony. This relates chiefly to entries made in shop books, and in other matter of similar character which are receivable in evidence in certain cases. To be admissible, they must have been made, in the performance of his duty, by one whose office or function it was to make them, and they must have been made under circumstances such as to negative the idea of falsehood or fraud. Formerly such entries were admitted only on proof of the death of the person who made them, but this rule has been modified, in recent times, in such a way as to admit considerable testimony of this character which was formerly excluded. "In the United States this

---

People, 57 Barber, 353; Com. *vs.* Keyes, 11 Gray, 323; State *vs.* Mahon, 33 Vt., 241; Smith *vs.* State, 41 Tex., 352; Kingen *vs.* State, 50 Ind., 557; People *vs.* Simonds, 19 Cal., 375.

principle has been carried farther, and extended to entries made by the party himself in his own shop books. Before the books of the party can be admitted in evidence they are to be submitted to the inspection of the court, and if they do not appear to be a register of the daily business of the party, and to have been honestly and fairly kept, they are excluded. If they appear manifestly erased and altered in a material part, they will not be admitted until the alteration is explained."[105]

Hearsay testimony is also admitted as to declarations made under oath in a previous trial, provided the litigant parties are the same. It is also receivable in matters of public and general interest. Under this head falls testimony relating to highways, easements, rights of way or of pasture or fishery, and the like. Such declarations must refer to ancient rights, and must have been made by a deceased declarant, and before the subject of declaration became an essential element in an action at law. Ancient documents, in the nature of deeds, leases, maps, and the like, may be received in evidence, their makers being presumed to be dead, and the instruments themselves not to have been made, or executed, with a view to subsequent litigation.[106]

THE BEST EVIDENCE

The Best Evidence.— The rule that the best obtainable evidence must be submitted is calculated to prevent fraud, and to enable the jury to base its finding upon the best attainable evidence in every case. All evidence, whether oral or written, is of various degrees, or orders, in point of primariness and originality. If a witness

---

[105] 1 Greenleaf, §§ 115, 118.

[106] 1 Greenleaf, §§ 141-145.

testify as to facts which he has heard or seen, or if the original of a document be produced, such testimony is, in the nature of the case, the best attainable, and is said to constitute *primary* evidence. If, on the other hand, the witness testifies to facts, the knowledge of which he has gained from another, or if a copy of a document be submitted, or if neither the original nor a copy be forthcoming and the contents of the paper be testified to orally, such evidence is not the best, and is said to be *secondary* or *derivative.* In some cases, as where the testimony is pure hearsay, it is rejected; in others, especially in the case of documents, it is accepted upon proof, by the party offering it, that it is the best evidence attainable; that is, that the original has been lost or destroyed, or is in the possession of the opposite party, or in that of a person beyond the jurisdiction of the court.

THE BURDEN OF PROOF

Burden of Proof.— The rules as to the burden of proof are necessary to the orderly and methodical presentation of evidence in actions at law. It has been seen that the issues referred to a jury for trial are decided in civil actions by a preponderance of proof, and in criminal cases by proof sufficient to establish guilt beyond a reasonable doubt. What is called the *burden of proof* — that is, the task of establishing the truth of a proposition outlined in the pleadings — rests primarily upon the one who alleges a fact or makes the contention that such fact exists. In every pleading by way of traverse or denial it will be remembered that the pleading concludes with a tender of issue, or an offer to prove the correctness of the facts alleged in the pleading, and it is this particular burden which is contemplated in the rule of evidence above stated.

Burden of Proof in Criminal Trials.— In a criminal action the burden rests upon the prosecution of establishing in evidence the facts constituting the offense as set forth in the indictment. The accused goes to trial with the benefit of the presumption that he is innocent, which attends him throughout the trial, but when the prosecution has succeeded in establishing the facts constituting guilt, by the testimony of competent and credible witnesses, the burden of proof shifts to the defense and he is required to meet and rebut, or disprove, the facts established in evidence by the prosecution. In collateral issues arising in the course of the trial as to the competency of witnesses, the admissibility of testimony and the like, the burden of proof rests upon the party who alleges incompetency or objects to the admission of particular testimony.

SUBSTANCE OF THE ISSUE. DEPARTURES

Substance of the Issue.— The substance of the issue only need be proved. By the *substance* is meant the material or essential part, as indicated in the pleadings upon which issue has been joined.[107] In the application of this rule a distinction is made between *matter of substance,* which pertains to an issue, and *matter of description.* The latter must be proved as alleged; the former, as to its legal or material part only. This rule is somewhat more strictly enforced in criminal than in civil actions, as personal rather than property rights are there drawn in question.

For example: A is charged with the larceny of a horse, the property of B. It is sufficient in the indictment

---

[107] *U. S. vs.* Howard, 3 Sumner, 12 ; U. S. *vs.* Foye, 1 Cush., 364; Wilson *vs.* Codman, 3 Cranch, 193.

to allege that a horse, the property of B, was feloniously taken by A, with intent to convert the same to his own use. If the indictment describes the animal as a black horse, the color must be proved; and if the horse proves to be white, the variance is fatal. So, too, if A be charged with the larceny of two bank-notes of a certain denomination, it is enough to allege the larceny of two bank-notes each of the denomination of five dollars and to prove the felonious taking. If, however, the notes be described by the names of the banks of issue, and the names and titles of the offices who signed them, such description will have to be proved as alleged. A departure from the allegations of a pleading in matters of description is called a *variance,* and is fatal unless aided by statute in the jurisdiction in which the trial is had.

JUDICIAL NOTICE

Judicial Notice.— There are certain facts of which all courts take what is called *judicial notice;* that is, accept them without proof, as they are alleged or referred to in pleading, or argument, during the progress of a trial.

This is done as to certain facts because the law requires it, and as to others because of their notoriety and general acceptance by the community at large. To the former class belong the laws which the court applies in the decision of the cases before it, including the Constitution, laws, and treaties of the United States, those of the State in which the court sits, the common law the law of nations, the custom of merchants, and the admiralty or maritime law of the world. They also recognize the great seal of the United States, those of the several States, the seals of courts of record when attached to their records, orders, and decrees, together with the seals of notaries public and the great seals of foreign States. Under the latter head they will take judicial notice of the ordinary divisions of time, of calendar and lunar months, of weeks and days, and of the hours of the day; of astronomical and physical facts; of the laws of nature, including their ordinary operations and consequences; of the government of the United States and the governments of the several States, with their principal officers; of the existence of foreign States and their rulers; of war and peace; and of the great facts of history as recorded in the works of writers of standard authority.[108]

DOCUMENTARY EVIDENCE. DOCUMENTS

Documents — Classification — Evidential Value.— A *document* is a statement of fact, in a written instrument, or anything upon which inscriptions, characters, or signs have been recorded, and which is susceptible of use as evidence. The term includes deeds formally executed under seal, all forms of written or printed instruments, together with maps, plans, and inscriptions upon monuments, buildings, churches, or headstones. The writing may be in any language or character, and may be expressed pictorially or in the language of signs. Written instruments are classified, according to their source and

---

[108] Marbury *vs.* Madison, 1 Cranch, 137; Course *vs.* Stead, 4 Dall., 22 ; Owings *vs.* Hull, 9 Pet., 607; Junction R. R. Co. *vs.* Bank of Ashland, 12 Wall., 226; Elwood *vs.* *F*lannigan, 104 U. S., 562: Lamar *vs.* Micou, 114 U. S., 218; Beaty *vs.* Knowles, 4 Pet., 152; Gardner *vs.* Collector, 6 Wall., 499; Carpenter *vs.* Dexter, 8 Wall., 513; U. S. *vs.* Perot, 98 U. S.. 428 ; Strother *vs.* Lucas, 6 Pet., 763 ; Armstrong *vs.* *U. S.,* 13 Wall., 154 ; U. S., *vs.* Wilson, 7 Pet., 150 ; Burke v*s.* Miltenberger, 19 Wall., 519 ; La Vengeance, 3 Dall., 297 ; Brown *vs.* Piper, 91 *U. S.,* 37 ; Terhune *vs.* Phillips, 99 *id.,* 592 ; King *vs.* Gallun, 109 *id.,* 99.

authority, into *public* and *private documents,* and, according to the formality attending their execution, into *specialties,* or *instruments under seal,* and *writings* or *documents not under seal,* a term which includes all other writings of whatever character.

From the point of view of evidence, a written instrument is regarded as of the highest authority upon the subject to which it relates. If executed under seal, no testimony will be received which is calculated to change its meaning or to modify its terms in the slightest degree, the presumption being that if a person reduces a proposition to writing under the sanction of a seal, the instrument so executed must be held to embody his fully considered views as to the subject so expressed in permanent and enduring form. For these reasons the rules of evidence attach the greatest weight to documentary evidence, and place peculiar safeguards about its introduction, with a view to give to this form of testimony its true evidential value.

PRIMARY AND SECONDARY EVIDENCE

Primary and Secondary Evidence.— Written evidence is derived from documents, and is said to be either *primary* or *secondary in* character or degree, depending upon its originality. *Primary evidence* consists in the production of the document itself. In the absence of the primary or original document, evidence called *secondary* may be admitted to prove its contents. This may exist in several degrees, consisting of copies of the original, or in parol testimony as to its contents, derived from witnesses who are familiar therewith. As between copies of a document produced by printing, photography, or by any facsimile process, all are primary as respects each other, but all are secondary in their relation to the instrument of which they purport to be copies. The production of written evidence is *voluntary* when done by a party in his own interest, and *compulsory* when required by the court in obedience to its order, rule, or subpœna. When a document is produced, the burden of identifying it, and of proving that it is the best evidence attainable, rests upon the party in whose behalf it is produced.

PUBLIC DOCUMENTS

Public Documents.— A *public document* is any written instrument originating in, or pertaining or relating to, any office or department of the Government. Under this head are included the statutes, resolutions, and other acts of the Legislature; the treaties, proclamations, orders, regulations, reports, and other utterances of the Executive; and the records, judgments, orders, and decrees of courts of justice. Every public document pertains to, or is said to be *of record* in, some public office, the chief of which is its legal custodian. Public documents are, as a rule, so far regarded as confidential that they are not subject to examination by the public at large without the authority of law or the consent of their legal custodian.

Production of, in Evidence, How Secured.— When it becomes necessary to produce a public document in court, secondary evidence of its contents in the form of a copy is usually furnished, and authenticated, in strict conformity with the requirements of statutes, by the seal of the office from which it emanates, this for the reason that the public business would be relayed and considerable inconvenience caused by the removal of such document from the files of the office to which it pertains. Copies so certified are given, by statute, the full evidential value of originals. For this reason all courts of record and the principal offices of the several Executive Departments are provided with seals of which the courts take judicial notice when attached to copies or exemplification of documents issuing therefrom. As has been said, all courts are required to take judicial notice of the laws which they apply in the decision of cases. In this way the public statutes of the United States, and of the several States, are recognized by courts when read from books purporting to have been published by authority. The fame rule applies to the public statutes of the several States of the Union. Foreign statutes and judgments are proved by copies under the great seal of the State to which they pertain, or by the certification of an officer authorized by law to execute copies and certify to their correctness. Acts of magistrates, and in some cases of notaries public, must be authenticated by the seal of the court of record within whose territorial jurisdiction they act.[109]

PRIVATE DOCUMENTS

Private Documents.— *Private documents* differ from public documents chiefly as to the kind and amount of testimony necessary to establish their identity, such burden of proof, in any case, falling upon the party in whose interest the paper is produced. In general the best evidence of the contents of a paper is that obtained by the production of the instrument itself. If it be a sealed instrument, its execution must be proved by the testimony of at least one subscribing witness, unless the document is in the hands of the opposite party, or be over thirty years

---

[109] U. S. *vs.* Johns, 4 Dallas, 412; U. S. *vs.* Amedy, 11 Wheaton, 392: Watkins *vs.* Holman, 16 Pet., 25; Gregg *vs.* Forsyth, 24 How., 179; Post *vs.* Supervisors, 15 Otto, 667; Savage's Case. 1 Ct. CIs., 170: Leathers *vs.* Salvor Wrecking Co., 2 Woods, 680; McCall *vs.* U. S., 1 Dak., 320.

old and comes from the proper custodian, in which case it is said to prove itself, the subscribing witnesses being supposed to be dead. When admitted subject to the foregoing conditions, no testimony will be received to vary its terms in the slightest degree.

How Produced — How Proved.— The production of a paper, if in the hands of the opposite party, is obtained by a formal *notice to produce;* if the paper be in the possession of a third party — that is, in the custody of one not a party in interest — its production is compelled by a *subpœna duces tecum.* When the means above described have been fully resorted to or upon satisfactory proof that the paper has been lost or destroyed, or that it is in possession of a person not within the jurisdiction of the court, secondary evidence may be submitted as to its contents. Such testimony may consist in written, printed, photographic, or letterpress copies, or in parol testimony as to the contents of the paper in question. When written copies are submitted, witnesses are called to prove handwriting, and they testify:

(1) from having seen the document written; (2) from having seen writings, personally admitted by the writer to be genuine; and (3) by a comparison of writings, the comparison being made between papers already in evidence before the court. In England comparison is authorized, by statute, of writings proved to the satisfaction of the court to be genuine, and a similar rule exists ill several of the States; in others, however, the comparison is required to be made of writings already in evidence, the reason being that the introduction of writings not pertinent to the case may give rise to fraud in the matter of selection, and so tend to prejudice the minds of the jury in reaching their finding.

CHAPTER IV

ALTERATIONS AND ERASURES

Alterations and Erasures.— When an alteration or erasure appears upon the face of an instrument, and its validity is drawn in question, the burden of explaining the change falls upon the party who produces the document. Alterations are usually in the nature of interlineations or erasures. *Interlineations* consist of words or clauses inserted between the lines of an instrument; *erasures* are effected by striking out words or clauses, usually by means of a line drawn through the matter to be omitted. As such alterations suggest fraud, it is incumbent upon the party who would benefit by the change to explain its cause and the time of its execution. The effect of a material alteration, unexplained, is to invalidate the instrument.[110] Alterations made at the time of execution of a legal instrument can be made valid by the insertion of a clause explaining them, immediately over the signatures of the parties.[111] In a sealed instrument and, when no ground of suspicion appears, in other writings as well, alterations are presumed to have been made prior to the complete execution of the document.[112]

---

[110] Morrill ex. Otis, 12 N. H., 466; Richmond Mfg. Co. *vs.* Davis, 7 Blackford (Ind.), 412; Boston *vs.* Benson, 12 Gushing (Mass.), 61; Davis *vs.* Carlisle, 6 Ala., 707.

[111] Ravisies *vs.* Alston, 5 Ala., 297; Boston *vs.* Benson, 12 Cush., 61.

[112] North River Meadow Co. *vs.* Shrewsbury Church, 22 N. J. Law (2 Zabriskie), 424; Matthews *vs.* Coalter, 9 Mo., 705 ; Beaman *vs.* Russell, 20 Vt., 205.

EXAMINATION OF WITNESSES

Examination of Witnesses — Oaths — Objections to Competency.— Witnesses are sworn before testifying by an officer of the court charged by law with the performance of that duty. While certain forms of oath, or affirmation, are prescribed by statute in the several States, any extra-statutory form may be used which a witness may regard as having special binding force. Objections to the competency of a witness are properly made before the administration of the oath, but will be considered at any stage of the trial, provided the cause of incompetency was not known to exist at the time the witness was sworn; if the objection be sustained, the jury will be instructed *to* disregard any testimony that the witness may have given prior to the discovery of his incompetency.

Order of Examination.— Witnesses are first examined in chief by the party in whose behalf they appear, and are then cross-examined by the opposite party. Considerable latitude is allowed a party in the examination of his witnesses, so long as the questions asked are relevant to the issue.

Leading Questions.— Leading questions — that is, questions which suggest their answers — are excluded if objected to by the opposite party. Questions merely introductory in character, questions asked for purposes of identification or to assist defective memory, and questions asked of a witness who seems to be hostile to the party introducing him are exceptions to this rule. The purpose of cross-examination is to test the credibility of the witness, and, to that end, leading questions may be put in cross-examination, together with questions not otherwise relevant, the purpose of which is to test his powers of observations, the accuracy of his memory, and his correctness of statement.[113]

PRIVILEGED QUESTIONS

Privileged Questions.— Witnesses are permitted to decline to answer certain questions and, in a proper case, will be sustained by the court in so doing. Such questions are said to be *privileged,* and are made so as a matter of public policy, with a view to prevent inquisitorial trials, or to forbid the disclosure of facts the discovery of which would affect injuriously the public business, or trespass unduly upon certain private relations the continued existence of which it is the policy of the law to secure. The principal cases of privilege are:

1. *State Secrets.*— This privilege extends to all departments of the Government, and has its origin in the belief that the public interests would suffer by a disclosure of certain facts relating to the administration of state affairs. It covers the statements of persons engaged in the discovery of crime, the deliberations of courts and of certain bodies, like grand and petit juries and boards of arbitration, the results of whose deliberations only the public has a right to know. It also extends to the transactions of legislative committees and to the deliberations of legislative bodies in closed session, and includes diplomatic correspondence and communications between the principal officers of the several executive departments, on matters of public business, together with the proceedings of commissions, courts-martial, and courts of inquiry, and, generally, all oral or written

---

[113] U. S. *vs.* Dickinson, 2 McLean. 325; Bevins *vs.* Pope, 7 Ala., 371; Green *vs.* Gould, 3 Alien (Mass.), 465; Burton *vs.* Kane, 17 Wis., 37.

communications in which the production of documents or oral disclosures of any kind is restrained by law or would, in the opinion of the executive, be detrimental to the public interests.[114]

2. *Attorney and Client.*— The disclosures made by a client to his counsel, or legal adviser, are privileged during the entire period within which the relation of attorney and client exists; and the privilege extends to the clerks, agents, stenographers, interpreters, and other employees whose services are necessary to an attorney or counselor in the transaction of his business. [115] Knowledge in relation to a cause of action, or to a criminal offense, obtained by an attorney as the result of his observations as a private individual, and not due, in any degree, to his professional relation to his client, may be testified to in any case and at any time. The same is true of information gained before his employment as counsel began or after it has ceased to exist. At common law this privil ege extends to attorneys and counsel only, as above explained, and any confidential communications made to physicians, clergymen, or others may be testified to unless specially privileged by statute.[116]

3. *Husband and Wife.*— The disability of the parties to a marriage contract, due to their identity of interest, has already been discussed. In addition to this, the law forbids either husband or wife to testify as to any confidential

---

[114] Greenleaf, § 251; Wharton, § 578; 2 Robertson's Burr's Trial, 501; U. S. *vs.* Six Lots of Ground, 1 Woods, 234.

[115] People *vs.* Atkinson, 40 Cal., 284; Alderman *vs.* People, 4 Mich., 414; People *vs.* Blakely, 4 Parker, 176.

[116] People *vs.* Stout. 3 Parker, 670; People *vs.* Gates, 13 Wendell, 311.

communications made during the continuance of the marriage relation, as opposed to public policy.

4. *Criminating Questions — By Whom Determined.*— At the common law a witness was privileged to decline answering a question when the effect of such answer was to criminate him or expose him to a penalty or forfeiture. The term "criminate" is here used in a technical sense, and means that the effect of a particular answer will be to expose the witness to a criminal prosecution or to a penal action. The question is one for the court to determine, in view of all the circumstances of the case, and if, upon such examination and consideration, it appears that the answer to a particular question will tend to criminate the witness — that is, if the answer, taken in connection with other facts, will be calculated to form a link in the chain of criminating circumstances — the court will instruct the witness to refuse to answer. A similar rule prevails in equity procedure.[117]

IMPEACHING CREDIT

Credibility.— The *credibility* of a witness may be attacked, as has been seen in cross-examination, or his testimony may be rebutted by the testimony of other witnesses. In addition, in a proper case, his reputation for troth and veracity may be impeached.[118]

---

[117] *U. S. vs.* McCarty, 18 Fed. Rep., 87; Richman *vs.* State, 2 Greene (Iowa), 532; Slate *vs.* Duffy, 15 Iowa, 425; Corn. *vs.* Braynard, Thacher (Mass.), Cr., 146: Floyd *vs.* State, 7 Fed., 215. But see *U. S. vs.* Burr, 1 Burr, Trial, 245; U. S. *vs.* Miller, 2 Cranch C.C., 247; Warner *vs.* Lucas, 10 Ohio, 306; Poole *vs.* Perritt, 1 Spears (S. C.), 128.

[118] Com. *vs.* Lincoln, 110 Mass., 410; Brown *vs.* State,

Reputation and Character.— It has been seen that the terms "reputation" and "character" are not synonymous. The character of a person, using that term in the sense of disposition, is known to no one but himself; the outward manifestations of character, however, as evinced by the life he lives and the reputation he enjoys in the community at large, are facts, and, as such, are susceptible of being established by the testimony of witnesses. One element of reputation pertaining to every person in a particular community is that of veracity in their communications with others. It is to this reputation for veracity that testimony impeaching credibility is usually addressed. When the reputation of a witness in this regard has been established in evidence, it is permitted, in some jurisdictions, to ask the witness whether he would believe such a person on his oath. This calls for an expression of opinion, not of fact, and the rules as to its admissibility are not uniform. In England and in some of the States of the Union the inquiry is permitted; in others such conclusions of fact are left to the jury for determination in attaching weight to the testimony of a witness whose reputation for truth and veracity has been shown to be bad.

Inconsistent Statements.— Witnesses may be shown, by their own testimony or that of others, to have made statements out of court not consistent with, and in some cases opposed to, those made in their sworn testimony. Such statements must have been relevant to the

---

24 Ark., 620; State *vs.* Hamilton, 83 Iowa, 572; State *vs.* Foye, 53 Mo., 336; Stephens *vs.* People, 19 N. Y., 549; Hamilton vs. People, 29 Mich., 133; State *vs.* Howard, 9 N. H., 485; Corn. *vs.* Billings, 97 Mass., 405; Keator *vs.* People, 32 Mich., 484; People *vs.* Tyler, 35 Cal., 563.

case, however, and fully identified by the admissions of the witness or the testimony of others.

REFRESHING MEMORY

Refreshing Memory.— A witness, while undergoing examination, may refresh his memory from notes made by himself at the time of the transaction to which he testifies, or made by another, if he can identify them as contemporaneous and can swear that they were read by him at the time when the events occurred. Such notes may be examined by the opponent's counsel and may be made the subject of cross-examination.

ADMISSION OF FACTS WITHOUT PROOF

Admissions.— The existence of a fact may, in a civil case, and to a limited extent in criminal cases also, be admitted by either party, or by an agreement or stipulation between both parties; and when so admitted in evidence no testimony in proof or disproof of such fact will be received.

NUMBER OF WITNESSES

Number of Witnesses.— As all matters affecting the credibility of witnesses are decided by the Jury, the question of attaching weight to particular testimony, which is an incident or consequence of their credibility, rests with, and is determined by, the jury. When the testimony is conflicting this task is frequently attended with difficulty, and is sometimes impossible of attainment, resulting in disagreement. It may be laid down as a general rule, however, that the testimony of a single competent and credible witness is sufficient to establish a fact in evidence unless the Constitution, a statutory provision, or a rule of the common law requires otherwise. The Constitution of the United Status provides that in case of *treason* the testimony of two witnesses to the same overt act, or a confession in open court, shall be necessary to a conviction, and it has been held that a confession out of court must also be substantiated by the testimony of two witnesses. In cases of *perjury,* also, the testimony of two witnesses is necessary to convict, as otherwise the oath of one man would be balanced against that of another. This rule has been relaxed in some jurisdictions, however, and the testimony of a single credible witness, supported by corroborating circumstances, is there held to be sufficient to establish guilt beyond a reasonable doubt.

Written Testimony, When Necessary.— In some cases written testimony is required to establish particular facts, and cannot be replaced by oral testimony. This is true as to certain cases arising under the Statute of Frauds.[119] In a similar manner the contents of an instrument under seal can only be revoked or modified by a sealed instrument of equal dignity; and the terms of a will can only be modified by a subsequent will or codicil in writing.

---

[119] Statute of 29 Charles II.. chap. 3, entitled "An Act for the Prevention of Frauds and Perjuries. It object was to prevent the facility to perpetrate frauds and the temptation to commit perjury, held out by the enforcement of obligations depending for their evidence upon the unassisted memory of witnesses, by requiring certain transfers of land and certain cases of contracts to be reduced to writing and signed by the parties to be charger therewith, or by their agents thereunto lawfully authorized in writing (Anderson's Law Dic.)

Cumulative Evidence.— When a fact has been conclusively established in evidence, and there is no conflict of testimony in regard to its existence, it is obviously unnecessary to consume the time of the court by introducing additional testimony in its support. Such testimony is called *cumulative,* and is, in general, rejected as superfluous and unnecessary.

Depositions.— In its provisions respecting civil and criminal trials, the law assumes that evidence will be obtained, as a general rule, from the testimony of witnesses, given under the sanction of an oath in open court. This is especially true of criminal cases, in which the accused is guaranteed the right of being confronted with the witnesses against him and of exercising the privilege of cross-examination. It is also essential to a just determination of the case that the jury should have the privilege of hearing testimony from the lips of the witnesses, in order that it may judge of their credibility and attach proper weight to their evidence. In some instances, however, this is impossible, and the testimony of such material witnesses as are sick or absent, or who reside out of the jurisdiction of the court and are not subject to its process, must be taken in writing under such conditions as are calculated to secure the best evidence obtainable under all the circumstances of the case. This is accomplished by written instruments called *depositions,* which the law places at the disposal of litigant parties for this purpose. A *deposition* may therefore be defined as a written declaration under oath, made upon notice to the adverse party for the purpose of enabling him to attend and cross-examine, or to make use of written interrogatories for that purpose.

Procedure.— In a proper case the questions, or *interrogatories* as they are called, are drawn up by the party who desires the testimony of the witness to be taken, and are submitted to the adverse party, who adds such *cross-interrogatories* as he may deem necessary. The interrogatories are prepared by the direction of the court, who decides all points that arise as to the relevancy or materiality of the questions submitted. The interrogatories are then sent to a person designated by the court to act as commissioner, or to some official authorized by law to act in such cases, to receive the testimony of the absent witness. The witness then appears before the commissioner and, after having been duly sworn, answers the questions in the same order as if he were giving his testimony in open court. As the matter of depositions is regulated by statute, the terms of the statute must be substantially complied with in preparing the interrogatories and in taking the testimony of the witness. The answers of the witness are taken down in writing, their correctness is certified to by the commissioner, and the deposition is returned to the court from which the commission was issued.

Competency of Deponent.— Questions of competency are determined as in the case of a witness who testifies in open court, and the deposition when received is read to the jury or, with the permission of the court, may be taken to the jury room, with a view to its examination by the jury in the course of their deliberations.

PRESUMPTIONS

Presumptions.— *Presumptions* are assumptions of fact, without proof of their existence, made with a view to dispense with, or defer, the introduction of testimony in their support, or to make it for the time being unnecessary.

Law and Fact.— *Presumptions* are classified *into presumptions of law* and *presumptions of fact,* and, in accordance with their operation or effects, into *conclusive* and *disputable presumptions. A presumption of law* assumes a certain fact or state of facts to exist, either absolutely or until the contrary has been proved. *Presumptions of fact* are mere inferences, or conclusions, as to the existence of a fact from the existence or nonexistence of other facts.

Conclusive Presumptions.— A *conclusive presumption* is one which assumes a fact or condition of fact to exist, and forbids all proof to the contrary. Such are the presumptions that a crime committed by the wife in the presence of the husband is committed by his direction or coercion, that a child under seven cannot commit crime, or that a boy under fourteen or a girl under twelve is incapable of matrimonial consent.

Disputable Presumptions.— A *disputable presumption* consists in the assumption of the truth of a fact until the contrary is proved. Such are the presumptions that an accused person is innocent until proved guilty, that an assault with a deadly weapon presumes an intent to kill, or that persons are sane, living, or competent to testify until the opposite has been established in evidence.

Effect of Presumptions.— Presumptions of law are arbitrary in their nature and assume certain rules of conduct to have been observed in the past. Some of them take the form of legal enactments — as in the case of statutes of limitation — others are customary or are derived from the common law. Presumptions of fact become operative only when the facts upon which they are based have been conclusively established in evidence and the inferences from them are so strong as to remove all doubt and uncertainty from the minds of those whose duty it is to draw them.

Presumptions are, as a rule, continuous and favor an existing status, and the burden of showing the opposite to be true rests upon him who asserts it. Hence a person is presumed to be living until seven years have elapsed since he was last heard from; he is then presumed to be dead until the contrary has been shown. A person having a legal residence or domicile is presumed to continue in such residence, and a similar rule applies to sanity, competency, and marriage. Presumptions also favor order, regularity, and good faith. The power of persons to contract, the legitimacy of children, the proper and regular execution of instruments, the validity of public acts, the constitutionality of laws, the correct performance of administrative duties, and the like, are examples of this class of presumptions. So, also, the possession of real or personal property presumes ownership, the acceptance of services presumes an agreement to pay for them, the mailing of letters, where a delivery exists, affords a presumption of delivery, while the fact of registration affords a very strong presumption of such delivery.

ESTOPPEL

Estoppel.— Where a person, by formal declaration or representation, or by his conduct, or in some cases by his silence as to facts within his knowledge, induces another to believe that such representations are true, and to act upon such belief, the law forbids him to assert the contrary in an action at law. The avowal or silence must have been intended to mislead, and must have actually misled the other party, in order to operate as an *estoppel.* When A, for example, represents to B that 0 is his agent, and induces B to enter into a contract in that belief and as a result of such representations, he is estopped from afterward denying the fact of such agency. Estoppel may exist by deed, in the case of a sealed instrument, or in fact, as in the case above stated; or may be of record, when it appears in the pleadings in an action at law.[120]

References.— Of the smaller books relating to this subject which have appeared in recent years, the Digest of Evidence, prepared by the late Justice Stephen, is in many respects the most useful to the student. Professor Greenleaf's work on Evidence, the last edition of which appeared in 1894, is still regarded as the standard authority in the United States. The American works of Wharton, Underhill, and Rice, and the English works of Starkie, Roscoe, Taylor, Best, and Phillips can be consulted with advantage, and are all accessible in relatively recent editions.

---

[120] Estoppel may be by deed, that is by a sealed instrument, by record or *in pais,* that *is* by the act or admission and the like, as above described. Branson *vs.* Wirth, 17 Wall., 32 ; Railroad Co. *vs.* Dubois, 12 Wall., 47 ; Ketchum *vs.* Duncan, 96 U. S., 659; Morgan *vs.* Railroad Co., 96 U. S., 716.

CHAPTER V

PERSONAL AND PROPERTY RIGHTS

Individual Rights, How Secured.— The individual rights which the State undertakes to guarantee and make effective, in behalf of its citizens, consist in general in the right to acquire, hold, and alienate or transmit property of all kinds, ill an immunity from interference in the quiet enjoyment of the same, in the privilege to participate in the suffrage to the extent authorized by law, and in such freedom of speech, movement, occupation, and opinion as is consistent with the exercise of a similar right on the part of others. Some of these rights are secured and protected by the enactment and enforcement of what are called criminal laws; others by the provision of appropriate remedies in the event of their infringement or denial; and still others by means of constitutional guarantees or statutory prohibitions.

Classification.— The individual rights which are susceptible of enumeration and definition may be arranged under the general heads of *personal rights* and *rights of property. Personal rights* may also be classified under the two heads of *political* and *civil rights.*

Political Rights.— *Political rights* are those which entitle their holders, being citizens, to participate in the suffrage and to be elected or appointed to office, under such restrictions as to age, intelligence, or other qualifications as are specified in the constitution and laws of the State which accords them. These rights are acquired, in part, by birth or naturalization, and become effective upon reaching a certain age, or upon the acquisition of citizenship, or upon proof of the possession of a certain amount of property, or of a certain degree of education, and, in nearly all cases, by the payment of a small personal impost called a *poll-tax,* and by residence in a particular locality for a specified period.

Civil Rights.— *Civil rights* are those which affect the safety or security of the person, or the power or capacity of the individual to transact business, and. acquire, enjoy, alienate, and transmit property of every description. Civil rights are defined, guaranteed, and protected by formal enactments embodied in the Constitution and laws of the United States and in those of the several States of the Union. The recognition of rights acquired, by the citizen in one State is secured to them elsewhere by Section 2 Article IV of the Federal Constitution, which provides that "the citizens of each State shall be entitled to all privileges and immunities of citizens in the several States."

Regulated by Law — Aliens.— As both civil and political rights are created by and pertain to citizens alone, the extent to which they shall be extended to and enjoyed by aliens is a matter which is regulated by statute in each of the States of the Union. For this reason, aliens, as such, cannot lay claim to any of the rights enjoyed by the citizens of a State, who owe it the allegiance of defense and contribute to its support, receiving in return the exclusive privileges and immunities of citizenship.

METHODS OF EXERCISE

The civil rights of individuals, in respect to property and contracts, may be exercised directly by the *individual,* or collectively through *corporations or partnerships.*

CORPORATIONS

Corporations.— The term "person" has been used thus far in relation to human beings, or natural persons; but the law recognizes, in addition to the living beings who constitute its citizenship, another form of entity called corporations. A *corporation* may be defined as a body, consisting of one or more natural persons, established by law, usually for some specific purpose, and continued by a succession of members.[121] From the point of view of the law, corporations are regarded as artificial persons, having some, but by no means all, of the characteristics of natural persons; their existence may be indefinitely prolonged, by succession of membership, but they are incapable of committing crime, or holding public office, or of exercising the right of suffrage; nor, as a matter of strict right, can they extend their operations beyond the territory of the State from which their charters are derived. The individual citizen, save for the few exceptions already referred to, may select a residence, choose any calling in life, and may change either at pleasure; the corporation, on the contrary, can engage only in the business specified in its charter, and may exercise its franchise only in the State which created it.[122]

---

[121] Bouvier's Law Dict.

[122] Corporations are classified, according to their membership in point of numbers, into aggregate corporations and corporations sole; according to their

Partnership.— Another form of individual association recognized by law, and which remains to be described, is that of partnership. The *partnership* relation is based on contract, and may be said to exist where parties join together their money, goods, labor, or skill for the purposes of trade or gain, and where there is a community of profits.[123] A *partnership* differs from a *corporation* in that the community of interests is limited in point of time and is created by contract of the parties, and is not a continuing body called into being by a charter issued by the authority of the State. They differ in their methods of management as well; the affairs of a corporation being managed by its duly authorized officers and agents, the individual shareholders being merely units in the body corporate and not authorized, as such, to speak or act in its behalf; partners, on the other hand, are the active managers of the affairs of the firm, each acting in the joint interest of his copartners.[124] A *partnership* differs

---

religious or secular character, as ecclesiastical and lay; according to their objects and the nature of their franchises, into public and private. The State itself is a corporation, as are counties, towns, and cities in the several States, the latter being known as municipal corporations.

[123] Ward *vs.* Thompson, 22 Howard, 323 ; Perry *vs.* Butt, 14 En. Ga., 699 ; Gregory *vs* Dodge, 14 Wendel, 593 ; Vassar *vs.* Camp, 14 Barber, 341. See, also, Anderson's Law Dictionary, title "Partnership."

[124] Kimbro *vs.* Bullitt. 22 How., 256 ; Crawford *vs.* Welling, 4 Dallas, 286 ; Le Roy *vs.* Johnson, 2 Pet., 186 ; Rogers *vs.* Batchelor, 12 *ibid.,* 221; Imperial Refining Co. *vs.* Nyman, 38 Fed., 574; Cutlin *vs.* Gilders, 3 Ala., 262; Bradley *vs.* Camp, Kirby (Conn.). 77 ; Fitch *vs.* Stamps, 7 Miss., 487.

from an *agency* in that each partner has a definite interest in the objects of the association; an agent, as will presently be shown, having no such interest.

Kinds of Partnerships.— Where the partners merge all their business relations in the undertaking, the resulting association is called a *general partnership;* where the agreement is for a special branch of business, or for a particular enterprise, it is called a *special partnership.* A *limited partnership* is one authorized by statute, in which either the liability of the association or that of each individual member is restricted in a manner strictly in accordance with law. The creation of such a partnership is accompanied by such notice to third persons, or the general public, as will make known its limited character.

Partners.— The parties to a contract of partnership are called *partners,* and it is a fundamental principle of such an undertaking that the acts and admissions of each member of the association bind all copartners. A *dormant partner,*[125] the term being used to distinguish such a member from an *active partner,* is one who takes no part in the control or management of the partnership business; an *ostensible partner* is one who exhibits himself to the public as connected with a partnership and interested in its business.

As a partnership is formed for joint purposes, the members assume joint risks and incur joint liabilities. Hence all the members sue and are to be sued, but each is liable for the firm debts, except in limited associations.[126]

---

[125] Winship *vs.* *U. S.* Bank, 5 Pet., 529.

[126] Buzard *vs.* Bank of Greenville, 67 Tex., 89; Berthold *vs.* Goldsmith, 24 How., 536 ; Farr *vs.* Johnson, 25 111., 522 ; Moore *vs.* Bare, 11 Iowa, 198 ; Gallot *vs.* McCluskey, 18 La. Ann., 259; Cochran *vs.* Cunningham,

Partnerships are dissolved by the expiration of the contract of partnership, by voluntary dissolution, by the insolvency or bankruptcy of the association, or by the death of a member; but in the latter case a member may, by will authorize a continuance of the relation without subjecting his general assets to joint debts.[127]

---

16 Ala., 448; Dob *vs.* Halsey, 16 Johns. (N. Y.), 34.

[127] Burwell *vs.* Mandeville, 2 How., 576; Smith vs. Ayer, 101 U. S., 320 ; Jones *vs.* Walker, 103 *ibid.,* 444.

CHAPTER VI

PROPERTY RIGHTS IN GENERAL

Property.— As all property, or ownership, as that term is now understood in the civilized States of the world, is created by the law, and only exists so long as it has such legal protection and recognition, it follows that the word property, in its most general sense, may be defined as anything which, under the sanction of the law, may be made the subject of individual ownership. The term *hereditament* is nearly synonymous with property, and may be defined as a thing owned by, or a right vested in, an individual which may be transmitted by him to his descendants. A *tenement,* or *holding,* is anything of a permanent character which may be lawfully owned or held by an individual or corporation. The holder, whose title or ownership the law recognizes and protects, is called the *tenant,* and the instrument which describes the terms and conditions in accordance with which the estate or tenement is held is called a *grant, lease,* or *conveyance.* Property is classified, according to its nature and character, into real and personal.

Real Property.— *Real property* consists in land, together with the buildings erected thereon, and of all things growing upon or permanently attached thereto. The term also applies to certain rights issuing out of, annexed to, and exercisable upon land, the nature and extent of which will be explained hereafter. As now used, the word has precisely the same meaning as real estate.

Personal Property.— *Personal property* includes all chattels, or things of a movable character, which may be made the subject of individual ownership. For example, farms, together with the land, buildings, forests, waters, roads, fences, walls, and growing crops attached or belonging thereto, are real property; furniture, money, merchandise, all articles of commerce, tools, fruits, crops that have been gathered, and all products of the soil which have been severed therefrom, are personal property.[128]

---

[128] 2 Kent's Com., 340 ; Walker, 62, 801; Crouch *vs.* Smith, 1 Md. Ch., 401; Turner *vs.* Fenner, 19 Ala., 355 ; Woolsey *vs.* Judd, 4 Duer (N. Y.), 379.

CHAPTER VII

REAL ESTATE. ESTATES IN LAND

Common-law Theory of Ownership — Fiefs or Fees.— By the common law of England, all real property was presumed to be held from the king, in whom a title vested which was paramount to any estate which could lawfully be held by a subject. This view of ownership had its origin in the feudal system, under which a superior, or overlord, granted to a vassal a *feudum, or fee,* as a reward for services rendered or as a condition of services to be rendered in the future. The *fee,* or *fief,* consisted in an estate in land which was conferred upon a grantee and gave him the right to make such use of the land as he saw fit, to create estates therein of less dignity or value than his own, and to enjoy such benefits or profits as he was able to derive therefrom. Upon the death of the grantee, or upon the forfeiture of the fee for breach of any of the conditions of the grant, the land reverted to the superior and was by him re-granted to another upon such conditions as he saw fit to impose.

Character of Grant.— It will thus be seen that the thing granted, in any case, was a conditional right to the beneficial use of certain lands rather than absolute ownership of the soil, as that term is now understood. As time passed, however, and the feudal system began to adapt itself to the requirements of an advancing civilization, particular holdings came to be bestowed upon the heirs of a first, or original, grantee upon the fulfillment of certain conditions, consisting usually of burdens in the way of rents, fines, or services which accrued, or became due, upon the passing of the fee from the original grantee to his heirs or descendants. In England such estates descending in the male line and, by preference, to the eldest of the heirs male, with a view to retain the estates in particular families, gave rise to the system of *primogeniture,* which still prevails in most counties of the United Kingdom, and forms part of the common law in all its provisions which relate to the inheritance and ownership of real estate.[129]

Tenures in the United States — Escheats — Eminent Domain.— Although feudal tenures have long since disappeared in England, and although they have never existed in the United States (save in a few instances in colonial times, and then in a greatly modified form), the theory remains that the ultimate ownership of land is in the State, and that all titles thereto issue from and are protected by its authority. This is shown by the fact that the land and other property of an individual escheats, or reverts, to the State upon his death without legal heirs. It is also shown by the recognition, on the part of the United States and that of the several States of the Union, of what is known as the right of *eminent domain,* by which the land of a person, or, strictly speaking, the right to use such land, may be taken for the public use upon the payment of just and reasonable compensation. The lands so taken may be appropriated to a public use, as for streets, highways, and the like, and, in certain cases, by private persons or corporations, for the construction of roads, canals, railways, dams, and other works for the benefit of the community at large.

ESTATES

Estates — Classification.— The word *estate* is derived from the Latin *status* — the state or condition in which an owner stands with reference to his landed

[129] 3 Kent's Com., 487, 501 ; Walker, 308.

possessions[130] — and implies the degree, quantity, nature, and extent of interest which a person has in real property. This word has several meanings. In its most extensive sense it is applied to anything of which riches or fortune may consist, and includes real and personal property; hence we say personal estate, real estate, etc. In its more limited sense the word *estate* is applied to lands. It is so applied in two senses. The first describes or points out the land itself, without ascertaining the extent or nature of the interest therein, as, "My estate at A," etc. The second, which is the proper and technical meaning of the term, is, as above mentioned, the extent of interest which one has in real property, as, an estate in fee, or an estate for life, or for years. Estates are classified, in accordance with their tenures, into estates in possession, in reversion, and in remainder. An *estate in possession is* one in which the tenant is in actual occupation, or in receipt of the rent and other advantages accruing therefrom. An *estate ill remainder* is one which takes effect on the termination of a previous estate, created by the same instrument, called a *particular estate.* When a person grants a less estate than he himself holds, the portion so granted, on its determination for any cause, reverts to the original grantor; and the estate which thus returns to a grantor is called an *estate in reversion.*

REMAINDERS

Vested and Contingent Remainders.— Remainders are either vested or contingent. A *vested remainder* is one by which a present interest passes to a person, to be by him enjoyed in the future, after the termination of a particular estate created at the same time as the remainder. An estate to A for twenty years, with the remainder to B

---

[130] 2 Crabb, Real Property, p. 2, sec. 942.

for life, is a vested remainder. A *contingent remainder is* one so limited as to depend upon an event or condition which may never happen or be performed, or which may not happen until the preceding estate has determined. An estate to A for life, with remainder to the eldest son of B, in fee, is a contingent remainder, the uncertain event being that of a son being born to B. The instant a son is born, however, the remainder is no longer contingent, but vested. Had A died before the birth of a son to B, there would have been no remainder, as the estate would have determined before the remainder could vest. A remainder may also be contingent as to an event where the person is certain; an estate to A for life, and, in case B survives A, with remainder to B, in fee, is a contingent remainder, the doubtful event being the survivorship of B.

The Particular Estate.— It was the rule of the common law that there must be a precedent estate to support the remainder, or residual estate. This was called the *particular estate,* and both estates were required to pass out of the grantor at the same time and by the same instrument: this because of a requirement that all transfers of real estate must be in accordance with a formal ceremony of transfer known as *livery of seisin. As* there could be no estate at common law greater than one in fee simple, a particular estate and a remainder combined could not exceed in amount an estate in fee simple.[131]

ESTATES IN FEE SIMPLE

Fee Simple.— The highest estate in land known to the law is *a fee simple,* or *freehold,* and applies to the case of absolute ownership of the soil, with unlimited power of

---

[131] 4 Kent's Com., 197-262 ; Walker, 335, 811.

alienation.[132] Such ownership includes not only the land, buildings, forests, waters, etc., on the earth's surface, but also mines and mineral products obtained from beneath the surface, and extends indefinitely upward and downward.[133] Such an estate may be granted or conveyed away at pleasure, and can be devised by will, or, in the event of the death of the tenant without a will, will be transmitted by operation of law to the legal heirs of the deceased. The word simple in this connection has no other meaning than to imply the complete absence of qualification or condition in the ownership of the estate.[134]

ESTATES FOR LIFE

Estates for Life — Freeholds.— An *estate for life* is a freehold estate, not of inheritance, which is held by the tenant for his own life or for an indefinite period. It may endure for the life or lives of persons in being, but not beyond the duration of the life or lives for which it is granted. When the measure of duration is the tenant's own life, it is called simply an estate for life; when such measure of duration is for the life of another person or persons, it is called an estate *per autre vie.* Estates for life

---

[132] With a view to prevent perpetuities, it was a rule of the common law that no limitatation could be attached to an estate which did not become vested or void within a life or lives in being and twenty-one years. This rule, with some qualifications, has been generally adopted in the United States. (4 Kent's Com., 5.)

[133] For the hereditaments which are attached to and pass with estates, see pages 105.

[134] An estate tail is one which descends to a particular class of heirs: for this reason it is less absolute, as an estate, than a fee simple.

may be created by the law, or by the act or agreement of the parties. The principal estates for life, created by law, are estates of dower, estates by curtesy and jointures, and estates tail after possibility of issue extinct.

Dower — Curtesy — Jointures.— An *estate of dower* is a life estate created by law out of the property of the husband in behalf of his widow. An *estate by the curtesy* is a similar estate to which a husband becomes entitled, at the death of his wife, in the lands and tenements possessed by her during marriage, provided there has been lawful issue, born alive and possibly capable of inheriting her estate. A *jointure* is a joint estate, limited to both husband and wife, with remainder to the survivor. It was intended to afford a livelihood to the wife, in lieu of dower, and was to take effect immediately upon the death of the husband. This estate must consist of at least a *freehold* — that is, of an estate for life or in fee simple. It must be created before marriage and must vest immediately upon the death of the husband. The term *estate for life* is also applied to all estates of indefinite duration, less than estates in fee simple, to distinguish them from an estate of definite duration, presently to be described, called an "estate for years."

Incidents of Life Estates.— The incidents, or essential elements, of an estate for life have chiefly to do with the uses to which the lands may be put, the benefits that may be derived from them, and to certain rules that become effective at its sudden termination, with a view to regulate the incidents and diminish the hardships of its abrupt transfer at the termination of the life upon the continued existence of which it is conditioned. A life tenant may therefore cut such timber as is necessary to keep old buildings in repair, or to construct new ones from time to time as needed. He may also cut a reasonable amount of fuel, and may, by lease, confer a similar right upon tenants holding under him, provided no substantial injury is done to the inheritance. Such right to fuel was called at common law *estovers*. A tenant for life is bound to maintain the estate in substantially the same condition as that in which he received it. He cannot commit *waste;* he is obliged to make repairs, but not to undertake permanent improvements. If buildings are burned through his carelessness or neglect, he is bound to replace them within a reasonable time and at his own expense. If he receives the estate subject to a mortgage or other incumbrance, he must keep down the interest, but is not expected to clear off the incumbrance itself, which goes with the estate to the remainderman.

Political Privileges.— As a life estate constituted a freehold at common law, a tenant for life was invested with certain important political privileges, and could hold political office, sue in the courts, serve as a juror, and was, as a freeholder, entitled to vote for members of Parliament.[135]

ESTATES FOR YEARS

Estates for Years — How Created.— It has been seen that an estate for life was indefinite in extent by reason of the uncertainty as to the duration of the life or lives upon which its continuance depended. The next estate in dignity and importance was one of exact duration, called an *estate for years.* These tenures, prior to the reign of Henry VIII., were so precarious in character as to give them but little value. A statute[136] enacted during the reign of that monarch, however, gave them such permanence that they came to be used for the purpose of

---

[135] 4 Kent, 73.

[136] 21 Henry VIII.

raising portions for children, in family settlements and by way of mortgage.[137] An *estate for years* may be defined as an interest in lands, created by a contract for their possession for a term of years. The instrument which creates the estate and defines and determines the conditions of its tenure is called a *lease,* the parties to a lease-being known as the *lessor* and *lessee.*

Duration.— A lease may run for any number of years — a thousand, for example, at one extreme or for a part of a year at the other — the length of time covered by the lease being less important than the exact expression of its duration.[138] An estate for years may thus be created which shall far exceed in point of time any possible duration of human life. Estates for years differ also from freeholds, or those of inheritance, in that they can be created to begin in the future. No express words are necessary for the creation of an estate for years. The terms "demise," " grant," and "to farm let" are the most common, but any form of words indicating an intention to transfer the possession of an estate for a definite time is sufficient.

Assignment and Underletting.— A lessee for years may assign his whole interest unless restrained from doing so by the terms of the lease, and he may sublet for a less number of years than be himself holds; he may also encumber the estate to any limit, not exceeding his interest therein. An alienation of the entire interest of a tenant is called an *assignment,* a grant for a less term than his own is called an *underlease,* and there is a reversion in favor of the tenant for years. It has been seen that, by reason of the uncertainty which attended the termination of estates for

---

[137] 4 Kent, 86.

[138] 4 Kent, 94.

life, the law stepped in to protect the interest of the life-tenants and those holding under them from such hardships as arose from the sudden and abrupt termination of their holdings. As all estates for years terminate at the expiration of definite periods of time, lessees and tenants for years need no such protection, as the terms of the lease itself give them full and sufficient notice of the termination of their respective holdings.

How Terminated.— An estate for years may be terminated by the expiration of the lease, by eviction on the part of the lessor due to breach of condition, as for default ill payment of rent, subletting or assignment, or by release or surrender. The destruction of a leased building by fire did not operate to cancel the lease at common law, but this provision has been modified by statute in many of the States in such a way as to make void the obligation to pay rent so long as the leased premises are not in an inhabitable condition due to fire or other casualty.[139]

ESTATES UPON CONDITION

Estates upon Condition — Conditions Precedent — Conditions Subsequent.— An estate upon condition is one of uncertain duration, its tenure depending upon the happening of an event which will operate to enlarge or diminish the estate, or to transfer it to another person. The conditions upon which such estates depend are either precedent or subsequent. A *condition precedent* is one which must happen or be performed before the estate can vest. A *condition subsequent* is one the happening or performance of which will operate to enlarge or defeat an estate already vested, or to transfer it to another. An estate to A for life upon his marriage with B is a condition

---

[139] 4 Kent, 95.

precedent, the estate becoming vested in A upon the performance of the condition. An estate to A for life provided she does not remarry, A being a widow, or an estate to B so long as he continues to reside in a certain place, are examples of conditions subsequent. In the first case A forfeits the estate upon her marriage; in the second the estate of B determines and reverts to the grantor whenever B ceases to reside in the place named in the deed of conveyance.

MORTGAGES

Mortgages — Parties.— The principal estate upon condition known to the common law was the mortgage. A *mortgage* is, in form, a conditional grant or conveyance of land for a term of years which, upon the performance of the condition, becomes void; in default of such performance, however, the conveyance becomes absolute, and operates to create an estate in fee simple in favor of the grantee. The parties to a mortgage are the *mortgagor,* who is the grantor, or borrower, and the *mortgagee,* who is the grantee, or lender. A mortgage includes not only a deed of conveyance of the estate mortgaged, but also contains the added condition that the estate shall revert to the mortgagor upon the payment of the money loaned, otherwise the estate will vest in the mortgagee. As this stipulation, if carried into effect, is calculated to terminate or defeat the estate, it is called the *condition of defeasance.*

Present Use.— In its original form the mortgage was in fact, as well as in form a conveyance of land. The lender entered and took possession of the estate and continued in the enjoyment thereof until he had reimbursed himself for his debt out of the rents and profits of the land, when it was returned to the borrower. This condition no longer exists, and mortgages, as a result of the action of courts of equity, have so completely changed in character as to have become simply a high form of security for debt; conferring upon the creditor the right to obtain eventual ownership of the land, or the right to have the land sold in satisfaction of his debt if it is not paid at maturity.

Foreclosure — Equity of Redemption.— This is accomplished in behalf of the creditor by the issue of a decree of foreclosure, which gives him possession of the estate upon the failure of the mortgagor to satisfy the debt at its maturity.[140] As the transaction in its original form worked considerable hardship to the debtor — since the value of the land in most cases largely exceeded the amount of the loan — the courts of equity interposed and gave to the borrower a right to redeem his land within a limited time after it had passed by foreclosure into the hands of his creditor. This was called the equity of redemption. The conditions of foreclosure and the nature and extent of the equity of redemption are regulated by statute in several States of the Union. Mortgages are capable of assignment and transmission in the same manner as other chattel interests, being regarded as personal property in the hands of a mortgagee or his representatives.

Mortgages of Personalty.— Articles of personal property may also be made the subject of mortgage, or they may be pawned or pledged as security for money loaned. A mortgage of personalty differs from one of

---

[140] In this case it is termed a strict foreclosure: if it simply direct the sale of the premises and the satisfaction of the mortgage debt out of the proceeds, it is called an equitable foreclosure—strict foreclosure having been abolished in some of the States.

realty chiefly in one particular, namely, as to the party who shall have possession of the property during the existence of the mortgage. As possession of personalty is *prima facie* evidence of ownership, and as there are no records of personalty where titles can be traced and encumbrances ascertained, it is the policy of the law, in order to prevent fraud upon third persons, to give the mortgagee possession of the thing mortgaged. If third persons are not actually defrauded, however, the mortgage is valid as between the parties, although the mortgagor retains possession. In other respects the rights and remedies of the parties are nearly the same as with respect to mortgages of realty.[141]

ESTATES AT WILL

Estates at Will.— A small number of estates of less dignity than freeholds or estates for years were known to the common law and are still of considerable importance. These estates were of indefinite duration, not because they were terminated by the happening of a particular event, as is the case with life estates and remainders, but because their continuation depended upon the will of an individual grantor. Under this head fall estates at will and estates upon sufferance.

Tenure: How Terminated — How Created.— An *estate at will* is a holding of land at the will of the lessor. As the use of lands for agricultural purposes lay at the

---

[141] Walker's American Law, p. 353; 4 Kent, 136-194. In some of the States mortgages of personalty may be recorded, and where tins is the case the mortgaged chattel may remain in possession of the owner. Iii ninny of the States the subject of the foreclosure of chattel mortgages is also regulated by statute.

base of all conveyances and leases, the lessee of an estate, at will acquired such rights as would enable him to cultivate the soil to advantage. For this reason, while the estate was considered as held at the will of both parties, neither could terminate or determine the lease to the disadvantage of the other. The lessor could not bring it to an end to the prejudice of the tenant at will, who was entitled to reap what he had sown, and was allowed a reasonable time to remove his family after the crop had been harvested. Nor could the tenant terminate the estate before the day of payment of rent had arrived, so, is to cut off the landlord from his rent. Estates at will may be created by agreement or by parol leases, which, under the statute of frauds, are declared to be estates at will. They may also arise when a person enters upon the land of another under a contract for conveyance, or an agreement for a lease. So, also, when a man is placed upon land as a mere occupant, without any terms prescribed, he becomes a tenant at will[142]

ESTATES FROM YEAR TO YEAR

Estates from Year to Year.— It has been seen that the chief value of land, from the point of view of the common law, lay in its agricultural use, for which purpose its uninterrupted possession for at least one year was necessary. As the creation of estates terminable in less than a year gave rise to considerable litigation, estates at will gradually fell into disfavor, and were changed by the

---

[142] Walker's American Law, p. 353; 4 Kent, 136-194. In some of the States mortgages of personalty may be recorded, and where tins is the case the mortgaged chattel may remain in possession of the owner. Iii ninny of the States the subject of the foreclosure of chattel mortgages is also regulated by statute.

slow process of judicial decision into holdings of more definite duration, called estates from year to year.

Tenure: How Created and Terminated.— An *estate from year to year* is a tenancy of indefinite character as to its ultimate duration, but definite as to the constantly recurring periods of which it is composed, which are determined as to length and frequency of recurrence by the rent paid or the amount of notice required to terminate the tenancy. These estates are created by leases annually renewable, or by a tenant for years holding over after his estate has expired, his annual rental in such case being the same as that paid during his estate for years. These estates are terminated by either party upon due notice.

Estates upon Sufferance: How Created and Terminated.— An *estate upon sufferance* is the interest of a tenant who has come rightfully into possession of lands by permission of the owner and continues to occupy them after the period for which he is entitled to occupy them has expired. If the holding over is with the permission of the landlord, the estate becomes a tenancy from year to year. This estate may be terminated by an action of ejectment, or, if the tenant has had reasonable time to remove, the landlord may enter and take possession of the premises and may make use of such force as is necessary to accomplish that purpose.

LEASES

Leases — Character and Operation.— The transfer or temporary alienation of the use or possession of property is effected by means of instruments called leases. A *lease* is a contract for the possession or profits of lands or tenements, either for life or for a certain number of years, or for a portion of a year, or during the pleasure of the parties. All kinds of property, real or personal, may be made the subject of lease, subject always to the qualification that a lessor cannot dispose by lease of an estate greater than his own.

Parties — Effects — Rent.— The parties to a lease are the *lessor,* or *landlord,* who rents or leases the property, and the *lessee* or *tenant.* By the contract of lease the lessor transfers the use and possession of certain real or personal property to the lessee, for which the latter agrees to pay a stipulated sum called *rent,* either annually, quarterly, or monthly, as may be determined by the conditions of the tenancy.

How Created.— No particular form of words is necessary to constitute a lease, so long as it can be gleaned from the instrument, or agreement, that the intention of the parties was to transfer the use and possession of property from one to the other in consideration of the payment of rent. The form of words ordinarily made use of to accomplish this purpose is: "hath granted, demised, leased, and to farm let and, by these presents, doth grant, lease, and to farm let."

Forms of Leases.— Leases may be in the form of deeds under seal, and in some of the States this form is obligatory. If made orally, or in writing not under seal, they are called *parol leases.* They may be for life, for a term of years, or for a single year or a part of a year, or may terminate at the will of either party, upon reasonable notice. The leased premises should be accurately described in the lease, together with its exact duration, the date upon which it becomes operative, the conditions of tenure, whether for life or years, or from year to year; the times when the rent becomes due and payable and, if terminable upon notice, the form and length of notice required to terminate the tenancy. All statutory provisions on the subject of leases, in the jurisdiction in which the leased premises are situated, must be strictly complied with. When the term of the lease has expired, either at the time stated in the instrument or at the expiration of the notice, the landlord becomes entitled to immediate possession. He may also enter, upon the breach of any of the conditions, or covenants, on the part of the tenant, as for failure to pay rent, and the like.[143]

CONDITIONS AND COVENANTS

Conditions and Covenants.— A *condition* is a qualification inserted in a lease or other instrument which modifies or affects its operation. Conditions are either *precedent* or *subsequent,* depending upon whether they are to be fulfilled before the lease becomes operative or during its continuance. An agreement upon the part of the landlord to make certain improvements before the tenant enters is a condition precedent. A condition subsequent is one the failure of which defeats the estate and determines the lease. Conditions are binding upon both parties, and, in this respect, differ from covenants which bind only the party whom they affect, or who is to perform them. *Covenants* are clauses inserted in leases, or other instruments under seal, by which a party assumes certain obligations, or undertakes to perform certain duties for the benefit of the other. If formally stated in words, they are called *express covenants;* if deduced from the terms or conditions of the lease or conveyance, they are known as *implied covenants.* If they affect the property leased, they are called *real covenants* and are said to run with the land, and, as such, bind the covenantor and his heirs; if they are obligatory upon the maker only, they are said to be *personal covenants.* The most important of the real covenants are those which relate to the title of the leased

---

[143] 4 Kent's Com., 105.

premises and guarantee the tenant in the enjoyment thereof. Covenants relating to easements, commons, and the like are real, and, like all such undertakings, pass, with the land, to the heirs or representatives of the grantor.

Boundaries.— Estates in land are limited in extent by natural or artificial lines called boundaries, and every grant or conveyance of real estate should contain a description of its extent and boundaries sufficiently accurate in detail to enable a particular tract to be identified and separated from adjoining tracts or estates. Natural boundaries comprise such objects of a permanent character as are susceptible of accurate description and of recognition, in place, by the terms of such description in a grant or lease. Rivers, the snores of the sea, or of gulfs, bays, lakes and ponds, trees, rocks, streets, highways, and the like, are frequently made use of for this purpose. Artificial boundaries consist in monuments, walls, fences, and the like, erected by man for the purpose of marking the limits of estates or tracts of land. Natural objects, if well selected, are generally preferred to artificial boundaries, on account of their more permanent character.

Rivers as Boundaries — Changes.— If a non-navigable river forms a boundary, the limiting line is the mid-channel, and the boundary changes with all gradual changes of the current. Acquisitions of soil by accretion go to the owner of the lands upon which they are deposited, and similar losses are sustained by the owner of the land from which they are taken by the gradual action of the tide or current. Sudden and extensive changes due to movements of the channel leave the ownership unchanged, as the property can still be identified, which is not the case with gradual accretions. On the shores of the sea or of tidal or navigable rivers individual ownership ends at average high-water mark. The title to the shore proper, between high and low water mark, and to the beds of navigable rivers, and to the bottom of the sea, is in the State, as trustee for the public. On this principle, grants of the public lands in the United States, when made to individuals, end at the high-water mark; if made to States or to political corporations, they extend to the mid-channel, or, in case of the sea, to the limit of shore fisheries.

HEREDITAMENTS

Hereditaments, Corporeal and Incorporeal.— The term *hereditaments* has already been defined as an article of property, or a right, owned by or vested in a person which may be transmitted by him to his descendants. They are susceptible of classification, according to their nature, into —

1. *Corporeal hereditaments,* including those of a visible, tangible character which may be perceived by the senses. Lands, buildings, heirlooms, and the like are corporeal hereditaments.

2. *Incorporeal hereditaments,* including all rights issuing out of or exercisable upon land. They are not the objects of sensation, can neither be seen nor handled, are creations of the mind, and exist only m contemplation. Thus a man may have a right of common of pasture upon, or a right of way over, the lands of another; such common of pasture and right of way are incorporeal hereditaments. Corporeal hereditaments have already been described under the head of property. The principal incorporeal hereditaments known to the common law which have received recognition in the United States are the following:

COMMONS

Common of Pasture.— At an early stage of the practice of granting large tracts of lands to individuals in feudal tenures, it became important to devise some means of obtaining such income or return from them as would secure to their holders the means of providing for the cost of the military aid which they were obliged to render to the overlord from whom their estates were derived. To this end tenants in chief sometimes cultivated the soil themselves, but more frequently granted their lands to others at fixed rentals, and it was by this class of subordinate holders or tenants that the soil was chiefly tilled. The lauds comprised in the *manors, as* the estates of the principal tenants were called, were divided into plow land and pasture, certain definite tracts of the former being allotted to each tenant by metes and bounds. The fee of the pasture lands remained in the lord of the manor, but with each portion of arable land he granted the right to graze certain animals on the waste or pasture lands of the manor. This right was called *common of pasture;* it was *appendant* when it gave the tenant the right to pasture such beasts as were necessary to plow and manure the land. Common *appurtenant* was a right of pasture of a more general character, which could be created by grant or will, or could be acquired by prescription.

Common of Estovers was a right of similar origin, which gave to a tenant the privilege of cutting wood on the manor lands for fuel or for agricultural purposes. The rights of common above described have obtained but little, if any, prevalence in the United States.

Rights of Common in the United States.— In the early settlements of the colonies, and to an appreciable extent in the occupation of the public lands of the United States, the word "common" came to be applied to the less valuable lands in particular settlements, which for that reason were the last to be granted to or taken up by individuals. So long as they remained unappropriated they were used, by common consent, for pasturage by all holders of land or owners of cattle in the township. They ceased to be common, however, when they were appropriated by or granted to an individual. There are instances in which such lands have been granted, as common lands, to the community at large, and similar reservations of land were made for public uses by townships in various portions of New England. These were named "commons" because of their being specifically set apart to the public use.

Common of Fishery.— The right of fishery in the high seas, which is regulated by international law, is there held to be common to all the world. The foe simple of the shore, between high and low water marks, which is covered by the ebb and flow of the tide, is vested in the State adjacent thereto, and the right of fishery on the shores of the sea, or in gulfs, bays, or tidal rivers, vests in the same authority, by whom it may be held for the common use of all its citizens, or may be granted to individuals. A similar rule was applied, in the common law, to navigable rivers in which there was an ebb and flow of the tide. In non-navigable rivers the rights of fishery, like those of ownership, were vested in the riparian proprietors, and common of fishery could be granted to tenants and could be acquired by prescription. In the United States the right of fishery on the shores of navigable waters, including the sea, gulfs, bays, tidal rivers, and in some navigable rivers in which there is no ebb and flow of the tide, vests in the several States. The ownership of the soil, together with the right of fishery in non-navigable waters, including fresh-water streams, brooks, ponds, and small lakes, is vested in the proprietors of the soil adjacent thereto.

EASEMENTS

Easements and Servitudes — How Created and Extinguished.— An *easement, or servitude* as it was called in the civil law, consists in an obligation on the part of the owner of land to permit the public, or another person, to exercise certain rights thereon not inconsistent with his general rights of ownership. To constitute an easement there must be two tenements owned by several proprietors — the *dominant,* to which the privilege is attached; the *servient,* upon which it is imposed. Easements usually consist in rights of way, common of pasture, or fishery; or in rights to take wood, timber, stone, or minerals from the land of another; or to receive air, light, or heat from or over other land. They are created by a grant or agreement, express or implied, of the owner of the servient tenement, or by prescription extending over twenty years or more, to the extent of the easement claimed, and from which a grant is implied. Easements are extinguished by agreement or release; by merger, when the two estates are united in the same person, and by nonuser, or cessation of enjoyment in a case in which the easement originated by prescription, the nonuser creating a presumption of release when the abandonment has continued for a period at least as long as the uninterrupted use from which the right arose.

URBAN SERVITUDES

Urban Servitudes.— In addition to the *rural easements* already described, there are a number of *urban servitudes* which are enjoyed under similar conditions, and are created and terminated in the same manner. The principal of these are rights of *drip, drain,* and *way, structural support, party walls, rights to light and air,* and privileges to obtain water from wells, or other sources of water-supply, situated upon the lands of another. Most of these servitudes explain themselves, and all of them originate in grants, save in a small number of cases in which there has been a use for a sufficient number of years to create the presumption of a grant. The right of *structural support* consists in a privilege to rest house timbers or girders on the walls of another's building. The *right of drain* is a privilege to carry water in pipes or ditches over or through the lands of another. The *right of drip* is an obligation to allow the water from the roof of a building to drip or fall upon one's land. The *right of way* is precisely the same ill character and obligation as the corresponding rural servitude.

Party Walls — Rights of Owners.— A *party wall* is a wall erected upon the line separating two adjoining parcels of land belonging to different owners and used for the mutual support of adjacent buildings. The subject is regulated by statute in the several States, and their provisions usually require the wall to be built equally on the lands of the adjoining owners and at their joint expense. When but one owner desires to use such wall, it is built at his expense, and when the other wishes to make use of it he pays one half of its value. Each owner has the right to place his joists in the party wall and to use it to support his roof. When a party wall has been built, and the adjoining owner is desirous of having a deeper foundation, he has the right to undermine the wall, using due care and diligence to prevent injury to his neighbor, and, having done so, he is not answerable for any consequential damage that may ensue.

Fences — Common-law Rule.— At the common law the tenant of a close was not bound to fence against an adjoining close, unless by force of prescription; and if bound, by prescription, to fence his close, he was not bound to fence against any cattle but such as were rightfully in the adjoining close. If not bound at common law to fence his land, he was nevertheless bound, at his peril, to keep his cattle on his own grounds and prevent them from escaping. In the United States the subject is regulated locally by statute. In those States and Territories in which the grazing and farming interests are both considerable, the statutes on this subject depend upon and, to some extent, measure the predominance of either interest. Statutes enacted in jurisdictions in which the farming interest predominates do not, as a rule, require cultivated lands to be fenced, and impose severe penalties upon owners who permit cattle to range without sufficient provision in the way of borders. In those localities where there is a formidable grazing interest the statutes usually require agricultural lands to be inclosed with fences, the minimum standard of which is therein specified, and cattle which break through such an inclosure may be held until the damage committed by them has been repaired or its amount reimbursed.

Light and Air.— The common law recognized a right of property in light and air to exist in favor of the first to build upon land adjoining that of another. To acquire this privilege, the lights must have been ancient — that is, must have existed without obstruction for at least forty years. In modern times the period of prescription or limitation has been shortened, and the uninterrupted and exclusive enjoyment of window-lights for twenty years has been held to raise a presumption of title to the unobstructed enjoyment of that protection. In the United States, on account of the rapid growth of towns and the frequent changes that take place in the character and construction of buildings, the right is less generally recognized than in England, and in some jurisdictions is forbidden by statute. In some of the States, however, the principle continues to be recognized in behalf of earlier proprietors not only to the enjoyment of light and air, but to an exemption from injury due to the pollution of the air from causes originating within the premises of another. Such pollution constitutes a nuisance, for which the law provides an appropriate remedy.

WAYS

Right of Way.— A way is a right of passage over the lands of an individual existing in behalf of the public, for a public use, or in behalf of an individual. Ways originate in grants from the owners of the soil, or may arise by prescription, or immemorial usage, or by uninterrupted enjoyment for twenty years under a claim of right. They may also arise by necessity, as where a man purchases land accessible only over land of the grantor, or sells, reserving land only accessible over lands of the grantee, in which case he shall have a way of necessity over the land which gives access to his purchase or reservation. The necessity for this right of way must be absolute, and when the necessity ceases the way ceases with it.

Highways.— Highways are roads or other means of communication of a public character, the use of which is open to all. Tinder this head fall carriage-ways, roads, horse-ways, footpaths, and navigable rivers. They may arise by immemorial prescription, or may be acquired by the State under its inherent power to take private property for public use, called the *right of eminent domain.* When the use only is taken, the ownership of the soil remains in the grantor, subject to the conditions of the easement; and full rights of ownership revive when the land ceases to be used as a highway or is devoted to another and different use. When the fee simple of the land is taken, however, the title vests in the State, county, or other body politic to whose use it has been appropriated.

Characteristics of Easements.— Easements, like other incidents of estates in land, are either appendant or appurtenant; they are appendant when they arise by prescription, or are annexed to an estate in land as a component part thereof, and, when so created, they are said to be assignable and pass with the land by alienation or by descent; they are appurtenant when they are purely personal in character and are created by license or by permission; in such cases they are not assignable and become void at the death of the licensee.

RIGHTS OF NAVIGATION

Navigability of Waters, How Determined.— In its technical sense, the term navigable, at common law, is only applied to the sea, to arms of the sea, and to rivers which ebb and flow with the tide; in other words, to tidewaters the bed or soil of which is the property of the State. All other waters are, in this sense of the word, non-navigable, and are *prima facie* strictly private property. But in England even such waters, if navigable, in the popular sense of the term, are either of common right, or by dedication subject to the use of the public as navigable highways, the fee of the soil remaining in the riparian proprietors. The rule of the common law by which the ebb and flow of the tide was made the criterion of navigability, has never been adopted in the United States, or, if adopted, it has been in a form modified and improved to fit the country and the wants of its inhabitants. According to the prevailing rule administered in the courts of tills country, all rivers which are found of sufficient capacity to float to market the products of the mines, the forests, or the tillage of the country through which they flow, or which are capable of use for the floating of vessels, boats, rafts, or logs, are subject to the free and unobstructed navigation of the public, independent of legislation. It is not necessary that the stream should be navigable all the year round.[144]

Navigation, How Regulated in the United States.—The general authority to regulate the public use of navigable waters is in the States, subject to the paramount authority of Congress, when particular waters constitute highways of commerce with foreign nations or between the States. This fact does not exclude State regulation, if Congress has not exercised its power, or if the regulations of the State do not conflict with Congressional enactments.[145] Subject, therefore, to the paramount power of Congress to regulate interstate commerce, the several States may construct works of river or harbor improvement, may authorize the construction of bridges, dams, and ferries in or upon such waters, and may impose regulations in respect to the navigation of the same. Over waters or other ways lying entirely within its territorial limits and not forming, with other avenues of communication, a route of interstate commerce, a State has exclusive jurisdiction.[146]

---

[144] The Montello, 20 Wall., 430, 11 *ibid.,* 411: The Daniel Ball, 10 *ibid.,* 557; Withers vs. Bulkley, 20 How., 84; Escanaba Co. *vs.* Chicago, 107 U. S., 678.

[145] The Montello, 20 Wall., 430, 11 *ibid.,* 411: The Daniel Ball, 10 *ibid.,* 557; Withers vs. Bulkley, 20 How., 84; Escanaba Co. *vs.* Chicago, 107 U. S., 678.

[146] The Montello, 20 Wall., 430, 11 *ibid.,* 411: The Daniel Ball, 10 *ibid.,* 557; Withers vs. Bulkley, 20 How.,

WATERCOURSES

Watercourses.— A *watercourse* is a stream of water flowing through the land of a proprietor, with a current varying in strength and volume at different seasons of the year. The right of ownership in watercourses extends to the soil lying under them and to a qualified use of the water itself as it passes through the land. Such use by an owner, however, must not result in a diminution of the normal flow of water at any season; nor cause it to overflow, or otherwise injure the lands of adjoining owners; nor can he detain it and convert the entire volume of the stream to his own use, unless he has an exclusive right thereto, based upon prescription. The right of an owner, in this respect, is not to the water itself, but to its beneficial or economic use, as it passes through his lands, and be must return it to its course, unimpaired in volume, when it issues from his estate.[147]

84; Escanaba Co. *vs*. Chicago, 107 U. S., 678.

[147] 3 Kent, 497, 516. See also Angell on Watercourses. Wadsworth *vs*. Smith, 11 Me., 278 ; Gillett *vs*. Johnson, 30 Conn., 180 ; Luther *vs*. Winnissimmet Co., 9 Cush., 171; Curtis *vs*. Kessler, 14 Barber (N. Y.), 511; Hill *vs*. Newman, 5 Cal., 445 ; Kelly *vs*. Natoma Water Co., 6 *ibid.,* 105.

CHAPTER VII

THE ACQUISITION, ALIENATION, AND TRANSMISSION OF REAL PROPERTY

Title to real property may be acquired in several ways:

I. TITLE BY OCCUPANCY

Title by Occupancy — Discovery — Soil by Accretion.— Where property of any kind is without an owner, it fairly belongs to the first person who takes possession. This is a dictate of the law of nature, and if there ever was a time when there was no such thing as exclusive individual property, occupancy must have given the first title. This, too, is the foundation of title by discovery. At present, however, there is so small an amount of property which has not a legal owner that the right of acquiring property is of very little consequence. But there are some cases in which tins right is even now called into exercise. It is settled that if soil be formed from the sea or a river by gradual accretion it is the property of the adjacent owner. If an island be formed in a river it belongs to the owner of the nearest bank, or if the middle line of the river passes through it, the portions on each side of this line belong, respectively, to the owners of the adjacent banks. Again, with regard to the use of air, water, and light as connected with the ownership of land, great weight is always given to prior occupancy. The doctrine is, that he who has made the first appropriation of either of these elements to a particular use is entitled to protection in the enjoyment of that use; but this doctrine is modified by so many considerations growing out of the increase of population and public policy that it is difficult to lay down any precise rules on the subject.[148]

Acquisition of Personalty.— It is easier to acquire personalty by occupancy than realty, on account of possession being stronger evidence of ownership. It is a general rule, as will be shown hereafter, that the ownership of realty must be evidenced, not only in writing, but by record; whereas personalty does not usually require written evidence of ownership. The consequence is that personalty is more frequently acquired by occupation than realty. The most common instances are as follows: (1) The finder of things lost is entitled to them unless the original owner appears to claim them, and still more if there be no such owner; (2) the captor of wild animals, including all those on land or water, which have not been domesticated is entitled to them, provided that in taking them he does not trespass on the rights of others; (3) the increase of value by accession is referred to this head the general rule being that if a thing in the possession of another receive an accession of quantity or value by natural or artificial means, as by the growth of vegetables, the pregnancy of animals, or the application of mechanical labor and skill, such increase belongs to the possessor; (4) the acquisition of value by invention, discovery, or authorship, *in* science, art, or literature, comes likewise under this head; (5) in speaking of the confusion of goods, the rule is, that if goods belonging to different persons become mixed or confounded together, by mutual consent, the owners have a proportional interest therein; but if done by one without the consent of the other, the latter has the whole.[149]

---

[148] Walker's American Law, § 155 ; Banks *vs.* Ogden, 2 Wall., 57.

[149] Walker's American Law, § 156.

II. TITLE BY MARRIAGE

Marriage — Dower — Curtesy.— One of the consequences of marriage, after the death of one of the parties, is to give the survivor a life estate in a part or the whole of the realty owned by the deceased. If the husband dies, the title thus acquired by the wife is called her dower. If the wife dies, the title so acquired by the husband is called his curtesy.[150] These are life estates, and are subject to all the incidents that attach to estates of that character.

III. TITLE BY DESCENT

Descent — Intestacy — Heirs.— When the owner of land dies without making formal disposition thereof, the law makes it for him. Leaving no will *(festamentum,* testament), he is said to die intestate, and in legal phrase is called the intestate. The persons to whom by the law his real property passes are called his heirs, and he is their ancestor; and the title by which the heirs take the property is called *title by inheritance* or *descent.* The distribution of the personal property of the intestate is effected by the common law, as modified by statute in the several States, or by the operation of laws enacted for the purpose called *statutes of distribution.* But before the property of an ancestor can avail his heirs there are certain prior claims to be satisfied. In the first place, the rights of dower or curtesy, if either exist, take precedence of heirship and cannot be affected by the law of descent. In the next place, the claims of creditors must be satisfied. The heirs succeed by descent to the residue, or, rather, at the instant of the

---

[150] *Ibid.,* § 157.

ancestor's death his property vests in his heirs encumbered by these prior claims.[151]

Rules of Descent.— The rules of descent vary considerably in the different States, but all agree in departing from the English law so far as to promote equality among the heirs. It is proper to observe that realty alone is strictly inheritable. Technically speaking, personalty does not, in any case, descend to the heirs, but on the death of the owner vests in the executor or administrator and is by him distributed. Those who take the residue after payment of debts are said to take, not as heirs, but as distributees, and are called personal representatives, to distinguish them from heirs, who are called real representatives.[152]

Distribution to Heirs — Rules of the Civil and Canon Law.— The share of an heir in the estate of an ancestor is determined by his relationship to such ancestor by blood, heirs of the whole blood being preferred to those of the half-blood in every case. In determining degrees of kindred two methods have been sanctioned, one ill accordance with the canon law, which prevails in England, the other in accordance with the civil law, which prevails generally in the States of the Federal Union.[153] These systems differ in their application to a particular case by one step or degree of kindred. The canon law, beginning at the common ancestor, reckons downward to a particular intestate and his descendants; the civil law goes back from the intestate and his heirs to the common ancestor, and through such ancestor to the particular intestate and his descendants. When the heirs are all of the same class or

---

[151] *Ibid.,* § 159.

[152] Walker's Amer. Law, § 159.

[153] *Ibid.,* § 159.

degree of descent they are said to take per capita, or by the head; when they are of different degrees they take per stirpes, by branches, or by representation, and, in each branch, per capita. Three sons of an intestate, for example, take per capita, or in equal shares; had one of them died prior to the death of the intestate, leaving three children, they would have been entitled, per stirpes, to the father's share, each taking a third of such share or portion.

Rule in the United States.— The general rule in the United States may be thus stated: The property of an intestate descends first to lineal descendants, then to parents, brothers and sisters, and their descendants, and to grandparents, according to their several degrees of kindred. If all stand in equal degree of consanguinity to the intestate, they take per capita; if in unequal degree, they take per stirpes or by representation. On failure of heirs under the preceding rules, the inheritance descends to the next of kin, when such kindred can be ascertained and identified. In the absence of kindred the inheritance reverts to the State, from which, by legal intendment, it is presumed to have been originally derived.

IV. TITLE BY DEVISE

Title by Devise.— It will be observed that the title to property transferred in accordance with any of the methods thus far described has passed by operation of law. Property of all descriptions, whether real or personal, may also pass at the discretion of its owner, as expressed in an instrument voluntarily executed by him, called a *will* or *testament.*

Power to Dispose of Property by Will.— As the estates recognized by the feudal system did not at first extend beyond the life of the tenant, it was not until tenures greater than life-estates came to be recognized that it was possible to devise property by will or testament. Indeed, real estate could not be disposed of by will in England until the year 1543, and then only under considerable restrictions. At present, however, subject to the claims of creditors and of dower and curtesy, every person capable of acting for himself is free to dispose of his property by will to whomsoever he pleases. There is an idea prevailing among the more ignorant classes that a father, in making a will, must give something, however little, to each of his children, or the will will not be good; but this opinion is without foundation. A man may give his property to whomsoever he pleases, to the complete exclusion of his children, and, however unnatural and inhuman this may appear, it will not affect the validity of the will. Indeed, it may be laid down as a general proposition that all restraints upon alienation of property are in opposition to the prevailing spirit and policy of our institutions.[154]

Parties to Wills.— When a person dies, leaving a will, he is called a *devisor* or *testator;* the property disposed of by will is called a bequest, legacy, or devise, and the persons who take it are known as legatees or devisees. The person appointed in the will to settle the estate is called an *executor,* the term being used in contradistinction to the term *administrator* who is a person appointed by the court, in accordance with law, to perform a similar duty in respect to the estate of a person dying intestate, or who has left a will which has been

---

[154] The creation of future estates by will is subject to the common-law rule against perpetuities, and no limitations can be imposed upon an estate created by will for a longer period than a life or lives in being and twenty-one years. See also Walker's. American Law, § 164 ; 4 Kent, 502-506.

found to be defective in some essential respect, or which has been contested for good reason and declared invalid. *Executors* and *administrators* perform their duties under the supervision of courts created for the purpose and endowed with what is called probate jurisdiction.[155]

Wills.— Power to Make Wills.— A *will,* or *testament,* is the formal statement of a person, in writing, as to the disposition he wishes to have made of his property after his death.[156] The provisions of the will are carried into effect by persons named therein, called *executors,* who perform their duties under the direction of courts having jurisdiction in such cases. Any person of full age and sound mind and memory, and not under restraint or tutelage, can make a will and can make such disposition of his property therein as he may desire. Married women, infants, insane persons, and others under restraint or tutelage can make wills only when especially authorized to do so by statute. Married women and aliens may be devisees, however, as may infants, idiots, and insane persons, whose portions pass to guardians or trustees who hold them in trust for their especial benefit. Subscribing witnesses to a will, on account of their peculiar relation to the testator, are generally disqualified from inheriting under a will signed by them in that capacity; their competency as witnesses, however, is restored in many jurisdictions by a rule declaring void any

---

[155] Walker, 164.

[156] A form of disposing of personalty was recognized at common law, especially in behalf of soldiers and sailors in active service, called a *nuncupative* will. The will was not in writing, the wishes of the testator being gleaned from his ante-mortem declarations, and was not sufficient to pass a title to real property. It has fallen into disuse in the United States, if indeed it has not become obsolete.

beneficial interest they may have in a will in which their names appear as subscribing witnesses.[157]

Testamentary Capacity Presumed — Codicils.— Capacity to make a will and freedom from restraint in making it are generally presumed, and want of testamentary capacity and undue influence, if alleged by a party in interest, must be proved by one who would contest its validity upon either ground. A will that operates upon personal property is sometimes called a *testament,* and one operating upon real property a *devise;* the latter term, however, relates rather to the disposition of real property by will than to the instrument itself. A *codicil* is a testamentary provision supplemental to a will, but executed at a later date and under the same formalities, for the purpose of modifying one or more of its provisions. When properly authenticated, it is regarded as a part of the will and is treated as such by the courts. A transfer of real property by will is called a *devise;* a similar transfer of personal property is called a *bequest* or *legacy.* The beneficiary in the former case is called a *devisee,* and in the latter a *legatee.* Any natural person, and, unless forbidden by statute, a corporation as well, may receive property under the provisions of a will.[158]

Forms of Wills — Revocation.— The form of a will is not mandatory, and technical forms of speech are not necessary to its valid execution. It must be in writing, signed by the testator, the signing to be attested in the presence of the testator by three subscribing witnesses, unless a less number is required by the law of the place in which the instrument is executed. It is not necessary that wills should be sealed in most States of the Union. A will may be revoked, wholly or in part, by implication of law,

---

[157] Walker, § 164-167.

[158] Walker, § 164-167.

or by act of the party, as by the cancellation, tearing, destruction, or obliteration of its contents, or by the execution, of a codicil, or by a new instrument of later date. A subsequent marriage, with birth of issue, operates to revoke a will by implication of law, unless provision be made therein for the second wife and her issue. The will of a single woman is revoked by her marriage.[159]

When Operative.— A will becomes operative, as a conveyance, at the death of the testator, and relates to property then in his lawful possession and ownership; but it cannot become effective as a transfer of real or personal property until probate has been made; that is, until the instrument has been proved in accordance with the forms of law in a tribunal haying jurisdiction for that purpose. As wills are made by persons not familiar with the technicalities of legal verbiage, they are usually construed liberally, and the courts will give effect to their provisions when the wishes of the testator are clearly shown by the terms of the instrument.[160]

IV. TITLE BY PURCHASE

Purchase — Livery of Seisin.— The transfer of personal property, by reason of its movable character, has always been effected by simple delivery of possession, without form or solemnity of any kind. This has not been the case, however, with real property, the transfer of which in relatively recent times has been attended with extreme difficulty. The transfer, or *alienation,* of freehold estates was effected at common law by a ceremony called *livery of seisin.* Few persons were able to write, and such written instruments as were executed were not required to be recorded in any public office, and a written transfer

---

[159] Walker, § 164-167.

[160] Walker, § 168.

standing by itself would have been defective, as not giving notice of a change of ownership to third persons. The transfer by livery was accomplished in the following manner: A formal deed of transfer having been executed, the parties went to the land, or in sight of it, and there, in the presence of as many witnesses as could be had, the grantor declared the contents of the deed, and then made a symbolical delivery of the land to the grantee by actually delivering a twig or turf taken from the soil. This completed the conveyance, the notoriety of which depended upon the number of persons who witnessed the ceremony of delivery. The corresponding conveyance of incorporeal hereditaments was termed a grant, which differed from the form of transfer above described in that there was no actual delivery — a thing in its nature impossible from the intangible character of the tiling itself.[161]

Alienation in the united States.— It may well be doubted whether the form of conveyance above described prevailed, to any appreciable extent, in any of the colonies prior to the outbreak of the war of the Revolution. A trace of the feudal system seems to have been brought to this country by the colonists; not extending, however, beyond the conception that lands were held by a tenure, not clearly understood, either as to its origin or sanction, from some sort of superior authority, whose office it was to make land titles secure and to guarantee them, as articles of property in the hands of their *bonn-fide* proprietors. Whatever this notion may, have been, it soon gave way to a very clear and precise conception of the State itself, representing the will of all its citizens, as the sovereign authority, from which, by a fiction of paramount ownership, all titles to property were derived, and to

---

[161] *Ibid.*, § 169; 4 Kent, § 480.

which, as the general heir, all property escheated or reverted upon the death of the owner without heirs or next of kin.

Acquisition and Alienation, How Regulated.— All questions relating to the acquisition and alienation of real estate are regulated, in the United States, by the governments of the several states, in all of which the utmost freedom of transfer is favored as a matter of enlightened public policy. Lands pass freely by descent in all of the States, and the formalities to be observed in their alienation are simple and easily understood. What are called *abstracts of title* are prepared usually by the grantor. These abstracts contain a brief history of all the transfers of which the particular parcel has been made the subject since its original grant from the Crown, or from the lord proprietor, or colonial government, or, in the case of the public lands of the United States, from the issue of the original patent from the Land Office in Washington.

Alienation by Conveyance.— Land is alienated and its ownership transferred at the present time by means of a sealed instrument called a *deed of conveyance.*[162] The parties to such a conveyance are the *grantor* who sells the land, and the *grantee* or purchaser. The grantor must be lawfully seized or possessed of the property which he proposes to convey, and cannot, of course, dispose by deed, or otherwise, of a greater estate in the land than he himself possesses.

Deeds of Conveyance.— While no particular form of words is necessary to constitute a conveyance by deed, the different parts or clauses of the instrument should be arranged in orderly sequence, and the words and phrases used must be such as to give complete effect to the

---

162 4 Kent, § 450; Walker, § 169.

intention of the parties. The instrument should therefore contain the names and titles or designations of the parties who are referred to throughout the instrument, the grantor as the party of the first part and the grantee as the party of the second part. Immediately after the names of the parties should appear the consideration for or in view of which transfer is made. Next in order comes the granting clause, followed by a detailed description of the premises by metes and bounds. The habendum and tenendum clauses follow the description of the premises, although the latter, in so far as it describes the tenure or holding of the grantor, is now inserted as a matter of custom merely, since feudal tenures, as such, have never been recognized in the United States. These clauses are followed by the covenants, if any there be, and the deed concludes with a mention of the date of execution and a recital of the facts of signature, sealing, and delivery. The date of the conveyance if omitted is not fatal to the validity of the transfer, but the signatures of tile parties and the fixing of their seals, where that formality is required, in the presence of the subscribing witnesses is essential to its legal operation. The grantors are also usually required to acknowledge their signatures to the deed before a notary public or other officer authorized to take acknowledgments, and the omission to comply with such requirement is fatal.

When Operative — Registry — Effects.— A deed becomes operative as a conveyance from the date of signature and delivery, and binds the parties thereto and all having a privity of estate with them. ln most jurisdictions deeds are permitted to be registered in a public office provided for that purpose, and in some States such registry is required. Deeds *so* registered are usually given special evidential value, and become notice to ill concerned of the transaction to which they relate; when not so registered they bind the parties to their operation, but not third persons who have no knowledge of their existence.

The Torrens System of Registration of Titles.— The existing system of alienating laud, although simpler in many respects than that prevailing in former times, is still a tedious and complicated process, and a purchaser can never be entirely sure of the completeness or validity of his title. Deeds of conveyance contain covenants of warranty, the purpose of which is to guarantee the title in the purchaser, but these can be made effective only by an action at law, and are of no avail unless the grantor is possessed of sufficient property to satisfy a judgment should one be rendered in favor of the grantee. While land constitutes one of the highest forms of security for debt, it is not quickly available for that purpose, as the same examination of title has to be made in case of a mortgage as would be necessary in the case of an actual transfer of ownership. The first steps looking to a modification of the common-law system of alienation was made in Australia at the suggestion of Sir Robert Torrens, and the method devised by him was adopted in that colony after thorough investigation, and is now in successful operation.

Purpose — Registry, How Effected.— The Torrens system consists, in substance, in the substitution of a system of registration of land titles for the elaborate record of deeds and other title papers, which are now essential to the validity of transfers of real estate. Its purpose is to enable a person to buy and sell land with the same facility and with as little trouble and delay as are encountered ill transfers of stocks, vessels, or shares in the public funds, which are now made the subject of legal record. To carry the scheme into effect, the abstract of title in the case of a particular parcel of land is examined by a board or commission of experts, and its conclusions as to the validity of the title, if favorable, are, after a short period of limitation, made final by statute. The system is not compulsory, and registration of title in any case is made only on the written application of the owner, and the title is not subject to registry unless it is found upon examination to be vested in one who has the power to appoint or dispose of the entire estate in fee simple. Land subject to incumbrance by way of mortgage, lien, or other charge may be registered, subject always to the contemporaneous registry of the incumbrance in connection with that of the land.

Alienation, How Accomplished.— Registry of titles is made in a public office provided for the purpose, and a certificate of registry is issued in the *case* of each parcel of land the title to which has been made the subject of legal examination. The registry so made becomes, by operation of law, conclusive evidence of ownership, and all future transfers are made subject thereto. When the owner desires to dispose of his land he surrenders his certificate, which is canceled, and a new certificate issues to the purchaser or transferee. If an owner desires to incumber a particular tract by a mortgage, the mortgage is filed in the office of the registrar, and a record of the fact is made on the certificate of title. This system, which has worked satisfactorily in several of the colonies of Australia, was authorized in England by act of Parliament in 1875, and has been adopted in Illinois by a statute permitting owners of real estate to register their holdings under a system closely resembling that in force in England and Australia.[163]

---

[163] The constitutionality of the Torrens Act has been drawn in question in Illinois and *e* now before the courts.

V. TITLE BY EXECUTION

Title by Execution.— The rules of the common law were not such as to favor the alienation of real estate, even in satisfaction of the owner's debts. It was possible, however, under that system for a creditor to obtain possession of a part, and in certain cases of the whole, of his debtor's interests in land, and to hold them in trust until his claim had been satisfied out of the rents and profits. "This limited remedy against the real estate of the debtor was not deemed sufficient security to the British creditors, in its application to the American colonies, and a statute was passed in the year 1732 (5 Geo. II., chap. vii) for their relief. It made lands, hereditaments, and real estate within the English colonies chargeable with debts and subject to like process of execution as personal estate. Lands were dealt with on execution precisely as was personal property, and it was, consequently, the practice of some of the States, and particularly in New York, before and since the Revolution, down to the year 1786, to consider lands as assets in the hands of executors and administrators, and to sell them as such." [164]

Practice in the united States.— "Partly as a result of the operation of the statute above referred to, and partly because of the tendency in all the colonies to favor the prompt alienation of real estate, the practice of selling real estate in satisfaction of judgment debts has become general in the United States, subject to such statutory regulations as are calculated to prevent abuse and hardship. The general rule in the several States of the Union at the present time is to require the creditor to resort in the first instance to the personal estate as the proper and primary fund, and to look to the real estate only after the personal estate shall have been exhausted. and found

[164] 4 Kent, § 429.

insufficient. A right of redemption within a specified time, usually one year, is reserved to debtors whose lands have thus been sold in satisfaction of debts. It is proper to observe that this was the rule of the Roman Law."[165]

VI. TITLE BY ESCHEAT

Title by Escheat.— This form of conveyance is an inheritance from the system of feudal tenures, which required, on the death of a grantee without heirs, that his fee should revert or escheat to the king, or other superior from whom it was held. "As feudal tenures do not exist in this country, there are no private persons who succeed to the inheritance by escheat; and the State steps in, in the place of the feudal lord, by virtue of its sovereignty, as the original and ultimate proprietor of all lands within its jurisdiction." [166]

References.— The subject of real estate is fully discussed in the standard works of Blackstone, Kent, and Walker. Apart from these the leading American writer on the subject is Judge Washburn, whose work on Real Property is still regarded as. a standard authority. In addition, Sharswood's Leading Oases, in four volumes, and the works of Willard and Ballard on Real Estate, of Hilliard, Tiedeman, Williams and Kerr on Real Property, and those of Curtis, Deane, Martindale, Jones, and Oliver on Conveyancing, may be referred to with advantage.

---

[165] 4 Kent, § 429.

[166] 4 Kent, § 424.

CHAPTER VIII

PERSONAL PROPERTY

Personal Property — Goods — Chattels.— The term *personal property* has already been defined. It comprises all kinds and forms of property in the nature of goods and chattels, not included in the description of real estate, including money, checks, or other representatives of money; all forms of business and commercial paper, patents, copyrights, merchandise, furniture; building materials; all products of the soil, when severed therefrom; ores and minerals when mined; all forms of raw material and manufactured goods; all tame animals that are susceptible of ownership, and such wild animals as have been reduced to subjection, and, in addition, certain rights or interests which can be reduced to possession only by a suit or action at law, called *choses in action.*

How Different from Real Estate.— The methods of acquiring personal property have already been described. It differs from real estate chiefly in respect to the importance attached to *the fact of possession,* which is always presumptive, and in most cases conclusive evidence of ownership, the registry of titles of personalty being a right of relatively recent origin, unknown to the common law, and created wherever it exists by local statutes of limited operation. As in the case of real estate, the right of ownership which the law recognizes and protects is the *estate in* or *title to* the article which vests in the individual owner for the time being, and such an owner can dispose of no greater estate or property in the article than he himself possesses. While in possession, estates may be created in personal property, remainders may be limited, it may be encumbered by liens or mortgages, it may be made the subject of lease or hiring, or may, by the addition of labor and in combination with other materials, undergo a complete change of form, passing from the state of a raw material to that of a manufactured article, and may acquire, as a result of such change, a sensible increase in value.

Locating of, at Domicile of Owner.— Unlike real estate, personal property has no situs, but is presumed to follow its owner wherever he may go, and is acquired, held, and disposed of in accordance with the law of his domicile. When actually found or located elsewhere, it becomes subject to the law of the place in which it is for purposes of taxation, distribution, and the like, and all local demands must be satisfied before it can be removed to another jurisdiction.[167] At the death of its owner personal property passes to the executor or administrator of the deceased, and is by him distributed in accordance with the terms of the will, or, in case of intestacy, in accordance with the local statutes of distribution. In the absence of such statutes the distribution will be controlled by the provisions of the common law.

BAILMENTS

Bailments — Parties.— The principal incidents affecting the use and ownership of personal property arise

---

[167] Walker, 801 ; Turner *vs.* Fenner, 19 Ala., 355 ; Johnson *vs.* Copeland, 35 *ivid.,* 521; Bridgeport Bank *vs.* New York, etc., R. R. Co., 30 Conn., 231 ; Warren *vs.* Hofer, 13 Ind., 167; Fouke *vs.* Fleming, 13 Md., 392 ; Swearingen *vs.* Morris, 14 Ohio St., 425 ; Noble *vs.* Smith, 6 R. I., 446 ; Holmes *vs.* Remsen, 4 Johns. (N. Y.) Ch., 460.

out of contracts or agreements, and may be classed under the general heads of bailment and sale. A *bailment is* a transfer of the possession of personal property from one person to another without transfer of ownership, the title remaining in the original owner. The parties to a contract of bailment are the *bailor,* or owner, and the *bailee,* to whom the possession is conveyed in trust. The most usual forms of the contract of bailment are —

1. Deposit.— This is a deposit or bailment of goods to be kept, without reward, for the use of the bailor, and delivered according to the object or purpose of the original trust.[168] The principal purpose of this form of bailment is to secure the safe-keeping or storage of the thing deposited, as of money, goods, furniture, or the like. If money be deposited and the identical notes or coins are to be returned, it is a *special deposit;* if interest be charged, the deposit becomes a *loan.* The deposit is terminated at a time agreed upon by the parties, or at the will of the bailor, by a demand for restitution of the bailed articles. As no title passes, the bailee, by disposing of the goods or appropriating them to his own use, becomes liable in an action for damages.

2. Mandate.— Mandate consists in the gratuitous transfer of goods to another, *in* order that he may perform some acts upon, or in reference to, the bailed goods.[169]

3. Commodatum is a gratuitous loan of property' or goods to be used by the borrower without paying for their use.[170]

---

[168] Story on Bailment, § 4.

[169] *Ibid.,* § 153.

[170] *Ibid.,* § 153.

Degree of Care.— During the time that the goods are in the possession of the bailee he is required to exercise care in their protection and preservation in proportion to the benefit that he derives from their use. The degree of care required in any particular case is determined by the contract of bailment. If it contains no provision on the subject, the matter is regulated by law, and is determined by the circumstances of each case.[171] Where the bailment is solely for the benefit of the bailor, the bailee is in general held to a slight degree of diligence only in the care of the bailed article. When the bailment is for the sole benefit of the bailee, he is held to a high degree of diligence. When it is for the mutual benefit of both parties, he is held to an ordinary degree of diligence.[172] The relation of the parties and the benefit that each or both may derive are not conclusive in the determination of the degree of care. The nature of the article bailed and other facts surrounding the bailment may also be important features in determining the degree of care required of the bailee.[173]

BAILMENTS FOR HIRE

Bailments for Hire comprise all those classes of bailments where the bailee hires the use of the bailed article; and also those where the bailor hires the bailee to store or carry the bailed article or to perform some work or act upon it.[174] The following are the principal cases of bailment for hire:

---

[171] *Ibid.*, §§ 220, 226.

[172] Story on Bailment, § 83.

[173] *Ibid.*, §§ 182, 186.

[174] *Ibid.*, §§ 370, 421, 422.

1. Carriers.— Carriers are classified, in accordance with the undertaking in each case, into carriers without hire, carriers for hire, common carriers, and carriers of passengers. As carrying without hire is an undertaking for the exclusive benefit of the bailor, the responsibility assumed by the carrier is that of a bailee only, and the degree of care required is less than that required of a common carrier whose legal responsibility is more nearly that of an insurer. A carrier for hire is one who undertakes to deliver goods for hire in a particular case, but who does not make such carriage a matter of public employment. His responsibility, though greater than that of the carrier without hire, is also less than that of the common carrier, and extends only to the exercise of ordinary care and diligence in the execution of his undertaking.

Common Carriers.— A *common carrier* is one who undertakes for hire to transport from place to place the goods of such persons as choose to employ him for that purpose. For a refusal to carry goods proffered for carriage, a common carrier is liable to an action at the instance of the aggrieved party, as his undertaking is to carry for all who apply for such service, in the way of transportation, as he publicly agrees or offers to render.

The *liability* of the common carrier is for the carriage of the goods, and for their safe delivery at the destination agreed upon by the parties. As he is responsible for such safe delivery, he practically insures them, while in his possession, against loss from any cause except acts of God and the public enemy. So long as he has room he must carry indifferently for all who apply and agree to his terms as to freight, description, classification of goods, and the like, and in most jurisdictions an action will lie for a refusal to carry goods so offered. A carrier may regulate his *charges* in accordance with the weight, bulk, or value of the articles to be transported, and may decline to receive certain articles on account of the danger incident to their transportation — powder and high explosives, for example — and may carry others of a perishable character at the risk of the owner or shipper. Such rules must apply equally, however, to all customers, and can contain no provisions limiting his liability for the negligence of himself or his employees.

Freight — Lien of Carrier.— The compensation due a carrier for transportation services rendered is called *freight.* At the common law, as the business of the carrier concerned the public, he was obliged to render similar or equal services for equal compensation, and was forbidden to make unjust discriminations in his rates of freight. This subject is now regulated by statute in the several States and by Congressional enactments in all transportation in the nature of interstate commerce. A carrier may require payment in advance, but if he receives goods of a consignor without insisting upon such prepayment of charges, he is held to waive his right in this respect, and must rely for compensation upon his lien for freight at the place of delivery. The lien for freight accrues when a complete delivery has been made to the consignee at the place agreed upon if the consignee refuses to receive the goods, and they are stored by the carrier, a lieu for warehousing accrues. The lien in both cases is specific, and attaches to the particular goods carried or stored, and cannot apply to back or unpaid charges or to a general account.

Stoppage in Transitu.— While goods are in the hands of a common carrier, the right of *stoppage in transitu* exists, and may be exercised by a consignor, who has sold goods on credit, against a consignee whose bankruptcy or insolvency has become known to the vendor prior to delivery. As the exercise of such right of stoppage is an interruption of the carrier's duty, he is entitled to express notice of the stoppage in time to give reasonable notice to his agent at the point of delivery, and the right of stoppage is defeated by the actual or constructive delivery of the goods to the vendee, or to his agent or servant.

Carriers of Passengers.— A carrier of passengers is one who undertakes to carry passengers for hire. His responsibility resembles that of the common carrier in respect to its public character and in the obligation to carry all who apply. It differs from it, however, ill that the carrier of passengers is not an insurer and has no lien upon the passenger himself for the transportation service rendered.

Liability.— The relation between carrier and passenger is created in part by contract, in part by statute, and in part by the common law. The carrier is held to a very high degree of care in the performance of his duty. He is responsible for injury to a passenger, due to his negligence or that of his agent or servant, acting within the scope of his employment, but not for; in accident due to the act of God or the public enemy, without fault on his part, or for unavoidable accident not due in any degree to his negligence, and such as no human foresight on his part could have prevented. The passenger is also held to the exercise of reasonable care, and cannot recover for an injury due to his own negligence, nor can he recover when, by reason of negligence oil his part, he has contributed to the injury or aided in its occurrence.

If a carrier accept idiots, insane persons, or invalids as passengers, he is held to a higher degree of care in their transportation than is shown in respect to persons who are physically able to care for themselves, and his responsibility for passengers carried free or at reduced rates is, in general, the same as for those who pay the regular rates of fare.

A large class of bailments for hire is composed of cases in which articles are delivered to bailees with a view to have work of some kind done upon the bailed article. The delivery of grain to a miller to be ground into meal or flour, of leather to be made into slices, or of cloth to be worked into a garment are examples of this class of bailments. The bailee is presumed to have the necessary degree of skill to perform the work which he undertakes, and is required to perform his task in accordance with the instructions of the bailor and to his satisfaction. He has a lien upon the goods for work done, but if the materials are reclaimed by the bailor, before the work is completed, his lien is for the work actually done and no more.

LIENS

Liens.— A *lien* is a charge against the property of another; it is based in most cases on money loaned or services rendered, and is generally secured by the possession of the property itself until the demand is satisfied, but may exist, by statute, independently of possession, as in the case of the lions of mechanics and materialmen for services rendered or materials furnished in the construction of buildings. *Mechanics' liens* are created by statute in the interest of the artisan class and as a matter of public policy. They are generally given precedence over all other forms of obligation, and for this reason are required to be filed within a period fixed by statute, at the expiration of which the right lapses by operation of law. The term *lien* is also applied, as has been seen, to the charge created by law in favor of *common carriers, innkeepers,* and the like, for services rendered to the public in connection with those occupations.

Pawns — Pledges — Chattel Mortgages.— A *pawn* or *pledge* is a bailment of goods to a creditor as security for money loaned. Delivery, either actual or constructive, is essential to the creation of the obligation, and forfeiture of possession operates to waive the security on the part of the pledgee. This form of bailment is terminated by repayment of the debt as security for which the chattel was pledged. If the debt be not paid at maturity, the pledgee may sell the pledge in satisfaction of the debt A mortgage of personalty is a conditional conveyance of the title to goods or personal property as a security for debt. If the debt is paid at maturity, the title revests in the mortgagor; otherwise it becomes complete in the mortgagee. The subject of pawning, pledging, and the mortgage of personal property is regulated by statute in the several States of the Union, with a view to secure fair dealing and an equality of rights as respects all parties to the undertaking.

INNKEEPERS

Innkeepers.— An *inn, hotel,* or *tavern* is a house for the lodging and entertainment of wayfarers or travelers. To constitute the house an inn, in the sense in which that term is used at common law, it must be a place for the entertainment of travelers generally, and not for a select class called lodgers. The *keeper* of such a common inn or tavern is called an *innkeeper.* A *guest* is a traveler or wayfarer who seeks lodging at an inn, the term being used in contradistinction to a townsman or inhabitant who resides permanently at an inn and who is called a boarder. The mere furnishing of food and drink to strangers does not vest in the proprietor the rights and duties of an innkeeper within the meaning of the common law; nor do the same rules apply to steamship and sleeping-car companies in respect to the accommodations which they furnish to such passengers as choose to avail themselves of the facilities afforded by them to the traveling public.

Obligations to the Public.— An innkeeper is required, in view of the public character of his undertaking, to receive all guests who apply for entertainment, and is responsible for the loss of or injury to any baggage, wearing apparel, or the like that the guest may bring with him. The innkeeper's responsibility begins, as to the guest, upon his arrival at the inn, and as to the baggage when it is received by himself or his agent; it terminates, as to the guest, when he pays his bill and departs, and as to the baggage at the departure of the guest or at its delivery at a station or train, if such delivery is undertaken by him.

Lien of Innkeeper.— A lien exists, in behalf of the innkeeper, upon the goods of the guest for the cost of his entertainment, and this independently of the ownership of such goods as are in possession of the guest during the period of his sojourn. A loss or surrender of possession on the part of the innkeeper operates as a waiver of the lien, unless aided by statute in the place where the business is carried on. An innkeeper may demand pay in advance, and may decline to receive intoxicated persons or those behaving in an indecent or boisterous manner. If the conduct of a guest be obnoxious to the innkeeper, or to other guests, he may be requested to depart, and, failing to do so, may be removed by force. The responsibility of an innkeeper is greater than that of a boarding-house keeper, as the latter is not required to entertain all who apply. Whatever lien exists in favor of the latter in a particular locality is created by statute, no such obligation being recognized by the common law.

CHAPTER VIII

SALES OF PERSONALTY

Sales.— A *sale of personal property* is an exchange of goods or chattels for money. As in the case of all other contracts or agreements, there must be a meeting of minds of the parties to constitute a valid sale, which is effected by the agreement of the parties, modified in some trades by usage or custom, and in some places by statutes which enlarge or restrict the common-law liabilities of the parties. As in the case of real estate, it is the *title* or *ownership* which is transferred by the fact of sale, and a person can transfer no greater estate in a chattel than he actually possesses at the time the transaction takes place. It is important to distinguish between a sale and an agreement for a future sale. Every actual sale is an executed contract, although payment and delivery may remain to be made. There may be an executory contract for sale, or a bargain that a future sale shall be made; but such a bargain is not a present sale, nor does it confer upon either party the rights or the obligations which grow out of the contract of sale.[175]

Essential Elements of a Sale.— To constitute a sale at common law there must be a mutual agreement or understanding as to the terms, based in every case upon a money consideration. The parties must be competent to contract, and there must be an absolute transfer of ownership in the article sold. Until an offer by one party has been accepted by the other, there is no agreement, and the sale is subject to revocation at the will of the vendor. The offer may be accepted orally, or by mail or telegraph, in which case it becomes binding upon the buyer when the letter or telegram passes from his control into that of the postal or telegraph authorities. The acceptance must

[175] Parsons, Laws of Business, 116.

exactly cover and conform to the terms of the offer, otherwise it is invalid and becomes the basis of a new agreement. As the vendor can dispose of no greater property in the article sold than he possesses, the vendee can acquire by purchase no better title than the vendor has. If there be unsatisfied liens or mortgages upon the article sold, the title passes subject to such incumbrances as exist at the moment of sale.

Consideration.— The contract of sale differs from other contracts in respect to the consideration, which must consist of money in every case. If the consideration be property, the transaction is an *exchange;* if there be no consideration, it is a *gift.* In all sales of personalty the rule of *caveat emptor* applies (let the buyer take care). The purchaser must examine for himself the article offered to him for sale, and exercise his own judgment respecting it. If he purchases without examination, or after a hasty examination, or in mere reliance upon the seller, and the article turns out to be defective, it is his own fault, and he has no remedy against the seller, unless the latter expressly warranted the article or made a fraudulent representation concerning it, or, knowing it to be defective, used some art to disguise it. This is a leading maxim of the law relating to the contract of sale; and its application is not affected by the fact that the price is such as is usually given for a sound commodity.[176]

Delivery — Lien of Vendor.— *Delivery* consists in the transfer of title or ownership to the buyer, and may be either actual or constructive. *Actual* or *real delivery* consists in the performance of some act on the part of the seller by which he transfers the commodity to the possession of the buyer or his agent; *constructive* or *symbolical delivery* is the transfer of some article which is

---

[176] Parsons,116-186.

a symbol or evidence of ownership, such as the delivery of the key of a warehouse containing the goods sold, or of a bill of lading of goods at sea, or of the bill of sale of a ship at sea.[177] If payment be deferred or credit given, the vendor has a lien upon the goods for the selling price and may retain possession until the price has been paid; forfeiture of possession, however, operates as a waiver of the lien unless otherwise provided by statute. So long as anything remains to be done to the goods by the seller, in the way of identification, separation, or ascertainment of quantity, as by weighing, measuring, or the like, title does not pass until such act or thing has been done. It is not in general the duty of the seller to send or carry the goods to the buyer; but delivery to a common carrier constitutes delivery of possession, and operates to transfer responsibility for loss or damage to the carrier. As has been seen, the goods while in possession of the common carrier are subject to an exercise of the right of *stoppage in transitu* on the part of the seller. For any breach of the contract of sale, by either party, the other may refuse to perform his part or may decline to receive or deliver the goods, and may maintain an action at law with a view to recover damages for the injury received.

---

[177] Steph. on Sales, §§ 304, 311; Parsons, 121-126.

CHAPTER IX

CONTRACTS

Contracts.— A *contract* is an undertaking, based upon certain *consideration,* voluntarily entered into by two or more competent parties, with a view to increase, diminish, or determine their mutual duties and obligations.

Forms Assumed.— The forms assumed by contracts are as various as the business relations which they are calculated to regulate, and depend in any case upon the character and importance of the transaction, the will of the parties, the circumstances attending the formation of the agreement, and, to a considerable extent, upon the policy of the law. They may take the form of sealed instruments, or may be oral, or in writing not under seal; so also the terms of an agreement may be gleaned from an extensive correspondence, or may be inferred from the acts or declarations of the parties. In certain cases, to be described hereafter, the law requires that particular agreements shall be reduced to writing,[178] and in certain other cases that

---

[178] There are certain simple contracts which under the law must be reduced to writing, such as promissory notes, bills of exchange, and the several undertakings mentioned in the fourth and seventeenth sections of the statute of frauds. The principal of these are promises by an executor or administrator to answer damages out of his own estate ; certain contracts of suretyship ; agreements in consideration of marriage ; contracts for the sale of lands, tenements, and hereditaments ; contracts not to be performed within the space of one year from the making thereof, and contracts for the sale of goods and chattels above the value of £10.

they be executed under the formality of sealing and delivery. With these exceptions, however, mere form is regarded as a matter of minor importance, and contractual relations may be expressed in any form or terms that may be agreed upon by the parties to a particular undertaking.

Nature of the Contract Relation.— It is essential to the validity of a contract that it should have been freely entered into, and that the several parties to its operation should have become such with entire freedom from external restraint. The contractual relation having been established, however, the law steps in and requires each party to perform the duty which he has thus voluntarily undertaken. In other words, the law does not in general make the contract. The formation of the agreement is an act of free will on the part of the individuals whose business relations are to be regulated by it; the office of the law is to ascertain and determine its obligation and to enforce its stipulations, or to award appropriate damages for their non-fulfillment.

Classification — Contracts of Record.— Contracts are classified, as to their form, into contracts of record, contracts under seal, and simple contracts. *Contracts of record* are created by operation of law, and consist in the judgments of courts awarding damages, and in what are called recognizances — that is, undertakings entered into before a court to appear and answer to a criminal charge, to defend an action at law, or to prosecute an appeal. As the parties to these contracts voluntarily subjected themselves to the jurisdiction of the court, or submitted their differences to it for decision, its judgment constitutes an obligation of the most binding character.

Contracts under Seal.— *Contracts under seal,* sometimes called *specialties,* are written agreements entered into under the sanction of sealing and delivery.

They represent the highest form of contract relations between individuals, and, having been executed under the formality of a seal, are conclusive as to the terms and conditions of the agreement of which they constitute the record, and are binding, not only upon the parties to their operation, but upon their heirs and legal representatives. The presence of a seal is said to *import consideration* — that is, to make it unnecessary to prove that consideration passed between the parties when the contract was entered into. These instruments become effective upon delivery, and can, as a rule, be released or modified in their operation only by a sealed instrument of equal dignity.

Simple or Parol Contracts.— *Simple* or *parol contracts* include all agreements and undertakings, of whatever kind, not executed under seal; they may be either written or oral, or partly written and partly oral. When a controversy arises in respect to a simple contract, the essential elements of the agreement are established by the production of the instrument itself, or by the testimony of witnesses. The written instrument is evidence of a high character as to the terms of the undertaking, but is not conclusive as to such terms, as is the case with an instrument under seal.

Executed and Executory Contracts.— Contracts are classified, as to then-time of performance, into *executed* and *executory contracts.* An *executed contract* is one the subject of which is performed or completed by the execution of the contract. A conveyance of land in fee simple, for cash paid on execution and delivery of the deed, is an example of an executed contract. An *executory contract* is one that is to be carried into effect in the future or is to have future operation. A agrees to build a house for B, to be completed in six months, and to be paid for on completion and acceptance by B. This is an example of an executory contract. A single instrument or undertaking may contain both executed and executory provisions, in which case it is said to be executed in part and executory in part.

Express and Implied Contracts.— Contracts are also said to be either express or implied, depending upon the method of their formation. An *express contract* is one the terms of which are openly or expressly made known at the time of its formation. An *implied contract* is one in which the contract relation is implied or inferred from the acts or declarations of the parties. A renders services to B, who accepts them; the law presumes that such services were rendered at the request of B. In implied agreements the law presumes or infers the existence of the obligation from the acts or declarations of the parties. In express contracts such obligations are declared or defined by the parties themselves.

Freedom of Parties from Restraint; Competency.— It is essential to the conception of a contract that it be entered into freely and without constraint by the several parties to its operation. They must also be competent to make agreements. A person under tutelage or restraint of any kind, not being a free agent, is incapable of making contracts, or makes thorn subject to certain restrictions, the degree and amount of liability in any case being determined by the law of the place in which the agreement is entered into or is to be carried into effect. Such is the case with married women, infants, persons of unsound mind, and those under duress.

Conformity to Law; Possibility of Performance.— As the aid of the law may be invoked to enforce compliance with the terms of an agreement, its subject-matter must be lawful, and for a similar reason must be neither immoral nor opposed to the public policy of the place where its enforcement is asked for. Nor will the courts give effect to an agreement the enforcement of which is impossible. It is otherwise, however, with a contract in which a party has undertaken a task that he has not the ability or capacity to perform; and such an agreement, if freely entered into, will be enforced by the courts, whatever may be the hardships inflicted upon him who has thus ignorantly charged himself with an obligation which he is unable to carry into effect.

MUTUALITY

Mutuality — What Persons Bound.— As at least two persons are necessary to the creation of a contractual obligation, and as the obligation itself is single, it follows that there must be mutuality in every contract — that is, its terms and conditions must not only be understood, but must be understood by all parties to its operation in precisely the same sense. In other words, there must be what is called *a meeting of minds* as to the several stipulations of which the agreement is composed; and the legal obligation, which the courts will enforce, is deduced from such mutual understanding of the terms and conditions of the contract. It is also evident that a contract binds only those who are parties to its operation. For this reason *third persons* are not only not bound by a contract to which they are not parties, but are not presumed to have any knowledge of its operation, or even of its existence.

OBLIGATION OF CONTRACTS

Obligation — Performance.— The *obligation* of a contract is its binding force, which is conferred by the law of the place in which it is proposed *to* carry it into effect. A particular agreement having been voluntarily entered into by two or more parties legally competent to contract, the law steps in and enforces the obligation thus freely assumed. The obligation resting upon each party is to faithfully perform the duty with which he has charged himself in the agreement. If *performance* by one party is conditioned upon prior performance upon the part of another, called a condition precedent, his obligation becomes effective upon performance of the prior condition. If he is the first to act, the terms of the instrument will determine the time and method of his performance — either at a date therein specified, or upon demand or notice by another party. If action lies within his discretion, then in accordance with such discretion; and performance may be at will or within a reasonable time.

CONSIDERATION

Consideration.— The law presumes that no sane person will assume an obligation or incur a liability, not in its nature a legal or moral duty, without some inducement to do so, or without receiving in return a corresponding benefit or advantage. Common sense and ordinary business prudence alike teach us that men will not part with their property without obtaining its equivalent in value, or render services without reasonable compensation therefor. Upon this doctrine, deduced from the experience of mankind, is based the idea of *consideration,* which forms an essential element of every contract, and which may be defined as the inducement offered by one party and accepted by the other, in exchange for which a promise is made or an obligation incurred. A bare promise has no legal binding force, and is not enforceable in a court of justice. There must be a mutual *quid pro quo,* something given and surrendered in return, to make the promise binding; and this may be either a benefit to the promisor or a detriment to the promisee.

Kinds of Consideration.— *Consideration* may consist in money paid service rendered, obligations canceled, or any act done, or omitted, from which another derives an advantage. Consideration is said to be either good or valuable. *Good consideration* is that of blood or affection between near relatives. *Sufficient* or *valuable* consideration consists, as above described in money paid, service rendered, or "in some right, interest, profit, or benefit accruing to one party, or some extension of time of payment, detriment, loss, or responsibility given, suffered, or undertaken by the other." The law recognizes a *moral* or *equitable consideration* which consists in a "duty *to* perform, voluntarily, an obligation which is no longer enforceable at law." Such consideration will support an executed contract, and is illustrated by the ratification of an infant's contract upon his attaining his majority. Consideration is also classified, according to the circumstances of the particular case, as *express* or *implied, legal or illegal, valid* or *invalid, entire or separable, nominal* or *impossible.* Consideration may also be *present* or *future, executed* or *executory,* but must not be *past.* Unless fraud be alleged a court will not inquire into the mere adequacy of consideration, save to assure itself that the consideration has a real or ascertainable value. A man may part with his property or services for less than their true value, but not without some recompense or reward in support of the promise made in return.

Questions as to Execution, Performance, etc.: How Determined.— Remedies.— The law of the place where the instrument is made will determine all questions as to the form of the instrument or the validity of its execution. The law of the place where it is to be carried into effect will determine any questions that relate to the operation of the contract and the performance of the various duties imposed. The law of the place where action is brought will determine the form of remedy and the application of the statute of limitations. A contract may be made in New York, to be executed in Mexico, and may give rise to an action at law in Illinois. The courts of Illinois in such a case will apply the remedy afforded by the local law, but will be guided by the laws of New York as to matters in respect to the execution of the instrument, and by the laws of Mexico in the determination of all questions arising as to performance.

FRAUD

Fraud, Actual and Constructive.— As good faith is essential to all business transactions affecting the property rights of individuals, it follows that a number of acts, in reverse of good faith, consisting of artifice, deceit, misrepresentation, and the like, which are grouped under the general head of fraud, will, if resorted to by a party with intent to deceive, vitiate any agreement of which they form an essential part. On account of the variety and diversity of the acts and omissions which constitute fraud, it is impossible to frame a definition that will have general application. At the common law no such definition was permissible, each case being determined by the facts in evidence. Fraud may be classified, however, as either actual or constructive. *Actual* or *positive fraud* involves moral turpitude or intentional wrong. It is therefore a question, of fact, and is ordinarily determined by the jury. *Legal* or *constructive fraud is* an inference of law, drawn from the acts or situation of the parties, or the facts in a case, and is determined by the court. The terms actual and legal fraud are not synonymous; actual fraud may exist without impairing the obligation of a contract, and legal fraud may be inferred from acts not in themselves immoral.

Effects of Fraud.— To vitiate a contract, fraud must consist in a false representation of fact made by one party, with a knowledge of its falsehood, or in reckless disregard of truth, and in a matter essential to the validity of the undertaking, and must have been accepted or acted upon by the opposite party. When so made, the party injured may affirm the contract and ask to have the representation by which he has been induced to enter into it made good as far as possible; or he may avoid the contract on the ground of fraud, and resort to an action at law upon that ground; or he may obtain a judicial avoidance of the contract in a court of equity. If with full knowledge, however, he accepts the situation, or proceeds with the undertaking, he is as completely liable as if no fraud existed, and he will not be permitted afterwards to question its validity.

MISREPRESENTATION

Misrepresentation.— A person may have been induced to enter into an undertaking as the result of statements made prior to the agreement, or at the time of its execution, by a party to its operation, and the statements or representations so made may subsequently prove to have been false or erroneous in point of fact. If such false representations are made with full knowledge, and with intent to deceive, or as the result of reckless ignorance on the part of the person making them, they constitute fraud and render the contract voidable at the option of the injured party. If innocently made, and not material in inducing the other party to contract, or if, in the opinion of the court, they are not material to the validity of the agreement, they have no legal effect. If, on the other hand, the representations form a substantive part of the contract, they are called conditions or warranties; and if false in fact, they operate to discharge the injured party from his obligation, or to give him the right of action at law for damages sustained.

Misrepresentation in Policies of Insurance.— While they may occur in any contract, they are most frequently encountered in policies of insurance. These are contracts in which, from the nature of the case, one of the parties must rely upon the statements made by the other, and is placed at a disadvantage as regards his means of acquiring knowledge of the subject. In the contract of marine insurance, the insured is bound to give the underwriter all such information as would be likely to determine his judgment in accepting the risk, and misrepresentation or concealment of any such matter, though unaccompanied by any fraudulent intention, avoids the policy. In the contract of fire insurance the description of the premises appears to form a representation, on the truth of which the validity of the contract depends, and the innocent nondisclosure of any material fact vitiates the policy.[179] The contract of life insurance differs from those of marine and fire insurance in this respect. Untruth in the representations made to the insurer as to the life of the insured will not affect the validity of the contract unless they be made fraudulently, or unless their truth be made an express condition of the contract.

---

[179] If questions remain unanswered in the application, and the company thereupon issues the policy, it will be held to have waived such requirement, so far as the questions remain unanswered, and the policy cannot be voided by the company on the ground that the answers are not full. (Lorillard Fire Insurance Company *vs.* McCullough, 21 Ohio, 179.)

ASSIGNMENT OF CONTRACTS

Assignment of Contracts.— The obligation assumed by one party to a contract cannot be assigned or transferred without the consent of the other. In this case, strictly speaking, no formal assignment is made, but a substituted agreement takes the place of the original contract. Consent to such transfer or assignment may be express, as is the case when a new agreement is made to which the original contractor and the assignee are parties, or it may be implied from the acts of the parties, as is the case when a lessor accepts rent from the assignee of the lessee. An assignment of *rights* in a contract may be made without the consent of the other parties thereto, and by statute in many of the States an assignee may sue in his own name.

NEGOTIABILITY

Negotiability.— There are several forms of simple contract which constitute exceptions to the rule above stated, in that they are not only negotiable, but are intended by their makers to have that character and to pass from hand to hand upon the performance of certain conditions which are essential to their negotiability. The contracts so transferable are called negotiable instruments, and a *negotiable instrument* may be defined as an undertaking to pay money which may be transferred by a sale evidenced by indorsement and delivery, or, in some cases, by delivery merely. To confer the quality of negotiability an instrument must be drawn payable "to order" or "to bearer," or their equivalents. If drawn to order, it passes by indorsement; if to bearer, title passes by mere delivery. The instruments recognized throughout the commercial world as having the quality of negotiability are the *bill of exchange* and the *promissory note.*

CHAPTER IX

BILLS AND NOTES

Bills of Exchange — Parties — Acceptance.— A *bill of exchange* is in form a written order drawn by A and addressed to B, directing him to pay to C or order, or to C or bearer, a certain sum of money. The words "to C or order" or "to C or bearer" give to the instrument its negotiable character. A is called the *drawer,* and his undertaking is to pay to C or any subsequent holder, for value, the sum of money named in the bill if B fails to accept it, or, having accepted it, fails to pay it at maturity. B before acceptance is called the *drawee;* after acceptance, which is accomplished by writing the word "accepted" over his name, across the face of the bill, B becomes the *acceptor,* and is charged with the payment of the bill at maturity, even though he has no funds of the drawer in his hands.

Indorsement.— Bills of exchange drawn to order are transferred by *indorsement,* which is, in substance, an order signed by the payee or holder in favor of a third person, called the *indorsee,* who may transfer the instrument in the same manner. The effect of indorsement is to assign to the indorsee the right to demand payment of the acceptor at maturity, or, in the event of his failure to respond, to hold the drawer responsible for the amount of the bill.

Promissory Notes.— A *promissory note* is a written promise to pay a specified sum, with or without interest, at a specified date in the future, or on demand. The rules relating to the negotiability of bills of exchange apply to promissory notes with equal force.

Notice.— Certain rights are called into being, and certain obligations are said to accrue, upon the receipt of what is called *notice,* that is, upon information of their existence being conveyed to and received by those persons who are to be affected by them. Certain leases, for example, contain provisions authorizing their termination at the will of either party, upon certain notice; or in some cases, where they contain no such provisions, they may be terminated by what is called *reasonable notice;* the obligation of an indorser of commercial paper accrues upon notice of default in payment on the part of a prior indorser.

Notice is said to be *statutory* when it is made so by enactment. It is *judicial* when a court takes cognizance of a fact without formal proof or upon a particular form of proof required by statute. It is said to be *actual* when express information of a fact is conveyed to and received by a person whose rights are affected by its existence. It is said to be *constructive* when such a state of facts exists as would put a reasonable man upon inquiry as to their existence, or as to their effects upon his rights or obligations.[180]

CHECKS AND DRAFTS

Checks and Drafts.— A *check* or *draft* is an order drawn upon a bank or individual by one having funds deposited with the banking house or person upon whom the check is drawn. Checks are drawn *to order* or *to bearer,* and require the payment of the sum named upon presentation. As checks are intended to have instant effect

[180] Gress *vs.* Evans, 1 Dak. Terr., 387; Wilson *vs.* Wall, 6 Wall., 83; *U. S. vs.* Sturges, 1 Paine, 525; Carr *vs.* Hilton, 1 Curtis, 390; Oliver *vs.* Piatt, 3 How., 333; IT. S. *vs.* Pinover, 3 Fed. Rep., 305; Hinde *vs.* Vattier, 1 McLean, 110; Boyce *vs.* Grundy, 3 Pet., 210; Dexter *vs.* Harris, 2 Mason, 531.

and to be payable on demand, they must be presented for payment within a reasonable time, any delay on the part of the bolder being made at his peril. What constitutes reasonable delay will depend upon the situation of the parties — their distance from the bank upon which the check is drawn, and the time consumed in the movements of the mails. Checks may be antedated or postdated, and may be transferred by indorsement or delivery, depending upon whether they are drawn to order or to bearer. A *certified check* resembles an accepted bill of exchange in that, by the act of certification, the bank sets apart an amount equal to the face of the check as a fund for its payment on presentation.

DISCHARGE

Discharge of Contracts.— Contracts may be discharged in several ways:

1. *By complete performance,* to the mutual satisfaction of the parties.

2. *By agreement of the parties.*— This is accomplished by an agreement that the contract shall no longer bind either party. This may be in writing under seal, or by parol, or in writing not under seal, and in some cases may be inferred from the acts or declarations of the parties.

3. *By breach, of contract.*— When either party to a contract fails to carry into effect a stipulation which is material to its complete performance, he thereby creates a right of action in favor of the other for damages due to such nonperformance. His failure may also operate to discharge the other party from his contractual obligation. In the event of such breach being made the subject of an action at law, the amount of damages awarded will depend on the pecuniary loss sustained by the injured party, the

general rule being that "where a party sustains a loss by reason of a breach of contract he is, so far as money can do it, to be placed in the same situation with respect to damages as if the contract had been performed, Damages in an action for breach of contract are by way of compensation, and not of punishment; hence, unless punitive or exemplary damages are authorized by statute, a plaintiff can never recover more than will reimburse him for the pecuniary loss that he has sustained as a result of the nonperformance of the other party."[181]

SPECIFIC PERFORMANCE

Specific Performance.— In addition to the common-law remedy provided for nonperformance of contracts and agreements, the courts of equity may be appealed to, in certain cases, to compel what is called *specific performance* — that is, by the issue of an appropriate decree to require the party in default to carry into effect the undertaking with which he has charged himself in the agreement; as to execute a deed of conveyance, or to deliver a particular article which, on account of its peculiar nature or character, cannot be represented in damages. The equitable relief above referred to will not be afforded in a ease to which an action at law will afford an adequate remedy, or to a case of performance over which the court cannot exercise an intelligent supervision. The remedy applied in equity must also conform to the particular kind of performance required. If an act is to be done, its performance must be compelled by a decree of specific performance; if an act is to be refrained from, the proper remedy will be afforded by way of injunction.

---

[181] Anson on Contracts, p. 301.

CHAPTER IX

IMPOSSIBILITY OF PERFORMANCE

Impossibility of Performance.— It has been seen to be not a valid excuse for nonperformance of a contractual obligation that the thing agreed to be done is beyond the means or capacity of the party — in other words, that he has undertaken a task beyond his ability to perform. In every such case the courts will require a party in default to respond in damages to the *extent of his resources* for the injury inflicted upon the other party by reason of his failure to carry into effect the terms of the agreement. Impossibility of performance, to avail as a defense, must be such that the thing to be done has, through no fault of the party, become legally or physically impossible of performance. Such impossibility exists in the following cases:

1. Change in the Law.— When a change in the law makes performance impossible. A agrees with B to ship a certain amount of nitroglycerine, by rail, at intervals of two weeks, for the period of one year. At the end of six months a statute, enacted subsequently to the execution of the contract, goes into effect prohibiting the shipment of high explosives by rail. This relieves A from the unexecuted portion of his agreement.

2. Continued Existence of Subject.— When the contract contemplates the continued existence of the subject of the agreement. A charters a ship for a voyage of two years. At the end of ten months the ship is lost at sea; such loss puts an end to the agreement from the date of its occurrence.

3. Death of Party.— A contract for personal services is discharged by the death or disabling illness of the promisor.

4. Public War and Act of God.— The occurrence of public war suspends and in most cases operates to discharge contracts to which citizens of the belligerent states are parties. The parties to a contract are also relieved from their obligation by an act of God. This term comprehends all misfortunes and accidents, arising from inevitable necessity, which human foresight could not foresee or prevent.[182]

CONTRACTS OF THE UNITED STATES

Contract Policy of the United States — Sec. 3709, R. S.— The contract policy of the Federal Government is largely regulated by the requirements of section 3709 of the Revised Statutes, which provides that "all purchases and contracts for supplies or services in any of the Departments of the Government, except for personal services, shall be made by advertising for a sufficient time previously for proposals respecting the same, when the exigencies do not require the immediate delivery of the articles or the performance of the services. When immediate delivery or performance is required by the public exigency, the articles or services required may be procured by open purchase or contract, at the places and in the manner in which such articles are usually bought and sold, or such services engaged between individuals." Statutes subsequently enacted modify the provisions of the section above cited in their application to the several Executive Departments, and in some cases as to the contract relations of particular offices or bureaus of the same Department, the purpose of such legislation being to provide a course of procedure in the event of emergencies,

---

[182] Railroad Co. *vs.* Reeves, 10 Wall., 176; Holladay *vs.* Kennard, 13 Wall., 254; Caldwell *vs.* Southern Exp. Co. 1 Flip., 85.

or in cases to which the terms of the general statute do not exactly apply.

Sec. 3744, R. S.— The requirement of section 3744 of the Revised Statutes, to the effect that "all contracts entered into by officers of the War, Navy, and Interior Departments shall be reduced to writing and signed by the contracting parties" has been held to operate as a statute of frauds, by requiring the contracts of those Departments to be expressed in writing, though not of necessity in the form of an instrument under seal.

Government Contracts, by Whom Made.— Government contracts are made by officers acting in behalf of the United States, whose power to contract is measured by the act of appropriation or other statute in accordance with which the agreement is made. Such statutes not only limit and define the powers of public officers to make contracts, but operate as a notice to the general public as to the existence and extent of such powers; and one who enters into an agreement with an officer or agent of the United States to furnish supplies or services not authorized by law does so at his peril, as the Government has been held not to be bound by the act of its agent in excess of his authority.

Advertisement — Proposals — Award.— When supplies or services are to be obtained for the use of the United States, advertisements are issued setting forth the articles needed, specifying their kind and amount, the times when and places where they are to be delivered, together with such conditions as to inspection, payment, and delivery as are necessary to guide bidders in the preparation and submission of their proposals, which are required to be in writing and are submitted in sealed envelopes on a day named in the advertisement. At the day and hour named in the advertisement the proposals are opened, in the presence of the bidders and others who may desire to attend, and the award is made, as a general rule, to the lowest responsible bidder for the best and most suitable article. Written contracts are then executed and delivered, and in support of such contracts as require that form of security, bonds are executed and filed with the instruments to which they relate.

Purposes — Fiscal Year.— The contracts so executed provide for the procurement of supplies or services, for the purchase or sale of land, the construction or repair of buildings, the establishment of works of public improvement, or the transportation of troops or supplies. The administrative year of the United States Government, which is called the *fiscal year,* begins on the first of July of each calendar year and ends on the thirtieth of June following.

Appropriations; Estimates.— The general appropriation bills relate to this period, and are intended to supply the funds needed for the service of the several Executive Departments during the fiscal year next succeeding their passage. Appropriations so made are, in general, only available for expenditure during the fiscal year to which they relate, and for this reason contracts are, as a rule, restricted in their operation to the fiscal year to which they pertain, within which the supplies must be furnished or the services rendered. Appropriations not so restricted to the service of a particular fiscal year, are called *permanent appropriations; indefinite appropriations* are those in which no sum is named: both of these forms of appropriation, however, are exceptional in character and, to be available, must be specifically authorized by Congress. The annual appropriation bills are based upon estimates submitted, annually, by the heads of the several Executive Departments, for the service of their departments during the fiscal year next succeeding the meeting of Congress. These estimates contain such information as will be calculated to make known to that body, not only the needs of the several departments for the ensuing fiscal year, but the laws or treaties upon which the annual estimates are based.

References.— Among the elementary works on this subject the American edition of Anson holds a deservedly high place, as do those of Smith, Wharton, and Benjamin. These test-books can be studied to the best advantage in connection with volumes of selected cases, of which Huffcutt and Woodruffs and that of Professor Langdell are the best and most available for this purpose. Parsons great work on this subject is still the standard in the United States. The English works of Chitty and Pollock, and the American works of Story, Wharton, Bishop, and Metcalf, are valuable books of reference on the subjects of which they treat.

CHAPTER X

TORTS

General Rule as to Remedies.— It is a well-established legal maxim that there is no wrong for which the law does not provide a remedy. The remedy may not always be adequate, or readily available to the injured party, but it exists and can be applied by the courts at the instance of the injured party. If the wrong be public and constitute a criminal offense, the remedy afforded is by a *prosecution* brought in the name of the State; if the wrong be of a private nature, arising out of a breach of contract, or a failure to perform an agreement, the remedy is by some form of the *action of contract,* while for all private wrongs, not in their nature breaches of the contract relation, a remedy is afforded by the *action of tort.*

Torts.— A *tort* may be defined as a private wrong, not in its nature a breach of contract, the effects of which upon the person, property, or reputation of the party injured are such as to give rise to an action at law for damages sustained. The term applies to a large number of causes of action, some of which so closely resemble actions on contract as to be distinguished from them only with great difficulty. Others constitute criminal acts, for which the offender has a double accountability — first, to the State in a criminal prosecution; second, to the party injured in an action for damages.

Principal Kinds of Torts.— The principal torts, or tortious acts, for which actions will lie are assault and battery, libel or slander, seduction, malicious prosecution, false imprisonment, all forms of trespass, with or without force, infringements of patents and copyrights, private nuisances, negligence in many forms; and, in general, an action will lie for any breach of duty the effect or consequence of which is to injure, deny, or trespass upon the legal rights of another.

LIABILITY FOR TORTS

Liability for Tortious Act — Corporations.— Any person, whether acting independently or under restraint, may be guilty of a tortious act, or become what is called a *tort-feasor* or wrongdoer. The legal responsibility of such wrongdoer will depend upon whether he is a free agent or under tutelage, and in the latter case upon the kind and amount of restraint to which he is subject, the rule being that if the inferior or subordinate is not directly accountable, the responsibility attaches to the legal superior, who may be called upon to respond in damages. In this way a master may become responsible for the torts of a servant, a principal for the wrongful acts of an agent, and in the same manner an owner of an animal for damage to the person or property of another, due to his negligence or want of care. Public officers are similarly liable for acts of oppression, or for excesses in the performance of their duties, by which injury is caused to individuals as a consequence of their wrongful acts. Corporations are capable of committing torts, and are as fully responsible for their harmful consequences as individuals would be in a similar case. Lunatics are liable for their torts, on the principle that tortious liability arises from the fact of injury or damage to another, and not from the capacity or intent of the tort-feasor.[183]

---

[183] Moore *v.* Crawford, 17 Vt., 499; Williams *v.* Hayes, 145 N. Y., 442.

DAMAGES

Damages — Measure of Damages.— Actions of tort are brought for the purpose of recovering compensation in the nature of damages for injuries done to one person by the wrongful act or omission of another. The question of damages being one of fact, is always determined by the jury, and the rule so applied in the determination of the amount of damages due in a particular case is called the measure of damages. The *measure of damages,* in any case, is a rule of law and is applied by the court in its charge to the jury at the conclusion of the trial. Damages are either *actual* or *compensatory* when they are precisely equal to the pecuniary loss or injury inflicted by a particular wrongful act; they are *vindictive* or *punitive* when they exceed such loss; and are *nominal* when they are so small in amount as to be inappreciable, and are awarded for the purpose of establishing the character of an act as wrongful or injurious. Damages are also said to be either *direct* or *consequential.* They are *direct* when the injury is due to the immediate consequences of the wrongful act complained of; they are *indirect* or *consequential* when they are awarded for injuries of a collateral character, but directly traceable to, and caused by, the act of the wrongdoer.

CHAPTER XI

THE DOMESTIC RELATIONS

The Family.— The interests treated of under this head have to do with certain legal rights and duties growing out of the institution of marriage, and pertaining to the several members of the social group called the family. All systems of law which have successfully endured the test of experience, for considerable periods of time, have not only made the family the basis of their social organization, but, in view of its importance, have undertaken to perpetuate the existence of the family relation by throwing such safeguards about it as seemed to them best calculated to accomplish that purpose. The common law regards the husband as the head of the family and vests in him the title to the family property, the power to control the services of the wife, and of such children as are of immature age, and the right to receive and enjoy the fruits of their labor; it charges him, however, with their protection, support, and maintenance, and with the expense of such education as is required by law.

Husband and Wife.— At the common law an unmarried woman above the age of twenty-one, or a woman in whose case the relation of marriage has ceased to exist, by the death or divorce of her husband, was regarded as having most of the civil rights incident to manhood; as a consequence of marriage, however, her legal personalty was merged in that of the husband, who acquired possession of all her personal property and of the income of her real estate, but became responsible for her ante-nuptial debts, and for her support and maintenance during coverture. The wife, in consequence of her marriage, became incapable of making contracts, incurring debts, or of alienating real estate in her own name. An injury to the wife was an injury to the husband, and an action for damages had to be brought in his name, as she was incapable of suing or being sued in her own right. With the exception of treason and murder, all crimes committed by the wife, in the presence of the husband, were deemed, to have been committed by his command or as the result of his coercion. As the husband was bound to provide for the support of the wife, he became liable for such purchases or contracts as she might make for necessaries. If she voluntarily separated herself from him, he ceased to be liable for her support during the period of separation, but his responsibility revived when she returned to his home. The property rights of the wife are thus seen to have been in abeyance during the period of coverture; they revived, however, at the death of the husband, when she resumed her separate legal existence and became capable of exercising the rights which she had enjoyed prior to her marriage.

Dower — Curtesy.— The right of dower, which is an estate created by law, exists in expectancy only during the lifetime of the husband, but becomes vested at his death, and consists, in most of the States, of a life interest in one third of the real estate of which he was lawfully seized during the entire period of coverture. Dower is barred by alienage or divorce, or by any conduct which is inconsistent with the marriage relation, as by elopement or adultery. Dower is also barred by a jointure — that is, by an estate settled upon the wife prior to the marriage and in lieu of dower — or by a similar provision, in. the husband's will. The rules of the common law in respect to dower have been considerably modified in the several States of the Union, generally with a view to secure to the widow such share in the property of her husband as is necessary to her support during widowhood. At the death of the wife, if there had been issue capable of inheriting, her entire estate in land vests in the husband as curtesy during the period of his life.

Marriage — Validity of, how Determined.— From a legal point of view marriage is regarded as a status or relation created by contract. To constitute a lawful marriage the consent of the parties and their capacity to marry are necessary. The contract is executed by marriage, and no religions ceremony is essential to its validity unless required by the law of the place where it is entered into. The formalities of registry and publication, or announcements of intention, are regulated, where they exist, by the same authority. A marriage may be declared void for want of legal, mental, or physical capacity on the part of either party, as in the case of an idiot or insane person, or of an infant under marriageable age, or where the husband or wife of either party is living. The validity of either a marriage or divorce is determined by the law of the locality where it took place, provided the parties were there resident at the time of its occurrence. Whether such marriage or divorce will be recognized elsewhere, is a matter to be determined by the law of the place in which its existence is asserted or its validity drawn in question.

How Terminated — Divorce.— Marriage may be terminated by the death or divorce of either party. Divorce is either absolute, in which case the parties resume their separate legal existence, or partial, which may be a voluntary separation merely, by agreement of the parties, or the result of legal proceedings terminating in a decree granting a qualified divorce, amounting, in fact, to a separation of interests only, some of the obligations of marriage continuing to exist, among them an incapacity to remarry. The power to grant divorces is strictly judicial in character, although in some of the States it has been assumed at times by the legislature. The power to hear and determine divorce cases is usually exercised by courts having equity jurisdiction, which have authority to award alimony and to make and enforce decrees in respect to the custody and support of children.

PARENT AND CHILD

Parent and Child.— The relation of parent and child is a status, recognized by the law, which regulates and defines the mutual rights and duties of which it is composed. The position of the child is that of an inferior and dependent, whose rights and duties vary both in kind and amount from year to year during the period of his minority. They are at a minimum at birth, increase through childhood and youth, and reach a maximum at majority, when the minor becomes invested with all the rights and privileges incident to manhood. The law in respect to legitimate children is in some respects similar to that regulating the status of the wife. It is made the duty of the father to protect, support, and educate his children; he is charged with their government, and is entitled to the benefit of their services during minority; when they attain their majority, however, they become free agents, and are endowed with all the rights and privileges of citizenship and become charged with all its duties and obligations.

Legitimacy.— A *legitimate child* is one born in lawful wedlock or within a reasonable time after the death of the husband. The presumption in the case of a child so born is in favor of legitimacy, and the burden of proving the contrary rests upon him who asserts it. The domicile of a child is that of the father, with which it changes, and he is incapable of acquiring a domicile separate from that of the father during the period of minority.

Capacity of Infants.— Infants, as such, are incompetent to make contracts, to hold office, to alienate real estate, to sue or be sued in their own names, or to exercise to their full extent any of the rights of manhood. An injury to the child, or a fraud committed against it, is actionable at the instance of the father only, upon the ground of the loss of the child's services or to its abduction or seduction. A contract entered into by an infant is void or voidable as a court may determine, depending upon whether the contract is or is not for its benefit. If voidable, it may be ratified by the infant upon attaining his majority.

Crimes of Wife and Child.— The rule that a crime committed by the wife in the presence of the husband is due to his coercion, based upon their identity of interest, does not obtain in the case of children, whose criminal responsibility is based exclusively upon their age and intelligence. Under seven years of age the indisputable presumption is that they are incapable of committing crime; from seven to fourteen the presumption is the same, subject to rebuttal by evidence that the child has sufficient intelligence and capacity to appreciate the consequences of its act; from fourteen to twenty-one the presumption is the same as that which applies to persons of full age, subject to rebuttal by evidence of want of knowledge or capacity, due to immaturity or inexperience. In the matter of torts or other injuries committed by them, the rule is quite different from that applied in the case of the wife. Children are suable for torts or injuries committed by them, and may sue by parent, guardian, or next friend, and recover damages for injuries received at the hands of others.

Illegitimacy.— Illegitimate children, or bastards, are those born out of lawful wedlock. Under the common law they had no right to an inheritable name, and, not being heirs at law, they could not inherit estates from either parent, except in accordance with the terms of a will; and could transmit only such property as they had themselves acquired to the heirs of their bodies. The domicile of an illegitimate child is that of its mother, who is bound to maintain it until it is able to support itself by its own exertions. The rights of illegitimate children in the United States are regulated by statute in the several States, the general tendency of which is to relieve their disabilities at common law, and to improve their situation in other important respects. In most of the States a subsequent marriage of the parents confers legitimacy upon the child; in some the mother and child can mutually inherit; in others it has a right to its mother's name.

Guardian and Ward — Appointment and Duties.— As the dependent condition of the child continues during minority, the law makes provision for the performance of the father's duty after his death by the appointment of a guardian who succeeds to and enforces the parental duties, the performance of which has been interrupted by death. The appointment of guardians is vested in courts specially charged with jurisdiction in such matters, and their duties are regulated by the law of the place in which the child resides or in which its property is situated. Guardians are also appointed to care for the interests of idiots, insane persons, spendthrifts, and others who are not deemed to have sufficient mental capacity, or self-restraint, to conduct their affairs without such assistance. In his personal relations to the ward the guardian stands, in most respects, in the place of the father; in respect to his estate he occupies the position of a trustee, and his acts, as such, are regulated by law, under the supervision of courts endowed with jurisdiction for that purpose.

MASTER AND SERVANT

Master and Servant.— The relation of master and servant is one created by contract, by which, in consideration of the payment of certain stipulated sums called *wages,* one person acquires the power to exercise a limited amount of authority over another during a definite period of time. The party in whom this power of control is vested is called the *master;* while the one upon whom the duty of obedience falls is called the *servant.* The relation between the parties is one of contract; that between the parties and the State is a status regulated by law, and resembling, in some respects, certain phases of the domestic relations, and in others that of principal and agent, into which it merges in the higher grades of employment. Under the general head of servants fall domestic servant, apprentices, laborers, and workmen.

Character of the Relation.— The tendency of the common law was *to* treat employees of this kind as a subordinate class, and English industrial legislation prior to 1824 leaned decidedly in favor of the master.[184] Since that date, however, in England, as well as the United States, the tendency has been to regard the relation as one of contract pure and simple, in which the parties appear on absolutely equal terms.

Hiring — Discharge.— The duties and obligations of masters and servants are therefore now regulated by the terms of the contract of hiring. As such hiring at common law had chiefly to do with agricultural operations, the term of service was, in nearly all cases, for one year; at present it may be by the year, month, week, day, or hour, at the option of the parties. Hiring by the month is the usual form in most trades; and the compensation is by the month, week, day, or hour, with payment of wages monthly or weekly, as may be agreed upon by the parties. The contract may be terminated by a month's notice, or, in a lesser period, by the payment of a month's wages. The

---

[184] Schouler, Dom. Rel., § 456.

causes which justify discharge are various, the principal of which, prior to expiration of term of service, are drunkenness, habitual negligence, improper behavior toward patrons or customers, immoral or disrespectful conduct, insubordination, or disobedience of orders. It may be said, in general, that an employer has no arbitrary power to discharge, save for good and sufficient reasons, the sufficiency of which in the last resort must be determined by a jury. A contract of service, like all other contracts, may be dissolved by mutual consent, or by the death or disability of either party or by the completion of the stipulated term.[185]

Injuries.— A master has a right of action for injuries done to a servant, by reason of the loss of his services, or to the impairment of his capacity to render them. When a servant transacts business in behalf of the master an agency is established, and the relations of principal and agent are called into being. The master is liable on the contracts made by the servant within the scope of his employment, and has a civil liability for his torts. For injuries due to his own negligence, the master is liable to the servant; he is not responsible, however, for an injury due to the negligence of a fellow-servant, to which he has in no way contributed. For criminal acts committed by the servant he alone is responsible.

Certificates of Character.— In the absence of a legal agreement to do so, a master is not obliged to give a servant a *certificate of character* on dismissal. If he does so in good faith, and if his statements in regard to the character of a particular servant are true, such statements *are privileged,* and cannot be made the subject of damages in an action at law.

---

[185] *Ibid.,* § 464.

Apprenticeship.— *Apprentices* are persons, usually minors, who are bound to service at a particular trade for a term of years. In the case of one under age the contract is usually for the period of minority. The conditions of service are regulated by the contract, which contains an obligation on the part of the master to support the apprentice, furnish him medical attendance, and to teach him an art or trade, and, on the part of the apprentice or that of his parent or guardian, to serve faithfully, and to receive and apply the instruction given by the master. These agreements, in the case of minors, are entered into for a term of years, and usually expire at the age of twenty-one in the case of males, and at the age of eighteen in the case of females.

AGENCY

Agency — Parties — How Created.— An *agent* is a person employed by another to act for him in a definite capacity. The contractual relation thus established is called an *agency,* the parties to which are the *principal* and *agent.* An agent who is empowered to transact all business connected with a particular trade or employment is called a *general agent;* one *who* acts in a single transaction only is called a *special agent.* Authority to act for another is always derivative in character, and is created by an exercise of authority called a power, which may be conferred by a written instrument, as in a power of attorney, or its existence may be inferred or deduced from the acts, declarations, or representations of either of the parties to the agency. To enable an agent to execute a sealed instrument, his authority must be under seal. In some cases arising under the statute of frauds the power must be in writing, but not necessarily under seal. When conferred in specific terms, whether in writing or otherwise, the power is said to be *express;* when deduced or inferred from the acts or declarations of the parties to an agency, it is said to be inferred or *implied.*

Capacity of Parties.— A principal must be one having full capacity to contract, and under no disability in respect to the exercise of civil rights. The capacity of the agent is determined largely by the character and scope of the agency. He must be sane, and mentally and physically competent to perform the duties imposed upon him by the existence of the agency.

Classes of Agents.— Agents are classified according to the extent and character of their employment as brokers, commission agents, factors, auctioneers, commercial travelers, shipmasters, attorneys at law, and the like, the scope and character of the agency not being the same in any two of the cases above cited.

Duties.— The act of an agent, done in the usual way and within the scope of his employment, serves to bind the principal. The agent's authority is limited, however, to the usual and ordinary means of accomplishing the business entrusted to him. On the other hand, acts in excess of his authority do not bind the principal unless ratified by him. Representations, admissions, and declarations of the agent respecting the subject-matter of the agency bind the principal, and may be proved in the same manner as if they had been made by him, and, when so proved have the same evidential effect. As there is a privity of interest between the parties to an agency, the knowledge of the agent is the knowledge of the principal, who is bound thereby. This rule is based on the principles of law that it is-the agent's duty to communicate to the principal the knowledge which he has respecting the subject-matter of a negotiation and the presumption that he will perform that duty.[186]

Ratification.— An act of the agent in excess of his authority may be ratified by the principal, who thus becomes responsible for it from the date of its execution or performance, and while he may enjoy any benefit accruing therefrom he becomes responsible for any obligation incurred by the agent in the performance of the act so ratified and adopted. No act is susceptible of ratification which is unlawful, or opposed to the public policy, or which is not performed by the agent, as such, in behalf of the principal.[187] Ratification may be express, or may be implied from silence or acquiescence, and such acquiescence will be presumed if the principal does not repudiate or disavow the act when it is brought to his notice.[188]

Termination.— Agency may be terminated by renunciation on the part of the agent, or by revocation of authority on the part of the principal, and becomes effective as between the parties from its date, but as to third persons only when they have had notice of such revocation or renunciation. The death or insanity of either party also operates to terminate an agency, as does an agreement between the parties limiting the existence of the agency in point of time or restricting its scope to a single undertaking.

---

[186] The Distilled Spirits, 11 Wall., 367.

[187] Cook *vs.* Tullis, 18 Wall., 338.

[188] Law *vs.* Gross, 1 Black, 533.

CHAPTER XII

EQUITY

Nature of Jurisdiction in Equity.— It has been seen that at common law *every* complaint or demand for redress had to be stated in accordance with one of the recognized forms of action, and if a particular cause of action was not susceptible of such statement the common-law courts were not able to furnish a remedy and the injured party was said to be without redress. In early times a party in this situation appealed to the king in person, who sometimes interposed, by an exercise of the royal prerogative, and rendered a decision upon the merits of the case in accordance with the principles of equity or natural justice. As such relief was, at best, but casual or accidental, and could in the nature of things be extended to but a small number of cases, the equitable jurisdiction of the sovereign came to be shared with and finally to be exercised by the chancellor, who, as the keeper of the great seal, had authority to issue writs of subpoena commanding a defendant to appear and make answer to a statement filed by a plaintiff, which alleged the existence of injuries for which there was no remedy at common law. The *petition* or *bill* of the plaintiff, after reciting the particular wrong or injury for which relief was asked, prayed that the defendant be required to appear in court and make discovery under oath of every fact and circumstance within his knowledge, information, and belief which was material to the case of the plaintiff as stated in his bill.

Discovery.— This right to enforce *discovery is* peculiar to equity jurisdiction and cannot be enforced by the common-law courts, in which the plaintiff must make out his case by the testimony of witnesses or the admissions of the defendant, as described in the chapter relating to the proceedings in an action at law. The right to this form of relief is not restricted to the plaintiff, and a defendant in equity may, by the institution of a *cross-suit,* as it is called, obtain discovery as to matters within the knowledge of the plaintiff.

Differences between the Jurisdiction of Law and Equity.— The jurisdiction exercised by courts of equity differs from that of the common-law courts in the following important respects: (1) No jury is provided, save in a few exceptional cases in which an issue of fact is to be tried, the court passing upon all questions of law and fact which are essential to a decision of the case; (2) the parties to the suit are not only permitted, but required, to testify; (3) such testimony as is received, appears in the form of depositions, oral testimony being excluded; (4) equity jurisdiction has chiefly to do with the obtaining of evidence by means of commissions and by the power of discovery with which courts of equity are endowed, with the perpetuation of testimony, the creation and performance of trusts and contracts, the re-execution and correction of instruments which have been lost or erroneously framed, and with the administration of remedial justice by the issue and enforcement of the extraordinary writs the use and office of which have already been described. In dealing with real property equity jurisdiction is restricted to questions relating to the ownership, care, and management of estates, such care being exercised through trustees, receivers, or others acting in a fiduciary capacity, under the orders of the court; equity courts are without power to afford redress for criminal acts or for civil injuries in the nature of torts.

Equity Jurisdiction in the United States.— The system of equity prevailing in England during the period of settlement and discovery was brought to this country by the colonists and was adopted, or continued in force, by the colonies on achieving their independence. Its development in the several States of the Union, however, has not been uniform, and the systems prevailing in the different jurisdictions are susceptible of classification under three heads: (1) Those which maintain a separate system of equity courts; (2) those in which equity jurisdiction, is administered by the common law courts, sitting, however, in equity and administering the rules of equity or chancery procedure in the decision of cases; and (3) those in which the distinction between law and equity has been obliterated by statute, the procedure in a particular case being determined by its nature and the proper form of relief to be afforded, or by the remedy to be applied. The equity jurisdiction of the Federal courts is conferred and regulated by statute, and the Supreme Court has provided that the procedure of the English high court of chancery shall form the basis of the equity procedure of the courts of the United States.

Suits in Equity, How Instituted — Original Bill.— A suit in equity is commenced by the filing of a petition in behalf of the plaintiff or complainant, setting forth the facts in his case and praying for relief. This petition is called a bill in equity, and, to distinguish it from other bills filed during the progress of the suit, it is called the *original bill.* The original bill consists of five principal parts: (1) the statement; (3) the charges; (3) the interrogatories; (4) the prayer for relief; (5) the prayer for process. These five technical divisions of a bill have their respective functions in the presentation of the complainant's case.

Statement of Case — Charges.— The bill must state the case in direct terms and with reasonable certainty. The allegations must be positive and not by way of recital, and must be of facts only and not law; and every averment of fact necessary to entitle the complainant to the relief sought must be contained in the stating part of the bill, which must also present a case upon which, if admitted by the answer, a decree in favor of the complainant can be based. The charging part of the bill is not essential to its completeness. It is, in fact, only a portion of the stating part, and consists of a statement of charges and pretenses.

Discovery — Interrogatories.— After the statement and the charges the bill next requires the defendant to make discovery — that is, to answer on oath in respect to the several matters specifically stated and charged,— and in the case of executors, trustees, and others administering property fiducially, to set forth accounts of property under their charge and to give a. list of books, accounts, and documents relating to the matter of the inquiry. With a view to this discovery of facts the bill contains an interrogating part, in which the statement of charges and pretenses are converted into a series of interrogatories, framed on the principle that, without the interrogatories, which must be answered specifically, the defendant would answer evasively.[189]

Prayer for Relief — Prayer for Process.— After the interrogating part the bill prays for the relief to which the plaintiff thinks that the case entitles him, and concludes with a prayer for general relief, under which any relief may be given to which a title is made out at the hearing. In conclusion, the bill prays process of subpoena against the defendant to compel him to appear and submit an answer in writing. The bill is signed by the plaintiff or his counsel, or both, and. is filed with the register of the court of equity. In accordance with the prayer of the bill, the clerk of the court of equity issues the writ, under the seal

---

[189] Mitford and Tyler, Equity, 64.

of the court, called a subpoena, by which the defendant is required to appear and answer the bill.[190]

Reply of Defendant.— If the defendant appears according to the requirement of the subpoena, he then makes his defense or reply, according to the forms established in equity pleading. In the defendant's reply, which is called the answer, he is required to answer fully, completely, and without needless prolixity as to the material facts alleged in the plaintiff's bill. The information so given includes not only all matters within the defendant's. knowledge, but such as he can acquire from his books and papers and from inquiries addressed to his agents and attorneys. Whatever information he has the right to possess the court will presume to be in his possession. A defendant in equity is privileged, however, not to make discovery as to matters tending to criminate him, or to expose him to a penalty or forfeiture, or to disclose legal advice given to him by his attorneys, or, if ho occupies an official station, to disclose state secrets or confidential matters relating to the administration of public affairs.

Demurrer.— If it shall appear from the complainant's statement of the case in the bill that there is nothing to warrant the interference of a court of equity, the proper course for the defendant is to demur to the bill for insufficiency, and demand the judgment of the court whether the suit shall proceed at all or the defendant make answer thereto. This mode of defense is called a demurrer.

Plea.— If the bill be sufficient in its statements and charges to warrant the interference of equity, but the defendant knows matters, not appearing on the face of the bill, which afford a reason why the suit should be either

---

[190] *Ibid.*, 65.

dismissed, barred, or delayed, it is the proper course for the defendant to meet the bill by a statement of these matters. Or, if some particular matter stated in the bill, which is essential to the plaintiff's case, be false, tills matter should be met by a denial. In such case the judgment of the court is demanded whether the defendant shall be compelled to answer further. This mode of defense is called a *plea.*

Disclaimer.— If the defendant has no claim, or disowns any, to the subject of the demand made in the bill, his proper course is to disclaim all right and title to the matter in demand, and pray judgment of the court that he be dismissed with allowance of costs. This mode of defense is called a *disclaimer.*[191]

Answer.— Where neither of the above forms of defense is available, the suit proceeds by the defendant answering the allegations and charges of the bill and demanding the judgment of the court on the whole case as presented on both sides. The defendant must answer distinctly, fully, and completely, without needless prolixity, positively and directly, and not by way of argument, to the best of his knowledge, information, and belief, every statement, charge, pretense, and interrogatory in the bill by either admitting, traversing, confessing and avoiding, or ignoring all the facts stated and charged. And the defendant must answer, not according to the information which he actually possesses at the time the bill is filed, but according to all the information which he has and can procure from his books, his agents, and other means under his control. This mode of defense is called an *answer.*

---

[191] Mitford and Tyler, Equity, 66.

Procedure after Answer.— After the answer is filed the plaintiff may, if he is satisfied with the defendant's answer, have the cause heard on the bill and answer, in which case he admits the answer to be true in all respects. Or he may file a replication, which is a general denial of the facts stated in the answer, requiring the fact to be proved. Or he may except to the answer for want of fullness, in order to compel further answer. After the replication the pleadings are ended, and the case is said to be at issue. The great aim in equity procedure is to procure from the defendant, as a sworn witness in the case, an admission of the case made by the bill, either in aid of proof or to supply the want of it, and to avoid expense. To this end an answer from the defendant is the great object to be obtained by a suit in equity as a means toward a decree of relief. Equity pleadings, therefore, center around the answer. The answer is what the plaintiff especially seeks and what the defendant especially avoids. The modern policy of equity pleading is to bring out the whole case in the bill and answer, and not to let the case run out into lengthened pleadings as at common law, which was the earlier practice in chancery. To this end mispleading in matter of form is never allowed to prejudice any party. Mistakes may be corrected, impolitic admissions suppressed, additional facts added, and all things done which are needful to insure a hearing on the substantial merits of the case as set forth in the bill and answer.[192]

Hearing.— The pleadings having been concluded, the next step in a chancery suit is the hearing. As has been seen, the court in. this form of procedure is made the judge of both the law and the facts, the jury being dispensed with, save in a few exceptional instances in which the court is given power to refer a particular issue

[192] Mitford and Tyler, 68, 69

to a jury for determination, in which event the finding of the jury is submitted to the court as a part of the proceedings in the case.

Masters and Receivers.— In dealing with the case at all stages of its progress the court is assisted by officers called masters and receivers. A *master in chancery* is a person appointed by the court to assist in taking depositions, stating accounts, estimating damages, investigating titles, and performing other services of a ministerial character. *Receivers* are persons appointed by the court to take charge of property in litigation, and to manage it under the direction of the court pending a decree as to its final disposition. These officers perform their duties under the orders of the court, and make formal reports from time to time as to the matters intrusted to their charge.

Evidence — Final Decree.— The testimony upon which the court bases its final decision is always in the form of depositions, in the taking of which the rules of evidence at common law are applied, save those relating to the incompetency of parties who in equity procedure are made competent witnesses and may be required to testify as to the merits of the case. The court, having all the evidence before it, in the way of depositions, reports, and the pleadings and answers of the parties, then proceeds to render a decision, called a *final decree,* which corresponds to the *judgment* in an action at law, and finally disposes of the case. If either party is dissatisfied with the decree, he may apply for a *rehearing,* corresponding to a new trial at common law; or he may take a formal appeal to a court having proper appellate jurisdiction, or he may obtain a revision of the decree in the court in which the case was originally tried by means of a bill of review — a proceeding analogous in some respects to that under the writ of error at common law.

The final decree, if not appealed from, bars all further litigation in equity upon the same subject-matter and between the same parties.

Equity Jurisdiction in General.— The extraordinary jurisdiction exercised by courts of equity, by the issue of what are called the prerogative writs, has already been explained, in general the jurisdiction of these tribunals extends to a class of cases over which the common-law courts either have no jurisdiction at all, or in which they are unable to afford an adequate remedy.

Jurisdiction in Equity, How Exercised.— The common-law courts must also have a case presented to them in such form as to be reducible to an issue, by an application of the rules of pleading, upon which the judgment of the court can be based. Courts of equity, on the other hand, have power to take judicial possession of the thing in controversy and, through appropriate agencies, to direct and supervise its management pending a decision as to its final disposition. This power, as has been seen, is exercised through receivers, trustees, and other persons acting, under the orders of the court, in a fiduciary capacity.

Contract — Specific Performance.— In actions of contract at common law the courts recognize the right of a plaintiff to demand specific performance, but they can only compel such performance by giving damages for nonperformance. Courts of equity, in proper cases, may decree *specific performance* — that is, they may require a defendant to do the precise tiling which he has agreed to do in his contract with the plaintiff. This power extends, however, only to contracts in which such performance is essential to justice, and if damages will fully indemnify the plaintiff, a court of equity will not interfere. The following cases will illustrate the application of the rule of specific performance: One Stuyvesant conveyed a large tract of land to the city of New York to be used as a public park. The conveyance contained a covenant on the part of the city to grade, curb, inclose, and otherwise improve the premises in such a way as to adapt them to use as a park; this the city failed to do, and the grantor brought a bill for specific performance, which was decreed.[193] A party entered into an agreement to build a hotel on the land of another, who was to receive several shares in the hotel company in payment for his land. The landowner cleared the land, removed some buildings therefrom, and otherwise prepared the ground for building. The builder began the construction of a hotel, but soon afterward abandoned the undertaking. The landowner applied for, and obtained, a decree for specific performance.[194] A court of law would have been unable to afford a remedy in either of the cases above cited, as it would have been impossible to place an estimate upon the damage sustained by the plaintiff.

Reformation of Contracts — Rescission and Cancellation.— Courts of equity may also reform contracts, in certain cases, where by reason of fraud or mistake the instrument does not express the real intent of the parties. Contracts may also be rescinded or canceled on the ground of fraud or mistake, or where undue influence, or want of capacity to contract is alleged, or where duress has been used, or a contract entered into through threats of personal violence. Courts of equity are slow to act in such cases, however, and they will require the fraud, misrepresentation, or mistake to be established in the strongest and clearest manner before they will interpose and afford relief to a complainant; acquiescence,

---

[193] Stuyvesant *vs.* New York City, 11 Paige, 414.

[194] Burchett *vs.* Boling, 5 Mumford (Va.), 442.

waiver, or unreasonable lapse of time will also operate to bar relief, unless fully explained or accounted for.

Trusts.— A trust is an obligation imposed upon a person arising out of a confidence reposed in him by another, or created by an act on his part which affects injuriously the rights of another. They consist in general of an equitable right or interest in property which another holds in confidence as the legal owner. The person in whom the confidence is imposed is called the *trustee;* the one for whose benefit the property is held is called the *cestui que trust.* Out of this confidential relation arise two estates in the property which is the subject of the trust — a legal estate in the trustee which consists essentially in an obligation, and an equitable estate in the cestui que trust which consists in right and beneficial enjoyment. Trusts are classified, according to the manner of their formation, into *express* and *implied trusts. Express trusts* are those which are created by deed or by the act of the parties; *implied trusts* are those which arise by operation of law, or are inferred or presumed by a court from the circumstances of the particular case. The creation, management, and dissolution of trusts forms a considerable part of the jurisdiction of courts of equity.

Fraud and Misrepresentation.— Fraud has already been discussed in its relation to the law of contract. It consists in any kind of artifice made use of by one person for the purpose of deceiving another; if with knowledge of the character and consequences of the act, and with intent to deceive, it is said to be *actual;* if it be an act, omission, or concealment which involves a breach of legal or equitable duty, and results in an injury to another, whatever be the intention, it is said to be *constructive fraud.* Constructive fraud is thus seen to be a conclusion of law, which courts will infer from acts and circumstances, whether the existence of a fraudulent purpose, in the strict sense, be proved or not. Misrepresentation is a false or erroneous representation in relation to a matter of fact. As has been seen, a misrepresentation as to any material fact voids a contract which has been entered into by another relying upon the truth of the fact so misrepresented. Fraud is never presumed, and must be proven by the clearest testimony, or inferred by the court from facts fully established in evidence. When so established, courts of equity may make such decrees and orders, or take such other remedial action as may seem to them warranted by the facts in the case.

Courts of equity also exercise an extensive jurisdiction in matters of account, partition of estates among tenants in common, assignment of dower, the prevention of waste by persons having a limited interest in property, and in the matter of deeds or other instruments which are alleged to have been lost, suppressed, or destroyed by parties claiming under them.

Other Jurisdiction of Equity Courts.— The aid of these tribunals is also frequently asked to supply defects in a suit prosecuted elsewhere, or to obtain evidence for use in a suit pending in a court of law. Such are *bills of discovery,* when used to obtain facts within the knowledge of a defendant, with a view to their use in the prosecution or defense of an action at law; *bills to perpetuate testimony,* in which the testimony of a material witness may be obtained, by deposition, which might otherwise be lost, as by his death or departure from the jurisdiction; and examinations *de bene esse.* To examine a witness *de bene esse is to* examine him out of court before the trial, subject to the contingency of his being able to attend court at the time fixed for the trial. If he be unable to attend, the deposition so obtained becomes competent, and may be read in evidence at the trial. If he be able to attend, however, the deposition is not valid, and he must be examined again at the trial in the usual way.

CHAPTER XIII

CRIMINAL LAW

Purpose of the Criminal Laws.— With a view to maintain peace within its territorial limits, to uphold morality, and to secure to its citizens an immunity from injury as to their persons and property, a State finds it necessary from time to time to forbid the occurrence of certain wrongful acts, the commission of which is calculated to endanger its safety, to impede the administration of the laws, or to affect injuriously the personal or property rights of individuals. This purpose is accomplished by the enactment of certain statutes called *criminal laws,* and the State vests in certain of its courts the power to apply them in the prevention and punishment of crime. The power thus granted to certain courts to execute criminal laws is called *criminal jurisdiction,* and it is exercised in a particular case in accordance with a set of rules, partly statutory and partly customary or derived from the common law, called *criminal procedure.*

The Peace of the Commonwealth.— The maintenance of good conduct, public order, and decorum within a community[195] constitutes the *peace of the commonwealth.* This condition of affairs is secured by the orderly and efficient administration of the criminal laws and by the application of appropriate remedies to injuries which constitute causes of action at civil law. With a view to prevent crime and to secure its prompt punishment, whenever and by whomsoever committed, it is made the duty of certain public officers, such as sheriffs, coroners, constables, and the like, to *preserve the peace,* that is, to

---

[195] Andersen's Law Dictionary, 161.

arrest offenders and to prevent violations of the law. For this reason such officers are called *peace officers,* and they are authorized in cases of emergency to call upon other citizens or bystanders to assist them in the performance of their duties. Offenses against the public peace are: threatening or demanding any valuable thing by letter; affrays, riots, routs, unlawful assemblies; forcible entry and detainer; going unusually armed; spreading false news; challenges to fight; libels. All criminal offenses are against the peace, and are so laid in indictments.[196]

Criminal Law, How Construed.— A *criminal law is* a statute declaring an act of commission or omission to be an offense against the State and forbidding its occurrence under appropriate penalties. As the effect of the operations of such statutes is to deny or otherwise abridge the personal rights of individuals, criminal laws are always construed strictly as to all those parts which make against defendants, but liberally as to those in their favor. " No person can be made subject to such statutes by implication, and when doubts arise concerning their interpretation such doubts are to weigh only in favor of the accused."[197]

---

[196] 4 Blackstone's Com., 142-152, 268. This is accomplished by the allegation in the indictment that the particular offense charged was committed " in the peace of the commonwealth." This because an offense committed in maintaining the peace of the commonwealth, such as the killing of an enemy in war, the execution of a criminal, or the taking of life in the performance of official duty, would not constitute a criminal offense. The old form of allegation was "in the peace of God and the Commonwealth." Bishop, Crim. Proc., §§ 57, 504.

[197] United States *vs.* Clayton, 5 Dill., 35.

CRIMES AND CRIMINAL OFFENSES

Crimes — Classification.— A *crime* is a wrongful act, of omission or commission, in violation of a law requiring it to be done or refrained from, and the occurrence of which is prohibited under specific penalties. As a wrongful act, crime affects society so directly that the State punishes it in its own name and by its own agencies. The effects of crime are so injurious to the community at large that the State takes the place of the individual who has suffered by its commission and treats the occurrence as an offense against its own dignity. Criminal offenses are classified, according to their gravity and importance, and in part on account of the forfeitures and other penalties consequent upon conviction, into *treason, felonies,* and *misdemeanors.*

Treason.— *Treason* is a violation of the duty of allegiance owed by the individual to the State of which he is the citizen or subject. As a State is an association of persons, the principal aim or purpose of which is mutual protection, it follows that treason is a violation of the fundamental duty of the citizen, amounting to a repudiation of his obligation of loyalty and allegiance. In the United States the crime of treason is defined in the Constitution, and consists in "levying war against them, or in adhering to their enemies, giving them aid and comfort."[198] The Constitution also provides that no person "shall be convicted of treason unless on the testimony of two witnesses to the same overt act, or on confession in open court."[199] Congress is given power in the same section to declare the punishment of treason, "but no

---

[198] Constitution of the United States, Art III, sec. 3.
[199] *Ibid.*

attainder of treason shall work corruption of blood or forfeiture beyond the life of the person attainted."[200]

FELONY

Felony — Status — Consequences.— In accordance with the present understanding of the term, a *felon* is a person who has been convicted of any one of several crimes which are regarded as felonious at the common law, or who has been adjudged guilty of a criminal offense, the punishment of which involves confinement in a state prison or penitentiary.[201] *Felony* is therefore a result of crime rather than a crime itself, and may be defined as the status of infamy or civil disability occupied by a person who has been convicted of a crime involving the punishment of death or forfeiture at common law, or of a crime which has been declared to be such by statute in the jurisdiction in which it was committed. In former times convictions of felony, in addition to the punishment of death, involved an attainder of blood; the felon forfeited all civil rights, became incapable of making contracts and agreements, of holding or transmitting property, and was not permitted to testify as a witness in a court of justice. The common-law disabilities above described have been modified or removed, by statute, in most of the States; but in those jurisdictions in which such modification has not taken place the rules of the common law still prevail, and a person incompetent by reason of infamy will not be permitted to testify in any action at law, civil or criminal.

As the United States has no common-law jurisdiction, none of the disabilities attaching to felony attend conviction of a crime against its authority, unless

---

[200] *Ibid.,* par. 3.

[201] *Ex parte* Wilson, 114 *U. S.*. 417, 427.

such disabilities are expressly imposed by statute; and it is only from the point of view of competency to testify that the subject has importance in the practice of the Federal courts. It has been authoritatively held that the rules of evidence applied by the Federal courts in criminal cases are those of the common law as they stood at the time of the adoption of the Constitution, as subsequently modified by enactments of Congress.[202] At the time of the adoption of the Constitution conviction of felony conferred the quality of infamy and deprived the felon of capacity to testify as a witness in any action at law, civil or criminal. What punishments shall be considered infamous may be affected by the changes of public opinion from one age to another. For more than a century imprisonment at hard labor in the State prison or penitentiary or other similar institution has been considered an infamous punishment in England and America.[203]

Classification.— Felonies are classified, according to their origin, into *common-law* and *statutory felonies. Common-law felonies* are acts which are in themselves wrong, and as such are condemned by the moral sense of the community; *statutory felonies* are those which are declared to be such in the statutes defining them, either expressly or by necessary inference from the nature of the punishment therein imposed.

Misdemeanors.— A *misdemeanor* is a public offense of omission or commission, less serious than felony, which is penal at common law or has been made so by statute. While some statutory offenses of this character are punished more severely than felonies, none of the consequences that follow conviction of felony are

---

[202] United States Reid, 12 How., 351 ; United States *vs.* Brown, 1 Sawyer, 531.

[203] *Ex parte* Wilson, 114 U. S., 417, 427.

involved in the punishment of misdemeanors. The term as now used covers a class of penal offenses the greater part of which are recognized as wrongful acts by the community at large, because they mischievously affect the person or property of another, or outrage decency, disturb the peace, injure public morals, or are breaches of public duty.[204]

THE ELEMENTS OF CRIME. THE INTENT

The Intent, How Established.— Every criminal offense is composed of, and can generally be separated in to, two elements, one outward and visible, or otherwise appreciable to the senses, the other inward or mental. The *external element* is made up of the facts constituting the particular crime as defined in the statute or as understood at the common law. The *inward element,* which is known to the law as the *intent,* varies in different crimes, in some amounting merely to a knowledge of the character and consequences of the act which is being committed; in others to a definite malicious purpose, formed in advance and deliberately carried into effect. The terms "intent" and "intention" are by no means synonymous. An intention, like other mental acts or states of mind, is known, as such, only to the person who cherishes it; it is made known to others by spoken words or other external acts. When, therefore, it becomes necessary to establish a particular intention in evidence, testimony must be submitted as to such acts or utterances as are calculated to prove its existence. These external acts are difficult to prove, and even when a considerable body of evidence has been adduced it is sometimes a matter of great difficulty to interpret them — that is, to place upon each its true meaning as an evidence of mental intention. It is not

---

[204] Kent.

necessary, however, in ordinary cases to prove the intent by evidence separate from that relied upon to prove the commission of the offense;[205] indeed, as will presently be seen, it is only in a limited number of cases that it is necessary to establish a separately cherished mental intention.

Presumptions as to the Intent.— It is a presumption of law that all persons of sound mind are familiar with the law — that is, they know what acts or omissions are criminal in character. The law also presumes that every sane person intends — that is, understands or appreciates — the natural and ordinary consequences of his acts.[206] As has been said, this knowledge alone in most cases constitutes the intent which is essential to the commission of every criminal offense, and when the facts constituting a particular criminal act have been established in evidence, the presumption that the accused acted with knowledge as to their consequences is applied, and it is not necessary to introduce testimony in its support.

Definition.— The *intent,* as an essential element of a criminal offense, may therefore be defined as the knowledge on the part of an accused person of the nature and consequences of his act or omission at the instant

---

[205] People *vs.* Beckwith, 103 N. Y., 360 ; U. S. *vs.* Baldrige, 11 F. R., 552 ; U. S. *vs.* Sanders, 6 McL., 598 : U. S. *vs.* Lee, 12 F. K., 816 ; U. S. *vs.* Taintor, 11 Blatchford, 374 ; U. S. *vs.* Shellmire, Baldwin, 370 ; U. S. *vs.* Imsand, 1 Woods. 581 ; U. S. *vs.* Bunton, 10 Fed. Rep., 730 ; U. S. *vs.* Nicholson, 3 Woods, 215 : U. S. *vs.* Leathers, 6 Sawyer 27 ; *U. S. vs.* Ulrici, 3 Dillon, 532 ; U. S. *vs.* Voorhes, 9 Fed. Rep , 143 ; U. S. *vs.* Libby, 1 Woodbury and Mason, 229.

[206] Commonwealth *vs.* Webster, 59 Mass., 306.

when the act was performed or the duty omitted. In some crimes of exceptional gravity — murder in the first degree, for example — *premeditation* or *malice aforethought* must be established in addition to the proof of the facts essential to constitute the crime. Proof of a particular intent is also required in certain statutory crimes. In such cases we must look to the terms of the statute for a definition of the crime and the kind and amount of proof that is necessary to establish the separate criminal intent.

Guilty Knowledge.— There are some offenses in which, from the nature of the act, the element corresponding to the intent in ordinary crimes is called *guilty knowledge.* Receiving stolen goods is an example of offenses of this class. Thus, goods were stolen by A with a particular felonious intent. If B, when he received them, was aware of their character, he is *said* to have acted with guilty knowledge, and so became liable to punishment as a receiver.

Criminal Negligence.— There are certain omissions which are said to constitute criminal negligence when they result in injuries to the person or property of another. For such wrongs the law affords a remedy, which consists in some cases of a criminal prosecution, and iii others of an action at law for damages. There is no specific offense known to the law as criminal negligence, unless in a particular jurisdiction certain acts are made such by statute. The offense consists, in general, of a negligent omission to perform a duty created by law or contract, the result of which is to cause loss of life, or injury to the person or property of another. The facts constituting the particular act of negligence will determine the offense committed, and the negligence itself forms, or, more properly speaking, replaces, the intent, which forms an essential ingredient of the criminal offense. For example:

A, a switchman, through negligence, fails to turn a switch; an accident results, causing the death of B. A has committed manslaughter.

CRIMINAL CAPACITY

Capacity to Commit Crime.— It has been seen that, from the point of view of criminal jurisprudence, all persons of sound mind are presumed to be familiar with the law, and are therefore held responsible for the consequences of their criminal acts.[207]

Insanity.— If there be mental unsoundness, or if the person is so deficient in intellect or understanding as not to be conscious of or capable of controlling his actions, his responsibility for them and for their harmful consequences either ceases to exist or is considerably modified. For acts over which he has no control, or as to which he is incapable of forming or cherishing an intention, he has no responsibility whatever. If he is dangerous to society, the law provides methods by which such restraint may be placed upon his movements as is necessary to the well-being of the community at large. If there be periods or occasions during which he is of sound mind, he is as to such periods fully accountable for his acts. If his mental faculties are merely impaired, the nature and extent of his responsibility is a question of fact to be determined by the jury, the presumption being in all cases that an accused person is mentally sound and therefore responsible for his acts, and the burden of proving the existence of mental unsoundness or incapacity lies upon the defense, and must be established by the testimony of witnesses.

Test of Responsibility.— The test of responsibility for crime lies in the capacity or power of the person to

[207] Com. *vs.* Webster, 59 Mass. 306.

commit the act; and the inquiry is whether the accused was capable of having and did have a criminal intent and the capacity to distinguish between right and wrong in reference to the particular act charged. The test of responsibility where insanity is asserted is the capacity to distinguish between right and wrong with respect to the act, and the absence of delusions respecting the same. If the accused knew what he was doing, and the act was forbidden by law, and he had power of mind enough to be conscious of what he was doing, he was responsible;[208] in other words. Had the accused the power to distinguish right from wrong, and the power to adhere to the right and avoid the wrong? If so, he is responsible for the consequences of his act.[209]

Intoxication.— The general rule is that drunkenness is no excuse for crime, and the person who is voluntarily in that condition takes the consequences of his own acts.[210] "So long as the offender is capable of conceiving a design, he will be presumed, in the absence of proof to the contrary, to have intended the natural consequences of his act."[211] If a man without provocation kill another, no degree of intoxication short of that which shows that he was at the time utterly incapable of acting from motive will shield him from conviction.[212]

---

[208] State *vs.* Nixon, 32 Kan., 205.

[209] Life Insurance Company *vs.* Terry, 15 Wall.. 590.

[210] Lanergan *vs.* People, 50 Barber, 266: Friery *vs.* People, 54 *ibid.,* 319; 2 N. Y. Ct. of App. Dec., 215; 1 Greene's Crim. Rep., 373.

[211] Kenny *vs.* People, 31 N. Y . 330.

[212] People *vs.* Rogers, 18 N. Y., 9; Lanergan *vs.* People, 6 Parker, 209; Hopt *vs.* People. 14 Otto, 631; *V. Q. vs.* Clarke, 2 Cranch, C. C., 158; Com. *vs.* Hawkins, 3

Married Women — Infants.— It has been seen that in the cases of married women and infants the responsibility for crime is considerably modified. The criminal acts of the wife committed in the presence of the husband are presumed to have been due to his direction and coercion. Children under seven are conclusively presumed to be incapable of committing crime; between seven and fourteen the presumption of law is against such capacity, subject to rebuttal by evidence showing proper intelligence, and knowledge of the character and consequences of the act in question; between the ages of fourteen and twenty-one the same presumption prevails as in the case of persons of full age.

Compulsion by Force.— Besides the case of marital coercion above alluded to, the law recognizes, as an excuse for crime, that its commission has been due to force, or to threats to kill ail offender, or to do him grievous bodily harm, in the event of his refusal to take part in a particular criminal act. For such a defense to avail, however, the threats must have been such as to place the accused person hi danger of imminent death or serious bodily harm, and must have been continuous during the entire period of the commission of the act in question.

PARTIES TO CRIME

Parties — Principals — Degrees.— The relationship of parties to a crime and their responsibility in connection with it are determined by their presence, actual or constructive, at its commission, or by their connection with it prior or subsequent to its occurrence. *Principals* are those present at the commission of an offense, and who

---

Gray, 463; Compiled Laws of Utah (1876), pp. 568, 569; Nichols *vs.* State, 8 Ohio N. S., 485; U. S. *vs.* Drew, 5 Mason, 28; O'Brien *vs.* People, 48 Barber, 274.

aid, procure, advise, assist, or otherwise take part in the wrongful act. A crime may consist of many acts, all of which must be committed in order to complete the offense, but each person present consenting to the commission of the offense, and doing any act which is either an ingredient of the crime or immediately connected with or leading to its commission, is as much a principal as if he had with his own hand committed the entire offense. *Principals* in crime are of two degrees: they are said to be of the *first degree* when they are the actual perpetrators of the offense; they are said to be of the *second degree* when they are present at its commission, aiding and abetting the act to be done. The distinction between principals is, at present, largely descriptive, as all persons participating in the commission of au offense are now held equally responsible for the criminal act.

Accessories.— *Accessories* are persons concerned in a criminal act who are not present at its commission, and whose connection with it, in point of time, precedes or follows the performance of the wrongful act. They are classified as accessories before and after the fact. An *accessory before the fact* is one who, not being present at the commission of the crime,. counsels or commands another to commit a criminal act. An *accessory after the fact* is one who, knowing a crime to have been committed, receives, relieves, comforts, or assists the criminal. In general, any assistance rendered to a criminal which is calculated to hinder his apprehension or to assist or facilitate his escape makes the person rendering it liable as an accessory after the fact. In former times accessories before the fact could only be tried jointly with the principals, or after they had been convicted, but this distinction no longer exists. Accessories after the fact are guilty of substantive crime and are liable to punishment therefor; their punishment is usually determined by statute, and is less in most jurisdictions than that awarded to principals. The distinction between accomplices is still important, as a matter affecting their competency to testify, when their testimony is relied upon to convict other participants.

Misprision.— *Misprision* is a form of criminal negligence, and consists in the concealment of knowledge that treason or a felony has been or is being committed. If there be assent in addition to concealment, the-offender becomes liable as a principal or accessory, depending upon the circumstances of the case.

Compounding.— *Compounding* consists in an agreement not to prosecute, entered into with the person by whom the offense was committed, by one who has suffered, in person or property, from the commission of a felony, the consideration being the return of goods stolen or the receipt of a bribe, or reward, on condition that there be no prosecution of the offense. Such an undertaking is in form a contract, but, being unlawful, its enforcement is impossible, and an attempt to compel performance may subject the parties to penal consequences.

ATTEMPTS; ASSAULTS

Attempts.— An *attempt* is an endeavor to commit crime, coupled with an overt act toward its commission, but desisted from or interrupted before the criminal act is begun. The offense of attempt is complete if the act, once begun, is abandoned because of surprise or discovery, or the like, before the crime is committed, and the overt act must be a cause, not a, preliminary condition. It is an attempt, for example, to take the impression of a key with intent to commit larceny in a house; but it is not an attempt, in a criminal sense, to purchase a deadly weapon or to procure poison, such acts not being in themselves unlawful. An attempt must consist in means suitable to accomplish the end desired, and must be made up of an act or acts which the accused could have carried into effect had he not been interrupted. Attempts may take the form of solicitations to commit crime, and the crime to which the attempt is preliminary may be impossible of commission; for example, a person may break open a trunk with a view to steal its contents, and find it empty; or he may insert his hand into a pocket which contains nothing, but the act would constitute an attempt in either case.[213]

Assaults.— *Assaults* resemble attempts, but when undertaken with intent to commit higher crimes are themselves criminal acts, and are punishable as such. At the common law an attempt to commit felony is a misdemeanor, and an attempt to commit a misdemeanor is itself a misdemeanor of less degree. In some States particular attempts are made criminal offenses by statute; in such jurisdictions the terms of the statute, in a particular case, will prevail in determining the offense and in imposing an appropriate punishment.

CONSPIRACY

Conspiracy.— A *conspiracy* is an agreement between two or more persons to do some unlawful act, or to do a lawful act in an unlawful manner. The agreement itself constitutes an offense, whether an act is done in furtherance of the object or not.[214] The evidence in proof

---

[213] Commonwealth *vs.* McDonald, 59 Mass., 365.

[214] United States *vs.* Watson, 17 Fed. Rep., 145: U. S. *vs.* Sacia, 2 *ibid.,* 754: State *vs.* Mayberry, 48 Me., 218; Com. *vs.* Hunt, 4 Metcalf, 111; Com. *vs.* Judd, 2 Mass., 337; State *vs.* Norton, 3 Zabriskie (N. J.), 33; People *vs.*

of the existence of a conspiracy will in general be circumstantial, and the existence of the conspiracy will be inferred from the facts as proved.[215]

CRIMINAL JURISDICTION

Criminal Jurisdiction in the United States.— In the United States the general authority to legislate, with a view to the preservation of the peace and the prevention and punishment of ordinary crime, is vested in the several States of the Union. To constitute a crime against the United States, an offense must have been made such by statute, and in certain cases must have been committed upon the high seas or upon territory over which the United States exercises exclusive jurisdiction.[216] The definitions of crime in the States are determined by the common law, or by statute in the State within whose jurisdiction an offense has been committed; the definitions of crime against the United States are determined in every case by statute, in the absence of which an act, however wrongful or injurious, is not punishable by the Federal courts.[217]

Mather, 4 Wendell (N. Y.), 259; U. *S. vs. Smith.* 2 Bond, 323; State *vs.* Ripley, 31 Me., 386.

[215] The Mussel Slough Case, 5 F. R., 680; U. S. *vs.* Mitchell, 1 Hughes. 439; *U. S. vs.* Coldberg, 7 Bissell. 175: *U. S. vs.* Sacia. 2 Fed. Rep., 754; U. S. *vs.* Smith, 2 Bond, 323.

[216] United States *vs. Fox,* 5 Otto, 670-673.

[217] *Ibid.*

CRIMES

Homicide.— *Homicide* is the general term applied to any act on the part of one person the result of which is to cause the death of another. Homicide is generally, but not always, a criminal act, and from the point of view of criminal responsibility is said to be either *felonious, justifiable,* or *excusable*- To constitute felonious homicide the person killed must have been in being, his death must have been the direct result of the injuries inflicted, and must have occurred within a year and a day thereafter. The homicide must also have been due to au act done with the intention to cause death or grievous bodily harm, or by an act of omission amounting to criminal negligence in the discharge of a duty imposed by law or contract, or to accident occurring in the performance of an unlawful act.[218]

Murder — Degrees.— *Murder is* the wilful killing of a human being, in the peace of the country, with malice aforethought either express or implied.[219] Although the definitions of murder differ somewhat in the several States, there is general concurrence as to premeditation, or malice aforethought, being an essential ingredient of the offense — that is, that there was a deliberately cherished intention to cause death or to inflict grievous bodily barm, or such reckless disregard of the consequences of a wrongful act as to warrant the inference of such an

---

[218] Steph. Dig. Crim. Law.

[219] *U. S. vs.* Outerbridge, 5 Sawyer, 620; U. S. *vs.* Carr, 1 Woods, 480; see also Sec. 5339 Rev. Stat., and, for a somewhat more comprehensive definition, the cases of U. S. *vs.* King, 34 Fed. Rep.. 302; *U. S. vs* Meagher. 37 *ibid.,* 875.

intention. There is also some difference as to the kind or amount of evidence necessary to establish premeditation; but it may be said, in general terms, that the malice aforethought may be established by independent testimony or may be inferred when "the fact of killing is proved by satisfactory evidence, and there are no circumstances disclosed tending to show justification or excuse, or where there is nothing to rebut the natural presumption of malice."[220] In some of the States the offense of murder is divided into degrees, depending upon the kind and amount of malice shown, as tending to aggravate the crime and to exclude considerations of justification or excuse. The distinction, wherever it exists, is statutory, not being recognized at the common law.

Manslaughter — Classification.— *Manslaughter* is the unlawful killing of a human being without malice, express or implied. It may be voluntary or involuntary. It is *voluntary* when committed with a design to kill, under the influence of sudden or violent passion, caused by great provocation, which the law considers such a palliative of the offense as to rebut the presumption of malice which would otherwise arise. It is *involuntary* when committed by accident or without any intention to take life.[221] "The crime of manslaughter is involved in that of murder; and so if a jury, in a prosecution for murder, finds that the homicide was without malice, they may find the defendant guilty of manslaughter alone."[222]

---

[220] Commonwealth *vs.* Webster. 59 Mass., 306.

[221] United States vs. Outerbridge. 5 Sawyer, 620-625: Gourko *vs. U. S.*, 153 U. S., 183.

[222] United States *vs.* Carr, 1 Woods, 480, 487: U. S. *vs.* Outerbridge, 5 *Sawyer,* 620; U. S. *vs.* Armstrong, 2 Curtis, 446; *U. S. vs.* Meagher, 37 Fed. Rep., 875; Collins

Justifiable Homicide.— *Justifiable homicide* consists in the taking of human life either in obedience to the law, as in the execution of a criminal or the killing of an enemy in war, or under such circumstances as to warrant the inference that the act was done without malice or criminal intention. The principal cases of justifiable homicide are —

1. *Homicide in Obedience to Law.*— Under this head fall the execution of criminals and the killing of enemies in war. The former case needs no explanation, save to say that it is an imperative duty, prescribed by the law, the performance of which cannot be avoided. The killing of an enemy is justifiable only when he is a part of the armed force of a belligerent State or is engaged in the performance of an act of war.

2. *Homicide in the Performance of Official Duty.*— When an officer of the law encounters resistance in the execution of lawful process, or in an attempt to make a lawful arrest, he may use sufficient force to overcome such unlawful resistance. The kind and amount of force used will depend upon the character of the resistance encountered. If the person arrested be unarmed, only such force will be lawful as is necessary to compel obedience; if he have in his possession a deadly weapon, extreme measures will be justified on the part of the officer making the arrest.[223] It is proper to observe, in this connection, that any opposition, obstruction, or resistance intended to prevent an officer from doing his official duty is an

---

vs.U. S., 150 U. S., 62. For a case of manslaughter due to criminal negligence, see U. S. *vs.* Knowles, 4 Sawyer, 517.

[223] U. S. *vs.* Rice, 1 Hughes, 560, 568 ; Cunningham *vs.* Neagle, 135 IT. S., 1 ; *U. S. vs.* King, 34 Fed. Rep., 302; State *vs.* Kirkpatrick, 42 *ibid.,* 689.

indictable offense at common law, the punishment of which is regulated by the nature of the offense.[224]

Excusable Homicide — Self-defense.— A man may repel force by force in the defense of his person, his family, or property against any one who manifestly endeavors by violence or surprise to commit a felony, as murder, robbery, or the like. The right to oppose force by force in such a case is founded upon the law of nature, and is not and cannot be superseded by the law of society.[225] To justify the taking of life in self-defense "the intent must be to commit a felony. If it be only to commit a trespass, as to beat the party, it will not justify the killing of the aggressor. No words, no question, however insulting and irritating, not even an assault, will afford such justification, although it may be sufficient to reduce the offence from murder to manslaughter. In the next place, the intent to commit a felony must be apparent, which will be sufficient, although it afterwards turn out that the real intention was less criminal, or was even innocent. This apparent intent is to be collected from the attending circumstances, such as the manner of the assault, the nature of the weapons used, and the like. And lastly, to produce this justification it must be apparent that the danger was imminent and the species of resistance used necessary to avert it."[226] By imminent danger is meant immediate danger — one that must be instantly met; one that cannot be guarded against by calling on the assistance of others or the protection of the law. And the species of resistance aged — that is, the means to prevent the

---

[224] *U. S. vs.* Outerbridge, 5 Sawyer, 620, 625.

[225] *U. S. vs.* Rice, 1 Hughes, 560, 568.

[226] U. S. *vs.* Wiltburger, 3 Wash., 521.

threatened injury — must be such as were necessary to avert it.[227]

Larceny.— *Larceny* is the unlawful taking and carrying away of things personal with the intent to deprive the owner of the same. To constitute the offense there must be an unlawful taking, which implies that the goods must pass from the possession of the true owner or of one having a qualified right of property therein and without his consent.[228] There must not only be a taking, but a carrying away. A bare removal from the place in which he found the goods, though the thief does not quite make off with them, is a sufficient asportation or carrying away.[229] The taking and carrying away must also be with intent to deprive the owner of the thing taken.[230]

Embezzlement.— *Embezzlement* is a species of larceny in the nature of a criminal breach of trust, and consists in the fraudulent conversion of property to his own use by an agent, clerk, servant, or in general by any

---

[227] U. S. *vs.* Lee, 12 F. R., 816; Alien *vs.* *U. S.*, 150 *U. S.*, 551 ; Starr *vs.* *U. S.*, 153 U. S., 614 ; People *vs.* Clark, 7 N. Y., 385.

[228] Hite *vs.* State, 9 Yerg., 198, 357; Com. *vs.* James, 1 Pickering, 375: Farrell *vs.* People, 16 III., 506; U. S. *vs.* Duffy, 1 Cranch, C. C., 164 ; *U. S. vs.* Mason, 3 Blatchforil, 360 : U. S. *vs.* Simms, 4 Cranch, C. C., 618.

[229] State *vs.* Wisdom, 8 Porter, 511; State *vs.* Jackson, 65 N. C., 305 ; Eckels *vs.* State, 20 Ohio, N. S., 508 ; Com. *vs.* Berry, 99 Mass. 428 ; People *vs.* Selden, 37 Cal., 51.

[230] Dodd *vs.* Hamilton, 2 Taylor, 31; State *vs.* Hawkins, 8 Porter, 461 ; Com. *vs.* Low, Thach. Crim. Cases, 477 ; IT. S. *vs.* Durkee, 1 McAllister, 196.

person acting in a fiduciary capacity. In order to constitute the crime, it is necessary that the property embezzled should have come lawfully into the hands of the embezzler, and by virtue of the position of trust he occupies in relation to the person whose property he takes.[231] In this respect it differs from the crime of larceny, in which the property is unlawfully taken and retained.[232]

Robbery — Force Used.— *Robbery* is the felonious taking of goods from the person of another or in his presence[233] by violence or by putting him in fear and against his will.[234] Robbery is thus seen to be larceny accompanied by intimidation and force, and the felonious intent in taking constitutes the offense.

---

[231] Com. v*s*. Hussey, 111 Mass., 432 ; Com. *vs*. Butterick, 100 Mass., 1; Com. *vs*. King, 9 Cushing. 284. The scope of the offense of embezzlement has been considerably extended, by Federal statutes, in its application to certain unlawful acts, respecting the public money and property, committed by public officers.

[232] Com. v*s*. Hussey, 111 Mass., 432 ; Com. *vs*. Butterick, 100 Mass., 1; Com. *vs*. King, 9 Cushing. 284. The scope of the offense of embezzlement has been considerably extended, by Federal statutes, in its application to certain unlawful acts, respecting the public money and property, committed by public officers.

[233] *U. S. vs*. Jones, 3 Wash., 209; U. S. *vs*. Wood, 3 *ibid.,* 440; U. S. *vs*. Wilson, Baldwin, 78 ; Com. vs. Holland, 1 Duvall (Ky.), 182 ; State *vs*. Gorham, 55 N. H., 152: McCloskey *vs*. People, 5 Parker, 299.

[234] *U. S. vs*. Jones, 3 Wash., 209; U. S. *vs*. Wood, 3 *ibid.,* 440; U. S. *vs*. Wilson, Baldwin, 78 ; Com. vs. Holland, 1 Duvall (Ky.), 182 ; State *vs*. Gorham, 55 N. H., 152: McCloskey *vs*. People, 5 Parker, 299.

Piracy.— *Piracy* may be defined as robbery committed on the high seas. It is an offense against the law of nations, and as such is punishable in the courts of the United States.[235]

Assault and Battery.— The offense of *assault and battery* is composed of the two elements named, which, taken together, constitute the complete offense. An *assault* is an attempt, with force and violence, to do corporal injury to another, as by striking at him with a weapon.[236] "The laying of a hand upon another, or seizing his clothing, if done in friendship or for a benevolent purpose, is not an assault; but if the act is done in anger or in a rude and insolent manner or with a view to hostility, it amounts not only to an assault, but to a battery. Even striking at a person, though no blow be inflicted, or raising the arm to strike, or holding up one's fist at him, if done in anger or in a menacing manner, are considered by law as assaults."[237] *Battery* is the unlawful beating or wounding of another.[238] A battery, from the nature of the offense, includes an assault, and is therefore charged as "assault and battery;" but there may be an assault without battery, which is regarded by the law as a criminal offense.

---

[235] *U. S. vs.* Durkee, 1 McAllister, 196 ; U. S. *vs.* Smith, 5 Wheaton, 153 ; Davison *M.* Sealskins, 3 Paine, 333: U. S. *vs.* Chapels, 2 Wheeler, 205 ; U. S. *vs.* Tully, 1 Gallatin, 247.

[236] *U. S. vs.* Hand, 2 Wash., 435 ; State *vs.* Morgan, 3 Iredell, 186; State *vs.* Bradley, 34 Tex., 95.

[237] U. S. *vs.* Ortega, 4 Wash., 531; *V. 8. vs.* Kierman, 3 Cranch. C. C., 435; People *vs.* Islas, 27 Cal., 680 : Smith *vs.* State, 39 Miss., 521 ; Lawson *vs.* State, 30 Ala., 14.

[238] Wharton's Law Dict.

Lawful Use of Force.— Not every species of violence, however, which is offered by one to another constitutes the offense above described. In the first place, the use of force may be in direct obedience to law, as in the execution of a criminal or in the killing of an enemy in war; in the next place, we may confidently lay down the broad general principle that, when any person is performing a public duty required of him by law, he is under the protection of the law. An officer of the law who has legal process in his hands is bound to execute it according to the mandate of the writ. If he is resisted in the performance of this duty, he must overcome such resistance by the use of such force as may be necessary for him to execute his duty. If necessary, the law authorizes him to resort to extreme measures, and if the resisting party is killed in the struggle, the homicide is justifiable. An officer is authorized to summon as many persons as may be necessary to assist him in the performance of his legal duties, and such persons are bound to obey such summons, and they are under the same protection afforded to officers, as they are for the time officers of the law. The law imposes upon private persons the duty of suppressing affrays, preventing felonies from being committed in their presence, and arresting such offenders and bringing them to justice; and such private persons, while performing their duties, are under the protection of the law.[239] The law, in its humanity and justice, will not allow unnecessary force to be used in the execution of its

---

[239] U. S. *vs.* Rice, 1 Hughes, 560 ; U. S. *vs.* Carr, 1 Woods, 480; U. S. *vs.* Jailer of Fayette Co., 2 Abbot, 279; Georgia *vs.* O'Grady, 3 Woods, 496 ; Burns *vs.* Erben, 40 N. Y., 463 ; Mandeville *vs.* Guernsey, 51 Barber, 99.

process. "The means used must be proportional to the end to be accomplished."[240]

Arson.— *Arson* is "the malicious and willful burning of the house of another." The word "house," as here understood, includes not merely the dwelling-house, but all outhouses which are parcel thereof. [241] To constitute the offense there must be an actual burning of the building or some part of it; but it is not necessary that it, or any part of it, should be wholly consumed.[242]

Perjury.— *Perjury* may be generally defined as false swearing, and includes the breach of the solemn sanction of an oath or the making of a false oath. When a witness, to whom a lawful oath has been administered in a judicial proceeding, swears falsely in a matter material to the issue, he is said to commit perjury. It is essential to the offense that the oath should have been duly administered by a person having authority to do so and in the course of a judicial proceeding. [243] In most jurisdictions there may be false swearing amounting to perjury in some forms of nonjudicial proceedings. Such an offense, however, is strictly statutory in character, and is not included in the

---

[240] U. S. *vs.* Carr, 1 Woods, 480; U. S. *vs.* Rice, 1 Hughes, 560 ; Oglesby *vs.* State, 39 Tex. 53 ; Com. *vs.* Carey, 12 Cushing, 246 ; State *vs.* Mahon, 3 Harrington, 568 ; Lewis *vs.* State, 3 Head, 127.

[241] Com. *vs.* Tucker. 110 Mass., 403 ; People *vs.* Butler, 16 Johns., 203; Com. *vs.* Van Schaick, 16 Mass., 105.

[242] People *vs.* Haggerty, 46 Cal , 354; Macy *vs.* State, 24 Ark., 44 ; State *vs.* Sandy, 3 Iredell, 570.

[243] Bishop, Crim. Law (7 ed.), § 1020 ; U. S. *vs.* Ambrose, 2 Fed. Rep., 556.

definition of the offense at common law. The false oath must be taken willfully, with some degree of deliberation, and with intent to impede or otherwise interfere with the due administration of justice. It must be taken positively and directly, and must in most cases relate to the existence or nonexistence of a material fact: for if a man swears to what he believes or remembers, he is not in general guilty of perjury; but if he swears that he believes a fact to be true which he knows to be false, he is guilty of perjury. The fact sworn to should be material; for if such fact have no bearing upon the issue, the administration of justice has not been affected injuriously, and there has not been perjury. *Subornation of perjury is* the offense of procuring another to take such a false oath as constitutes perjury in the principal.[244]

Forgery.— *Forgery* is the false or fraudulent making or alteration of an instrument with intent to defraud or to prejudice the right of another. The essence of the offense is the intent to defraud, and to constitute forgery there must have been a person in existence, at the time of the execution of the fraudulent instrument, who was capable of being defrauded thereby. The offense may consist in the forgery of an instrument, as in the case of a check, note, or bill of exchange, or of a signature only, or of an instrument partly engraved and partly written, like a bank-note, or of an instrument wholly engraved, as in the case of a railroad or steamship ticket.[245]

---

[244] U. S. *vs.* Bailey, 9 Pet., 238 ; U. S. *vs.* Moore, 2 Lowell, 232 ; U. S. *vs.* Stanley, 6 McLean, 409 ; U. S. *vs.* Perdue, 4 Fed. Rep., 897 ; U. S. *vs.* Mayer, Dearly, 127 ; U. S. *vs.* Smith, 1 Sawyer, 277 ; *U. S. vs.* Coons, 1 Bond, 1 : U. S. *vs. Wood,* 14 Pet., 430.

[245] State *vs.* Pierce, 8 Iowa, 231; State *vs.* Thompson, 19 *ibid.,* 399; People *vs.* Brotherton. 47 Cal, 388; U. S. *vs.*

Rape.— *Rape* is the violation or carnal knowledge of a woman, forcibly and against her will.[246] The offense must have been committed by a male person, with requisite physical capacity; for this reason a boy under fourteen is presumed to be incapable of its commission. In England the presumption of incapacity is conclusive; in some jurisdictions in the United States it may be rebutted by testimony showing capacity. There must be want of consent on the part of the woman, and the offense may be committed upon the person of a prostitute. Girls under a certain age, which is regulated locally by statute, are held to be incapable of giving consent. The fact of penetration is an essential ingredient of the offense, as is the use of force on the part of the offender. The force used may be either actual or constructive, but must be sufficient to accomplish the purpose.[247]

Burglary.— *Burglary,* at the common law, is the breaking and entering-of a dwelling-house by night with intent to commit a felony therein, whether such felonious intent be executed or not. The breaking is either actual, as where the person makes a hole in a door or opens a window, or in law, as where he obtains an entrance by threats, or fraud, or by collusion with some one in the house.[248] In the United States the English definition of

---

Jolly, 37 Fed. Rep., 108; *In re* Benson, 34 *ibid.,* 649; U. S. *vs.* Moore, 60 *ibid.,* 738, *id.,* 740.

[246] Charles *vs.* State, 6 Eng., 389; Cato *vs.* State, 9 Fla , 163.

[247] Cato *vs.* State, 9 Fla., 163; State *vs.* Burgdorf, 53 Mo., 65; Strang *vs.* People, 24 Mich., 1.

[248] Sweet, Law Dic.; U. S. *vs.* Bowen, 4 Cranch. C. C., 604. Larceny may be a lesser kindred offense where burglary with the intent to commit larceny is charged. U.

burglary has been so far modified by statute as to include offenses committed by day as well as by night, and in other buildings than dwelling-houses; various degrees of the offense have also been established.[249]

Riot — Rout.— A *riot* is an assembly of persons, to the number of three or more, with intent to forcibly disturb the peace in a tumultuous manner. The offense is equally riot if the assembly be with intent to commit one unlawful act, even if that act be desisted from and another unlawful act be committed.[250] If the unlawful assembly moves forward toward the execution of its design, it is a rout; an actual execution of the design is a riot. A rout, therefore, bears much the same relation, to a riot that an attempt to commit a crime does to the actual commission of the crime itself.

Mayhem.— At the common law the offense of *mayhem* consisted in the act of unlawfully and violently depriving another of the use of such of his members as might render him less able, in fighting, either to defend himself or annoy his adversary.[251] By statute in most of the States the scope of this of offense has been extended so as to include all malicious injuries to the person, and the original condition that the part injured should have been useful in fighting having been quite lost sight of. Before the Conquest such offenses formed an elaborate

---

S. *vs.* Dixon, 1 Cranch, C. C., 414; U. S. *vs.* Read, 2 Craach, C. C., 198.

[249] Archbold's Crim. Law, 1069.

[250] U. S. *vs.* Fenwick, 4 Cranch, C. C., 675; U. S. *vs.* Peace, *ibid.,* 601; U. S. *vs.* Stock-well, *ibid.,* 671; U. S. *vs.* McFarland, 1 *ibid.,* 140; U. S. *vs.* McFarlane, *ibid.,* 163.

[251] 4 Blackstone, 205; U. S. *vs.* Asking, 4 Cranch, C, C., 98; U. S. *vs.* Scroggins, Hemp., 478.

and extensive branch of the law, but the offenses were treated as torts rather than crimes. Some of the laws set forth with the utmost minuteness and particularity the compensation to be made for every sort of bodily injury. After the Conquest the offense of wounding seems to have been regarded rather as a crime than as a tort or civil injury, and to have been defined and punished as such.[252]

Many offenses are made such by statute that are either not offenses at common law, or extend the common-law liability for acts made criminal by that system of jurisprudence. They consist in offenses against the postal and revenue laws, offenses in connection with the obtaining or payment of pensions, offenses committed on the high seas or within the territorial waters of the United States, but not within the constitutional jurisdiction of a State, and, finally, offenses arising in the land or naval forces and in the militia when in active service in time of public danger.

References.— Bishop's Criminal Law and Criminal Procedure and Archbold on Criminal Procedure and Evidence are perhaps the most widely accepted authorities on this branch of the law. The History of the Criminal Law of England, by the late Justice Stephen, should be the foundation of all study of the criminal jurisprudence of England and the United States. Wharton's writings on this subject, of which the most prominent are his Criminal Law, Criminal Evidence, and Criminal Pleading, are works of great value to practitioners and students. The collections of criminal cases prepared and selected by Lawson, Hawley, Gibbons, and Green, together with Waterman's Criminal Digest of the United States, can be used with benefit in the study of the text-books already mentioned. Among recent text-books on this subject those

---

[252] III. Stephen Hist. Crim. Law, 108, and cases cited.

of Heard, May, Desty, Lawson, and Brown will be found of great value, especially in connection with the changes that have been effected by statute in the criminal jurisprudence of the several States of the Union.

Made in United States
Troutdale, OR
11/03/2026

56844501R00166